FINLAND

RUSSIA

ESTONIA

LATVIA

LITHUANIA

BELARUS

UKRAINE

MOLDOVA

ROMANIA

SERBIA

BULGARIA

MACEDONIA

GREECE

Aegean

an Sea

Black
Sea

GEORGIA

AZERBAIJAN

ARMENIA

TURKEY

CYPRUS

The Economist

POCKET EUROPE
IN FIGURES

The
Economist

=== POCKET ===

EUROPE
IN FIGURES

THE ECONOMIST IN ASSOCIATION WITH
PROFILE BOOKS LTD

Published by Profile Books Ltd,
62 Queen Anne Street, London W1M 9LA

First published by The Economist Books Ltd 1991

Copyright © The Economist Newspaper Ltd 1997

Material researched and compiled by Pamela Canetti,
Chris Coulman, Robert Eves, Carol Howard, Stella Jones,
David McKelvey, Nick Wiseman, Simon Wright

Design and makeup Jonathan Harley

Printed in Italy by
LEGO S.p.a. - Vicenza - Italy

A CIP catalogue record for this book is available
from the British Library

ISBN 1 86197 025 0

Contents

CONTENTS

CONTENTS

CONTENTS

Notes

In this first edition of *The Economist Pocket Europe in Figures* we present a detailed picture of Europe today: how its countries compare and how they have changed over recent decades. The contents list on the previous pages gives a full list of the hundreds of subjects covered in the 11 main sections. Some 48 countries are considered.

The research for this book was carried out during 1996, using the most up-to-date and most authoritative sources available. The sources used are listed at the end of the book.

The extent and quality of the statistics available varies from country to country. Every care has been taken to specify the broad definitions on which the data are based and to indicate cases where data quality or technical difficulties are such that interpretation of the figures is likely to be seriously affected. Nevertheless, figures from individual countries will often differ from standard international statistical definitions. Availability of data also varies, particularly for the transition economies.

Statistics do not yet fully reflect the changes that have taken place in the Czech Republic and Slovakia, the former Yugoslavia and the former Soviet Union. Serbia includes Montenegro. Macedonia is officially known as the Former Yugoslav Republic of Macedonia. Data for Cyprus normally refer to Greek Cyprus only. Data for the EU refer to its 15 members following enlargement of the Union on January 1 1995.

The all-important factor in a book of this kind is to be able to make reliable comparisons between countries. Although this is never quite possible for the reasons stated above, the best route, which this book takes, is to compare data for the same year or period and to use actual, not estimated, figures wherever possible.

Most countries' national accounts are now compiled on a GDP basis so, for simplicity, the term GDP has been used interchangeably with GNP.

Statistics for principal exports and principal imports are normally based on customs statistics. These are generally compiled on different definitions to the visible exports and imports figures shown in the balance of payments sections.

Definitions of the statistics shown are given on the relevant page or in the glossary below. Figures may not add exactly to totals, or percentages to 100, because of rounding or statistical adjustment. Sums of money have generally been converted to US dollars at the official exchange rate ruling at the time to which the figures refer.

A glossary explaining various terms is on the following pages.

Glossary

Balance of payments The record of a country's transactions with the rest of the world. The current account of the balance of payments consists of visible trade (goods), invisible trade (income and expenditure for services such as banking, insurance, tourism and shipping, together with profits earned overseas and interest payments) and current transfers (remittances from those working abroad, payments to international organisations, famine relief). Imports include the cost of "carriage, insurance and freight" (cif) from the exporting country to the importing. The value of exports does not include these elements and is recorded "free on board" (fob). Balance of payments statistics are generally adjusted so that both exports and imports are shown fob; the cif element is included in invisibles.

Comecon The former communist countries of central and eastern Europe.

Crude birth rate The number of live births per 1,000 population. The crude rate will automatically be high if a large proportion of the population is of child-bearing age.

Crude death rate The number of deaths in one year per 1,000 population. Also affected by the population's age structure.

Current prices These are in nominal terms and do not take into account the effect of inflation.

Enrolment Gross enrolment ratios may exceed 100% because some pupils are younger or older than the standard primary or secondary school age.

ECSC European Coal and Steel Community, established by the Treaty of Paris, signed April 18th 1951 and effective 1952.

Ecu European currency unit. An accounting measure used within the EU and composed of a weighted basket of the currencies of 12 EU members.

EEC European Economic Community, established by the Treaty of Rome, signed March 25th 1957, effective 1958. The European Atomic Energy Community (Euratom) came into effect at the same time.

EMU Economic and monetary union. Stages for implementation were proposed in the Delors report which followed the 1988 Hanover European Council meeting. The Maastricht treaty agreed in December 1991 laid out a timetable for progress towards EMU and the adoption of a single currency.

EC European Community. Merger of ECSC, EEC and Euratom signed April 8th 1965, effective 1967.

EU European Union. Following the treaty agreed at Maastricht in

December 1991 the EC was formally incorporated into a new and broader European Union. Until 1995 it had 12 members: Belgium, Denmark, France, Germany, Greece, Ireland, Italy, Luxembourg, Netherlands, Portugal, Spain and the United Kingdom. From January 1st 1995 membership increased to 15 as Austria, Finland and Sweden joined the Union.

Fertility rate   The average number of children born to a woman who completes her childbearing years.

Foreign direct investment   The purchase of assets in another country by a company or individual plus reinvested earnings and intra-company loans.

G7   The Group of Seven. Members are Canada, France, Germany, Italy, Japan, the United Kingdom and the United States.

GDP   Gross domestic product. It is the sum of all output produced by economic activity within that country. GNP (gross national product) includes net income from abroad eg. rent, profits. For simplicity, the term GDP has been used interchangeably with GNP.

Government   Finance and tax data may refer to central government only or to general government which includes central state and local government and the social security sectors.

Infant mortality rate   The annual number of deaths of infants under one year of age per 1,000 live births.

Inflation   The annual rate at which prices are increasing or decreasing. The most common measure is the change in the consumer price index. The producer price index tracks the prices of domestically produced goods when they leave the factory.

Invisible trade   Exports and imports of such items you cannot drop on your foot, that is, services such as shipping, insurance and banking plus profits, dividends and interest received by or from overseas residents.

Life expectancy   The average length of time a newborn baby can expect to live.

Market capitalisation   The value of a company or companies calculated by multiplying the number of issued shares by their market price at a given time.

Marginal tax rate   The rate of tax paid on an extra unit of income.

Money supply   A measure of the "money" available to buy goods and services. Various definitions of money supply exist. The measures used here are based on definitions used by the IMF and may differ from measures used nationally. Narrow money consists of cash in circulation and demand deposits; broad money also includes savings and foreign currency deposits.

OECD Organisation for Economic Co-operation and Development. The "rich countries' club" established in 1961. Now has 28 members: Australia, Austria, Belgium, Canada, Czech Republic, Denmark, Finland, France, Germany, Greece, Hungary, Iceland, Ireland, Italy, Japan, Luxembourg, Mexico, Netherlands, New Zealand, Norway, Poland, Portugal, Spain, Sweden, Switzerland, Turkey, United Kingdom, United States.

Population density The total number of inhabitants divided by the surface area.

Real terms Figures are adjusted to allow for inflation.

Relative humidity An indication of how much water vapour the air contains. A figure of 100 means the air cannot hold any more water vapour. Relative humidity varies inversely with temperature and is therefore normally highest just before dawn and lowest in the early afternoon.

Reserves The stock of gold and foreign currency held by a country to finance any calls that may be made for the settlement of foreign debt. Also used to buy and sell foreign currency to control fluctuations.

Trade-weighted exchange rates This measures a currency's depreciation (figures below 100) or appreciation (figures over 100) from a base date against a trade-weighted basket of the country's main trading partners.

Visible trade Exports and imports of things you can drop on your foot such as bricks, brass and bombs.

Part I

LAND
AND THE
ENVIRONMENT

Land and land use

Biggest countries

Land area, sq km

1	Russia	17,075,400	26	Lithuania	65,200
2	Turkey	779,450	27	Latvia	64,589
3	Ukraine	603,700	28	Croatia	56,540
4	France	551,500	29	Bosnia	51,130
5	Spain	504,780	30	Slovakia	49,500
6	Sweden	449,960	31	Estonia	45,125
7	Germany	356,910	32	Denmark	43,070
8	Finland	338,130	33	Switzerland	41,290
9	Norway	323,900	34	Netherlands	37,330
10	Poland	312,680	35	Moldova	33,700
11	Italy	301,270	36	Belgium	33,100
12	United Kingdom	244,880	37	Armenia	29,000
13	Romania	237,500	38	Albania	28,750
14	Belarus	207,600	39	Macedonia FYR	25,715
15	Greece	131,990	40	Slovenia	20,250
16	Bulgaria	110,910	41	Cyprus	9,251
17	Iceland	103,000	42	Luxembourg	2,586
18	Hungary	93,030	43	Andorra	468
19	Portugal	92,390	44	Malta	320
20	Serbia	88,361	45	Liechtenstein	160
21	Azerbaijan	86,600	46	San Marino	61
22	Austria	83,850	47	Monaco	2
23	Czech Republic	78,370	48	Vatican	0.44
24	Ireland	70,280			
25	Georgia	69,700		**Total Europe**	23,933,278

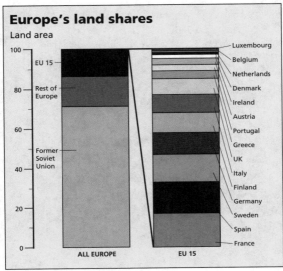

How agricultural?
Agricultural land as % of land area

1	Ireland	85		Switzerland		51
2	United Kingdom	77	25	Slovakia		50
3	Greece	71	26	Bosnia & Hercegovina		47
	Hungary	71	27	Belgium		46
	Lithuania	71		Turkey		46
6	Croatia	70	29	Luxembourg		45
	Ukraine	70	30	Armenia		44
8	Denmark	67		Belarus		44
9	Romania	65		Portugal		44
10	Liechtenstein	63	33	Austria		42
11	Spain	62		Macedonia FYR		42
12	Poland	60	35	Azerbaijan		41
13	Italy	59		Malta		41
	Moldova	59	37	Albania		40
	Netherlands	59		Latvia		40
16	Andorra	58	39	Estonia		33
17	Cyprus	57	40	Slovenia		32
	France	57	41	Iceland		24
	San Marino	57	42	Russia		13
20	Bulgaria	55	43	Sweden		9
	Serbia	55	44	Finland		8
22	Czech Republic	54	45	Norway		4
23	Germany	51				

How forested?
Forested area as % of land area

1	Finland	76	20	Switzerland		26
2	Sweden	64		Turkey		26
3	Slovenia	45	22	Serbia		25
4	Slovakia	41	23	Andorra		22
5	Portugal	40		Italy		22
6	Austria	39	25	Belgium		21
	Latvia	39		Luxembourg		21
8	Albania	38	27	Greece		20
9	Macedonia FYR	37	28	Liechtenstein		19
10	Bosnia & Hercegovina	36	29	Cyprus		18
11	Bulgaria	35		Hungary		18
12	Czech Republic	33	31	Lithuania		16
13	Estonia	31	32	Croatia		15
	Spain	31	33	Denmark		12
15	Germany	30	34	Netherlands		9
16	Poland	28		United Kingdom		9
	Romania	28	36	San Marino		8
18	France	27	37	Ireland		5
	Norway	27	38	Iceland		1

Natural facts

National high points
Metres

1	Russia	Elbrus	5,642
2	Georgia	Mount Shkhara	5,203
3	Turkey	Mount Ararat	5,165
4	France	Mont Blanc	4,808
5	Italy	Monte Bianco	4,808
6	Switzerland	Dufourspitze	4,634
7	Azerbaijan	Bazar-Dyuzi	4,480
8	Armenia	Transcaucasia	4,090
9	Austria	Grossglockner	3,797
10	Spain	Pico de Teide	3,715
11	Germany	Zugspitze	2,962
12	Andorra	Pia de l'Estany	2,951
13	Bulgaria	Musala	2,925
14	Greece	Mount Olympus	2,917
15	Slovenia	Triglan	2,863
16	Albania	Korab	2,764
17	Macedonia FYR	Korab	2,764
18	Serbia	Daravica	2,656
19	Slovakia	Gerlachovsky	2,655
20	Liechtenstein	Grauspitz	2,599
21	Romania	Negoiu	2,548
22	Poland	Mount Rysy	2,499
23	Norway	Glittertind	2,470
24	Bosnia & Hercegovinia	Maglic	2,396
25	Portugal	Ponta do Pico	2,351
26	Iceland	Hvannadalshnúkur	2,119
27	Sweden	Kebnekaise	2,111
28	Ukraine	Mount Goverla	2,061
29	Cyprus	Mount Olympus	1,951
30	Croatia	Troglav	1,913
31	Czech Republic	Sniezka	1,602
32	United Kingdom	Ben Nevis	1,342
33	Finland	Haltiatunturi	1,328
34	Ireland	Carrauntoohil	1,038
35	Hungary	Kékestetö	1,014
36	San Marino	Monte Titano	793
37	Belgium	Signal de Botranges	694
38	Luxembourg	Buurgplaatz	559
39	Moldova	Mount Balaneshty	429
40	Belarus	Dzyarzhynskaya	346
41	Netherlands	Vaalserberg	321
42	Estonia	Suur Munamagi	318
43	Latvia	Uidzeme	312
44	Lithuania	Jouzapine	294
45	Malta	Dingli Cliffs	253
46	Denmark	Yding Skovhoj	173

Highest mountains
Metres

1	Elbrus	Russia	5,642
2	Mount Shkhara	Georgia	5,203
3	Rustiveli	Russia	5,201
4	Dykh-Tau	Russia	5,198
5	Mount Ararat	Turkey	5,165
6	Kazbek	Russia	5,047
7	Mount-Blanc	France/Italy	4,807
8	Klyuchevskaya	Russia	4,750
9	Ushba	Russia	4,710
10	Dufourspitze	Switzerland	4,634
11	Dom	Switzerland/Italy	4,545
12	Bazar-Dyuzi	Azerbaijan	4,480
13	Matterhorn	Italy/Switzerland	4,478
14	Dente Blanche	Switzerland/Italy	4,357
15	Nadelhorn	Switzerland/Italy	4,327

Longest rivers
Km

		Outflow	
1	Volga	Russia	3,530
2	Danube	Romania	2,860
3	Dnieper	Ukraine	2,200
4	Don	Russia	1,870
5	Northern Dvina	Russia	1,860
6	Pechora	Russia	1,810
7	Kama	Russia	1,800
8	Oka	Russia	1,500
9	Belaya	Russia	1,430
10	Kura	Azerbaijan	1,360
11	Dniester	Moldova	1,350
12	Rhine	Netherlands	1,320
13	Vyatka	Russia	1,310
14	Vistula	Poland	1,200
15	Elbe	Germany	1,160

Longest coastlines
Km

1	Russia	37,653	14	Germany	2,389
2	Norway	21,925	15	Portugal	1,793
3	Greece	13,676	16	Ireland	1,448
4	United Kingdom	12,429	17	Estonia	1,393
5	Turkey	7,200	18	Finland	1,126
6	Croatia	5,790	19	Cyprus	648
7	Italy	4,996	20	Latvia	531
8	Iceland	4,988	21	Poland	491
9	Spain	4,964	22	Serbia	491
10	France	3,427	23	Netherlands	451
11	Denmark	3,379	24	Albania	362
12	Sweden	3,218	25	Bulgaria	354
13	Ukraine	2,782	26	Georgia	310

Saving nature

Protected areas
Total, 1994

1	Germany	504	**21**	Estonia	39
2	Spain	215		Romania	39
3	Sweden	214	**23**	Czech Republic	34
4	Russia	199	**24**	Croatia	30
5	United Kingdom	191	**25**	Portugal	25
6	Italy	172	**26**	Greece	24
7	Austria	170	**27**	Serbia	21
8	Denmark	114	**28**	Iceland	20
	Norway	114		Ukraine	20
10	Poland	111	**30**	Macedonia FYR	16
11	France	110	**31**	Georgia	15
12	Switzerland	109	**32**	Azerbaijan	12
13	Finland	82		Ireland	12
14	Netherlands	79	**34**	Albania	11
15	Lithuania	76		Belarus	11
16	Hungary	53	**36**	Slovenia	10
17	Bulgaria	46	**37**	Bosnia & Hercegovina	5
18	Latvia	45	**38**	Armenia	4
19	Turkey	44	**39**	Belgium	3
20	Slovakia	40	**40**	Moldova	2

Biosphere reserves
Total, 1994

1	Russia	15	**14**	Belarus	2
2	Spain	13		Finland	2
	United Kingdom	13		Greece	2
4	Germany	12		Ireland	2
5	Poland	7	**18**	Croatia	1
6	France	6		Denmark	1
7	Czech Republic	5		Estonia	1
	Hungary	5		Serbia	1
9	Austria	4		Netherlands	1
	Slovakia	4		Norway	1
11	Italy	3		Portugal	1
	Romania	3		Sweden	1
	Ukraine	3		Switzerland	1

Protected wetlands
Total, 1994

1	United Kingdom	73	**11**	Finland	11
2	Italy	46		Greece	11
3	Denmark	38	**13**	Czech Republic	9
4	Germany	31	**14**	France	8
5	Sweden	30		Switzerland	8
6	Spain	29	**16**	Austria	7
7	Ireland	21		Slovakia	7
8	Netherlands	15	**18**	Belgium	6
9	Norway	14	**19**	Poland	5
10	Hungary	13	**20**	Bulgaria	4

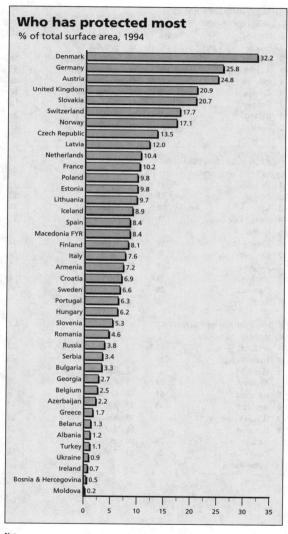

Who has protected most
% of total surface area, 1994

Country	%
Denmark	32.2
Germany	25.8
Austria	24.8
United Kingdom	20.9
Slovakia	20.7
Switzerland	17.7
Norway	17.1
Czech Republic	13.5
Latvia	12.0
Netherlands	10.4
France	10.2
Poland	9.8
Estonia	9.8
Lithuania	9.7
Iceland	8.9
Spain	8.4
Macedonia FYR	8.4
Finland	8.1
Italy	7.6
Armenia	7.2
Croatia	6.9
Sweden	6.6
Portugal	6.3
Hungary	6.2
Slovenia	5.3
Romania	4.6
Russia	3.8
Serbia	3.4
Bulgaria	3.3
Georgia	2.7
Belgium	2.5
Azerbaijan	2.2
Greece	1.7
Belarus	1.3
Albania	1.2
Turkey	1.1
Ukraine	0.9
Ireland	0.7
Bosnia & Hercegovina	0.5
Moldova	0.2

Notes
Protected areas are areas of at least 1,000 hectares that fall into the following
categories: scientific or nature reserves; national parks; natural monuments or
landscapes with some unique aspects; wildlife sanctuaries; other protected
landscapes or seascapes.
Biosphere reserves are those internationally recognised supporting, self-sustaining
and self-regulating ecological systems.

Air pollution

Carbon monoxide emissions
Kg per head, early 1990s

1	Norway	186	11	Iceland	113
2	Sweden	171	12	Portugal	110
3	France	168	13	Finland	109
4	Austria	165	14	United Kingdom	97
5	Italy	162	15	Hungary	82
6	Greece	142	16	Netherlands	58
7	Denmark	134	17	Poland	55
8	Ireland	127	18	Switzerland	51
9	Spain	126	19	Belgium	27
10	Germany	114			

Sulphur dioxides emissions
Kg per head, early 1990s

1	Hungary	81		Portugal	29
2	Poland	71	13	Finland	27
3	Spain	56	14	Luxembourg	25
4	United Kingdom	55	15	France	21
5	Ireland	52	16	Sweden	12
6	Greece	49		Turkey	12
7	Germany	48	18	Netherlands	11
8	Belgium	41	19	Austria	9
9	Iceland	34	20	Norway	8
10	Denmark	30		Switzerland	8
11	Italy	29			

Nitrogen oxides emissions
Kg per head, early 1990s

1	Iceland	87	12	Greece	32
2	Luxembourg	55		Spain	32
3	Finland	53	14	Belgium	30
	Norway	53	15	Poland	29
5	Denmark	51	16	France	26
6	Sweden	45	17	Austria	23
7	United Kingdom	40	18	Portugal	22
8	Germany	36	19	Switzerland	21
	Ireland	36	20	Hungary	18
	Italy	36	21	Turkey	8
11	Netherlands	35			

Emissions of volatile organic compounds
Kg per head, early 1990s

1	Norway	65	11	Spain	29
2	Sweden	57	12	Ireland	27
3	Luxembourg	50		Netherlands	27
4	Austria	48	14	Ireland	26
5	Italy	42	15	Greece	23
6	Finland	41	16	Portugal	21
7	United Kingdom	40	17	Poland	20
8	France	39	18	Denmark	18
9	Switzerland	38	19	Belgium	14
10	Germany	34	20	Hungary	13

Emissions of carbon dioxide from industrial processes
'000s tonnes, 1992

1	Russia	2,103,132	21	Bulgaria	54,359
2	Germany	878,136	22	Denmark	53,897
3	Ukraine	611,342	23	Portugal	47,181
4	United Kingdom	566,246	24	Switzerland	43,701
5	Italy	407,701	25	Finland	41,176
6	France	362,076	26	Serbia	38,197
7	Poland	341,892	27	Slovakia	36,999
8	Spain	223,196	28	Ireland	30,851
9	Turkey	145,490	29	Lithuania	22,006
10	Netherlands	139,027	30	Estonia	20,885
11	Czech Republic	135,608	31	Croatia	16,210
12	Romania	122,103	32	Bosnia & Hercegovina	15,055
13	Belarus	102,028	33	Latvia	14,781
14	Belgium	101,768	34	Moldova	14,209
15	Greece	73,859	35	Georgia	13,839
16	Azerbaijan	63,878	36	Slovenia	5,503
17	Norway	60,247	37	Armenia	4,199
18	Hungary	59,910	38	Macedonia FYR	4,100
19	Sweden	56,796	39	Albania	3,968
20	Austria	56,572	40	Iceland	1,777

Greenhouse gas emissions
Emissions of carbon dioxide, kg per head, 1992

1	Russia	14,110	14	Azerbaijan	8,760
2	Norway	14,030	15	Finland	8,210
3	Estonia	13,190	16	Austria	7,290
4	Czech Republic	13,040	17	Greece	7,250
5	Ukraine	11,720	18	Italy	7,030
6	Germany	10,960	19	Slovakia	7,000
7	Denmark	10,440	20	Iceland	6,850
8	Belgium	10,190	21	Sweden	6,560
9	Belarus	9,890	22	Switzerland	6,380
10	United Kingdom	9,780	23	France	6,340
11	Netherlands	9,160	24	Bulgaria	6,080
12	Poland	8,900	25	Lithuania	5,860
13	Ireland	8,870	26	Hungary	5,720

Waste and recycling

Total waste generation by sector

Agriculture, '000s tonnes, 1990

1	France	400,000	7	Netherlands	19,210
2	Spain	112,102	8	Norway	18,000
3	United Kingdom	80,000	9	Austria	880
4	Finland	23,000	10	Belgium	343
5	Ireland	22,000	11	Greece	90
6	Sweden	21,000			

Mining and quarrying, '000s tonnes, 1990

1	United Kingdom	107,000	7	Norway	9,000
2	France	100,000	8	Greece	3,900
3	Spain	70,000	9	Ireland	1,930
4	Sweden	28,000	10	Netherlands	391
5	Finland	21,650	11	Portugal	202
6	Germany	19,296	12	Austria	21

Manufacturing, '000s tonnes, 1990

1	Germany	81,906	10	Netherlands	7,665
2	United Kingdom	56,000	11	Greece	4,304
3	France	50,000	12	Denmark	2,304
4	Italy	34,710	13	Norway	2,000
5	Austria	31,801	14	Ireland	1,580
6	Belgium	27,000	15	Luxembourg	1,300
7	Spain	13,800	16	Switzerland	1,000
8	Sweden	13,000	17	Portugal	662
9	Finland	10,160	18	Iceland	135

Energy production, '000s tonnes, 1990

1	Germany	25,598	7	Belgium	1,069
2	United Kingdom	13,000	8	Finland	950
3	Greece	7,680	9	Sweden	625
4	Netherlands	1,553	10	Portugal	165
5	Denmark	1,532	11	Ireland	130
6	Austria	1,150			

Municipal, '000s tonnes, 1990

1	Germany	27,958	10	Finland	3,100
2	France	20,320	11	Greece	3,000
3	Italy	20,033		Switzerland	3,000
4	United Kingdom	20,000	13	Portugal	2,538
5	Spain	12,546	14	Denmark	2,430
6	Netherlands	7,430	15	Norway	2,000
7	Austria	4,783	16	Ireland	1,100
8	Belgium	3,410	17	Luxembourg	170
9	Sweden	3,200	18	Iceland	80

Other waste, '000s tonnes, 1990

1	United Kingdom	15,400	4	Belgium	2,830
2	France	9,800	5	Ireland	860
3	Sweden	3,850	6	Finland	150

Municipal waste
Kg generated per person, 1990

1	Finland	624	10	Italy	348
2	Austria	620		United Kingdom	348
3	Netherlands	497	12	Belgium	343
4	Denmark[a]	475	13	Germany	333
5	Norway	472	14	Spain	322
6	Luxembourg	445	15	Iceland	314
7	Switzerland	441	16	Ireland[a]	312
8	Sweden	374	17	Greece	296
9	France	360	18	Portugal	257

Nuclear waste
Tonnes of heavy metal, 1995

1	France	1,200	6	Belgium	120
2	United Kingdom	797	7	Switzerland	85
3	Germany	470	8	Finland	66
4	Sweden	250	9	Netherlands	15
5	Spain	160			

Paper and cardboard recovery rates
%, 1990

1	Spain	51.0	9	Austria[a]	36.8
2	Netherlands	50.3	10	Denmark	35.4
3	Switzerland	49.4	11	United Kingdom	31.0
4	France	45.7	12	Greece	30.0
5	Sweden	42.9	13	Norway	26.0
6	Finland	40.8	14	Belgium[b]	14.7
7	Germany	39.6	15	Ireland	3.0
8	Portugal	39.1			

Glass recovery rates
%, 1990

1	Netherlands	66.7	9	Finland	35.7
2	Switzerland	64.7	10	Portugal	30.0
3	Denmark	60.4	11	France	28.5
4	Austria	60.0	12	Spain	27.0
5	Belgium	55.0	13	Ireland	23.0
6	Italy	48.0	14	United Kingdom	21.0
7	Germany	45.0	15	Greece	15.0
8	Sweden	44.0			

a 1985.
b 1980.

Weather

Hot spots

Highest average temperatures, July, °C

1	Cyprus	Nicosia	37
2	Spain	Seville	36
3	Greece	Trikkala	35
4	Armenia	Erivan	34
5	Turkey	Izmir	33
6	Albania	Tirane	31
	Bulgaria	Plovdiv	31
	Georgia	Tbilisi	31
	Macedonia FYR	Skopje	31
	Russia	Astrakhan	31
11	Italy	Palermo	30
	Romania	Bucharest	30
13	Croatia	Dubrovnik	29
	France	Marseille	29
	Malta	Valletta	29
16	Hungary	Budapest	28
	Portugal	Faro	28
	Serbia	Belgrade	28
	Ukraine	Simferopol	28
20	Bosnia & Hercegovina	Sarajevo[a]	27
	Moldova	Kishinev	27
	Slovenia	Ljubljana	27
	Switzerland	Lugano	27
24	Andorra	Les Escaldes	26
	Monaco	Monte Carlo	26
	Slovakia	Kosice	26
27	Austria	Innsbruck	25
	Czech Rep.	Brno[a]	25
	Germany	Frankfurt	25
30	Poland	Cracow	24
31	Belgium	Brussels	23
	Lithuania	Vilnius	23
	Luxembourg	Luxembourg	23
34	Denmark	Copenhagen	22
	Finland	Tampere	22
	Latvia	Riga	22
	Netherlands	De Bilt	22
	Norway	Oslo	22
	Sweden	Stockholm	22
	UK	London	22
41	Estonia	Tallinn	20
	Ireland	Cork	20
43	Iceland	Reykjavik	14

Cold spots

Lowest average temperatures, January, °C

1	Russia	Perm	-20
2	Finland	Inari	-18
	Turkey	Kars	-18
4	Norway	Spitzbergen[c]	-15
5	Sweden	Pitea[b]	-14
6	Estonia	Tallinn[b]	-11
	Lithuania	Vilnius	-11
	Switzerland	Santis	-11
9	Spain	Madrid	-10
	Ukraine	Kiev	-10
	Latvia	Riga	-10
12	Armenia	Erivan	-9
	Austria	Klagenfurt	-9
14	Moldova	Kishinev	-8
15	Romania	Bucharest	-7
	Slovakia	Kosice	-7
	Poland	Przemysl	-7
18	Hungary	Debrecen	-6
19	Czech Republic	Brno	-5
	France	Embrun	-5
	Germany	Munich	-5
22	Bosnia & Hercegovina	Sarajevo	-4
	Bulgaria	Sofia	-4
	Slovenia	Ljubljana	-4
25	Denmark	Copenhagen[b]	-3
	Macedonia FYR	Skopje	-3
	Serbia	Belgrade	-3
28	Belgium	Virton	-2
	Iceland	Reykjavik	-2
30	Andorra		-1
	Georgia	Tbilisi	-1
	Luxembourg	Luxembourg	-1
	Netherlands	De Bilt	-1
34	Greece	Trikkala	0
	Italy	Milan	0
	Portugal	Braganza	0
37	Ireland	Dublin	1
	UK	York	1
39	Albania	Tirane	2
40	Cyprus	Nicosia	5
41	Croatia	Dubrovnik	6
42	Monaco	Monte Carlo	8
43	Malta	Valletta	10

a August.   b February.   c March.

Most rain

	Country	Place	mm rain	Month	Rainy days[a]
1	Switzerland	Santis[c]	302	Jul	18
2	Norway	Bergen	235	Oct	23
3	Albania	Tirane	211	Nov	16
4	Russia	Sochi	201	Jan	17
5	Croatia	Dubrovnik	198	nov	16
6	United Kingdom	Oban[c]	172	Dec	22
7	Ireland	Valentia[d]	168	Dec	21
	Portugal	Oporto	168	Dec	18
9	Spain	Santante	159	Dec	18
10	Slovenia	Ljubljano	151	Oct	14
11	Italy	Naples[d]	147	Nov	11
12	Germany	Munich	139	Jul	16
13	Austria	Innsbruck	134	Jul	19
14	Cyprus	Kyrenia	133	Dec	11
	France	Cherbourg	133	Nov	17
16	Greece	Trikkala	125	Dec	17
17	Monaco	Monte Carlo	123	Nov	7
18	Turkey	Izmir[d]	122	Dec	10
19	Romania	Bucher	121	Jun	12
20	Poland	Cracow	111	Jul	16
21	Malta	Valletta[d]	110	Dec	13
22	Andorra	Les Escaldes	105	May	15
23	Belgium	Virton	103	Dec	18
	Bosnia & Hercegovina	Sarajevo	103	Oct	12
25	Serbia	Belgrade	96	Jun	13
26	Iceland	Reykjavik	94	Oct	21
27	Ukraine	Kiev	91	Aug	12
28	Denmark	Fano	88	Sep	16
29	Bulgaria	Sofia[b]	87	May	13
	Netherlands	De Bilt	87	Aug	18
31	Sweden	Gothenberg	86	Jul	14
32	Lithuania	Vilnius	85	May	17
33	Luxembourg	Luxembourg	84	Aug	15
	Slovakia	Kosice	84	Jul	14
35	Czech Republic	Brno	81	Jul	14
36	Hungary	Debrecen	80	Jun	13
37	Estonia	Tallinn	78	Aug	15
38	Finland	Tampere	76	Jul	14
39	Georgia	Tbilisi	75	May	12
40	Latvia	Riga	70	Aug	16
41	Moldova	Kishinev	68	Jun	12
42	Macedonia FYR	Skopje	61	Oct	9
43	Armenia	Erivan	53	May	12

a Number of days with more than 1mm of rain.
b >0.2mm.
c >0.25mm.
d >1.0mm.

Relative humidity

Before noon, %

1	Austria	Klagenfurt	96	Oct
	Belgium	Virton	96	Jan
	France	Bordeaux	96	Oct
4	Luxembourg	Luxembourg	95	Dec
	Slovenia	Ljubljana	95	Sep
6	Ireland	Mullingar	94	Dec
	Italy	Milan	94	Dec
	Macedonia FYR	Skopje	94	Dec
9	Germany	Rostock	93	Oct
	Poland	Warsaw	93	Nov
11	Bulgaria	Plovdiv	92	Nov
	Denmark	Fano	92	Dec
	Netherlands	De Bilt	92	Nov
	Ukraine	Kiev	92	Nov
	United Kingdom	Belfast	92	Dec
16	Armenia	Erivan	91	Dec
	Czech Republic	Brno	91	Dec
	Finland	Helsinki	91	Oct
	Hungary	Debrecen	91	Dec
	Lithuania	Vilnius	91	Dec
21	Estonia	Tallinn	90	Nov
	Portugal	Braganza	90	Dec

Afternoon, %

1	Iceland	Reykjavik	67	May
	Monaco	Monte Carlo	67	Jan
3	Ireland	Mullingar	66	May
4	Belgium	Virton	61	May
5	Croatia	Dubrovnik	59	Jan
	Denmark	Copenhagen	59	May
	Malta	Vallette	59	Jul
	Netherlands	De Bilt	59	May
9	Luxembourg	Luxembourg	58	Apr
10	Lithuania	Vilanus	56	Jun
	United Kingdom	London	56	Apr
12	Estonia	Tallinn	55	Jun
13	Finland	Tampere	54	May
	Slovenia	Ljubljana	54	Jul
15	Latvia	Riga	53	Jun
	Sweden	Stockholm	53	May
17	Norway	Oslo	52	May
	Poland	Poznan	52	May
19	Germany	Frankfurt	50	May
20	Slovakia	Bratislava	49	May
21	Portugal	Libsbon	48	Jul
	Switzerland	Lugano	48	Jul
23	Hungary	Budapest	47	Jun

Part II

POPULATION

Population

From biggest to smallest
Population, m

	1994			2020	
1	Russia	148.37	1	Russia	140.28
2	Germany	81.14	2	Turkey	86.51
3	Turkey	60.77	3	Germany	77.94
4	United Kingdom	58.09	4	United Kingdom	60.94
5	France	57.73	5	France	60.92
6	Italy	57.15	6	Italy	53.65
7	Ukraine	51.47	7	Ukraine	49.13
8	Spain	39.55	8	Poland	41.09
9	Poland	38.34	9	Spain	38.35
10	Romania	22.74	10	Romania	21.95
11	Netherlands	15.39	11	Netherlands	16.29
12	Serbia	10.71	12	Serbia	11.36
13	Greece	10.41	13	Czech Republic	10.55
14	Czech Republic	10.30	14	Belgium	10.38
15	Belarus	10.16	15	Greece	10.08
	Hungary	10.16	16	Belarus	9.94
17	Belgium	10.08	17	Portugal	9.73
18	Portugal	9.83	18	Azerbaijan	9.71
19	Bulgaria	8.82	19	Sweden	9.59
20	Sweden	8.74	20	Hungary	9.47
21	Austria	7.92	21	Austria	8.27
22	Azerbaijan	7.47	22	Bulgaria	7.92
23	Switzerland	7.13	23	Switzerland	7.77
24	Georgia	5.45	24	Georgia	6.01
25	Slovakia	5.33	25	Slovakia	5.92
26	Denmark	5.17	26	Finland	5.39
27	Finland	5.08	27	Denmark	5.11
28	Croatia	4.78	28	Moldova	5.02
29	Moldova	4.42	29	Norway	4.67
30	Bosnia & Hercegovina[a]	4.38	30	Armenia	4.56
31	Norway	4.32	31	Bosnia & Hercegovina	4.48
32	Armenia	3.77	32	Albania	4.47
33	Lithuania	3.71	33	Croatia	4.28
34	Ireland	3.54	34	Ireland	3.88
35	Albania	3.41	35	Lithuania	3.80
36	Latvia	2.58	36	Macedonia FYR	2.53
37	Macedonia FYR	2.09	37	Latvia	2.36
38	Slovenia	2.00	38	Slovenia	1.86
39	Estonia	1.54	39	Estonia	1.44
40	Cyprus	0.73	40	Cyprus	0.90
41	Luxembourg	0.40	41	Luxembourg	0.44
42	Malta	0.36	42	Malta	0.42
43	Iceland	0.27	43	Iceland	0.33
44	Andorra	0.06			
45	Liechtenstein	0.03			
	Monaco	0.03			

a 1993.

Fastest growth
Annual average population growth, %

1985–94			1995–2020		
1	Andorra	4.2	1	Turkey	1.3
2	Turkey	2.1	2	Albania	1.1
3	Albania	1.6	3	Armenia	1.0
4	Armenia	1.5		Azerbaijan	1.0
5	Liechtenstein	1.4		Bosnia & Hercegovina	1.0
6	Azerbaijan	1.3	6	Cyprus	0.8
7	Monaco	1.3		Iceland	0.8
8	Cyprus	1.1	8	Macedonia FYR	0.6
	Iceland	1.1	9	Malta	0.5
	Macedonia FYR	1.1		Moldova	0.5
11	Luxembourg	1.0	11	Georgia	0.4
	Switzerland	1.0		Slovakia	0.4
13	Serbia	0.9		Sweden	0.4
14	Bosnia & Hercegovina	0.8	14	Ireland	0.3
15	Croatia	0.7		Luxembourg	0.3
	Netherlands	0.7		Norway	0.3
	Slovenia	0.7		Poland	0.3
				Switzerland	0.3

Slowest growth
Annual average population growth, %

1985–94			1995–2020		
1	Hungary	-0.4	1	Bulgaria	-0.4
2	Bulgaria	-0.2	2	Estonia	-0.3
3	Latvia	-0.1		Hungary	-0.3
4	Portugal	-0.1		Italy	-0.3
5	Czech Republic	0.0		Latvia	-0.3
	Estonia	0.0	6	Croatia	-0.2
	Ireland	0.0		Germany	-0.2
8	Denmark	0.1		Romania	-0.2
	Italy	0.1		Russia	-0.2
	Ukraine	0.1		Slovenia	-0.2
11	Belarus	0.2		Ukraine	-0.2
	Belgium	0.2	12	Belarus	-0.1
	Romania	0.2		Denmark	-0.1
14	Poland	0.3		Greece	-0.1
	Spain	0.3		Spain	-0.1
	United Kingdom	0.3	16	Portugal	0.0
			17	Austria	0.1
				Belgium	0.1
				Czech Republic	0.1
				Lithuania	0.1

Population density

Most crowded countries
Population per sq km

1950			1970		
1	Malta	987	1	Malta	958
2	Belgium	283	2	Netherlands	319
3	Netherlands	248	3	Belgium	316
4	United Kingdom	207	4	United Kingdom	228
5	Germany	192	5	Germany	218
6	Italy	156	6	Italy	179
7	Luxembourg	114	7	Switzerland	150
	Switzerland	114	8	Luxembourg	131
9	Czech Republic	113	9	Czech Republic	124
10	Hungary	100	10	Denmark	114
11	Denmark	99	11	Hungary	111
12	Portugal	91	12	Moldova	107
13	Austria	83	13	Poland	101
14	Poland	77	14	Portugal	98
15	France	76	15	France	92
16	Moldova	73		Slovakia	92
	Slovenia	73	17	Austria	89
18	Slovakia	71	18	Armenia	85
19	Serbia	70		Romania	85
20	Romania	69		Serbia	85

Most crowded EU regions
No. of people per sq km, 1993

1	Brussels	Belgium	5,884.2
2	Berlin	Germany	3,903.4
3	Hamburg	Germany	2,250.1
4	Bremen	Germany	1,692.4
5	Attiki	Greece	919.3
6	Ile de France	France	910.5
7	North West England	United Kingdom	873.4
8	South East England	United Kingdom	652.7
9	Madrid	Spain	626.8
10	West-Nederland	Netherlands	604.6
11	Nordrhein-Westfalen	Germany	520.1
12	Zuid-Nederland	Netherlands	462.7
13	Vlaams Gewest	Belgium	431.9
14	Saarland	Germany	422.0
15	Campania	Italy	419.9
16	West Midlands	United Kingdom	406.8
17	Lombardia	Italy	372.9
18	Madeira	Portugal	326.8
19	Yorkshire and Humberside	United Kingdom	325.4
20	Nord-Pas-de-Calais	France	321.1

1995

1	Malta	1,159
2	Netherlands	380
3	Belgium	331
4	United Kingdom	239
5	Germany	229
6	Italy	190
7	Switzerland	174
8	Luxembourg	157
9	Moldova	132
10	Czech Republic	131
11	Armenia	121
12	Albania	120
	Denmark	120
14	Poland	119
15	Hungary	109
15	Slovakia	109
17	Portugal	106
	Serbia	106
19	France	105
20	Romania	96
	Slovenia	96

2020

1	Malta	1,317
2	Netherlands	399
3	Belgium	340
4	United Kingdom	250
5	Germany	218
6	Switzerland	188
7	Italy	178
8	Luxembourg	170
9	Albania	156
10	Armenia	153
11	Moldova	149
12	Czech Republic	134
13	Poland	127
14	Slovakia	121
15	Denmark	119
16	Azerbaijan	112
17	Serbia	111
	Turkey	111
19	France	110
20	Portugal	105

Least crowded EU regions
No. of people per sq km, 1993

1	Oevre Norrland	Sweden	3.4
2	Mellersta Norrland	Sweden	5.6
3	Norra Mellansverige	Sweden	13.5
4	Manner-Suomi	Finland	15.0
5	Ahvenanmaa/Aaland	Finland	16.1
6	Smaaland Med Oearna	Sweden	24.1
7	Centro	Spain	24.3
8	Oestra Mellansverige	Sweden	38.6
9	Kentriki Ellada	Greece	47.0
10	Ireland	Ireland	51.7
11	Nisia Aigaiou, Kriti	Greece	57.1
12	Noreste	Spain	57.7
13	Vaestsverige	Sweden	58.1
14	Sud-Ouest	France	58.3
15	Voreia Ellada	Greece	59.3
16	Scotland	United Kingdom	66.4
17	Suedoesterreich	Austria	67.9
18	Sardegna	Italy	68.8
19	Bassin-Parisien	France	71.4
20	Mecklenburg-Vorpommern	Germany	79.9

City living

Capital facts

Country	Capital city	Ranking	Population, '000s
Albania	Tirana	37	244.15
Andorra	Andorra	44	16.15
Armenia	Yerevan	15	1,254.40
Austria	Vienna	13	1,560.47
Azerbaijan	Baku	17	1,149.00
Belarus	Minsk	11	1,654.80
Belgium	Brussels	39	136.49
Bosnia & Hercegovina	Sarajevo	35	415.63
Bulgaria	Sofia	19	1,114.48
Croatia	Zagreb	21	867.72
Cyprus	Nicosia	38	186.40
Czech Republic	Prague	16	1,216.51
Denmark	Copenhagen	27	619.29
Estonia	Tallin	33	447.67
Finland	Helsinki	30	505.05
France	Paris	9	2,152.33
Georgia	Tbilisi	14	1,268.00
Germany	Berlin	3	3,475.39
Greece	Athens	20	885.74
Hungary	Budapest	10	2,002.12
Iceland	Reyjavik	41	101.42
Ireland	Dublin	29	533.93
Italy	Rome	6	2,693.38
Latvia	Riga	22	865.23
Liechtenstein	Vaduz	46	4.90
Lithuania	Vilnius	28	581.50
Luxembourg	Luxembourg	42	75.83
Macedonia FYR	Skopje	32	448.23
Malta	Valletta	45	9.15
Moldova	Kishinev	25	667.10
Monaco	Monaco	43	27.06
Netherlands	Amsterdam	23	721.98
Norway	Oslo	31	473.45
Poland	Warsaw	12	1,654.49
Portugal	Lisbon	26	663.32
Romania	Bucharest	8	2,343.82
Russia	Moscow	1	8,526.75
San Marino	San Marino	47	2.79
Serbia	Belgrade	18	1,136.79
Slovakia	Bratislava	34	445.09
Slovenia	Ljubljana	36	281.82
Spain	Madrid	4	2,976.06
Sweden	Stockholm	24	684.58
Switzerland	Berne	40	129.69
Turkey	Ankara	5	2,782.20
Ukraine	Kiev	7	2,642.70
United Kingdom	London	2	6,904.60
Vatican	Vatican City	48	0.77

Note: Estimates of city populations vary according to where geographical boundaries are defined. As far as possible the data refers to the city proper.

Most urbanised countries
% of population living in urban areas

1980			1994		
1	Belgium	95	1	Belgium	97
2	United Kingdom	89	2	Netherlands	89
3	Netherlands	88		United Kingdom	89
4	Denmark	84	4	Germany	86
5	Germany	83	5	Denmark	85
	Sweden	83	6	Sweden	83
7	France	73	7	Spain	76
	Spain	73	8	Estonia	73
9	Norway	71		France	73
10	Estonia	70		Latvia	73
	Russia	70		Norway	73
				Russia	73

Least urbanised countries
% of population living in urban areas

1980			1994		
1	Portugal	29	1	Portugal	35
2	Moldova	40	2	Moldova	51
3	Turkey	44	3	Austria	55
4	Slovenia	48		Romania	55
5	Romania	49	5	Azerbaijan	56
6	Croatia	50	6	Ireland	57
7	Georgia	52	7	Georgia	58
	Slovakia	52		Slovakia	58
9	Azerbaijan	53	9	Macedonia	59
10	Macedonia FYR	54	10	Switzerland	61

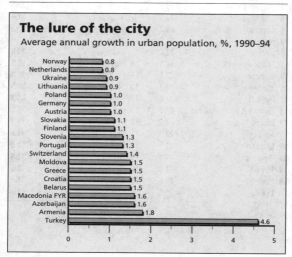

The lure of the city
Average annual growth in urban population, %, 1990–94

Norway	0.8
Netherlands	0.8
Ukraine	0.9
Lithuania	0.9
Poland	1.0
Germany	1.0
Austria	1.0
Slovakia	1.1
Finland	1.1
Slovenia	1.3
Portugal	1.3
Switzerland	1.4
Moldova	1.5
Greece	1.5
Croatia	1.5
Belarus	1.5
Macedonia FYR	1.6
Azerbaijan	1.6
Armenia	1.8
Turkey	4.6

Sex and age

Most male populations
No. of men per 100 women, 1995

1	Albania	105.0
2	Turkey	104.7
3	Macedonia FYR	101.3
4	Iceland	100.9
5	Cyprus	99.7
5	Ireland	99.7
7	Serbia	98.9
8	Switzerland	98.2
9	Netherlands	98.1
	Sweden	98.1
11	Norway	98.0
12	Bosnia & Hercegovina	97.9
	Malta	97.9
14	Denmark	97.7
15	Luxembourg	97.3
16	Romania	97.1
17	Greece	97.0
18	Armenia	96.9
19	Spain	96.6
20	Bulgaria	96.1

Most female populations
No. of men per 100 women, 1995

1	Latvia	85.7
2	Ukraine	86.8
3	Russia	88.3
4	Belarus	88.6
5	Estonia	88.9
6	Lithuania	89.9
7	Georgia	91.2
8	Moldova	91.4
9	Hungary	91.9
10	Portugal	93.4
11	Croatia	93.7
12	Slovenia	93.8
13	Italy	94.6
14	Finland	94.8
15	Poland	94.9
16	France	95.1
	Slovakia	95.1
18	Czech Republic	95.2
19	Germany	95.3
20	Austria	95.5

Youngest populations
% under 15

	1995			2020	
1	Turkey	33.9	1	Turkey	23.5
2	Azerbaijan	31.8	2	Azerbaijan	22.9
3	Albania	31.4	3	Armenia	22.5
4	Armenia	29.7		Moldova	22.5
5	Moldova	26.4	5	Albania	22.4
6	Cyprus	26.2	6	Ireland	20.9
7	Iceland	24.4	7	Cyprus	20.8
	Ireland	24.4		Georgia	20.8
	Macedonia FYR	24.4	9	Slovakia	20.5
10	Georgia	23.7	10	Poland	20.4
11	Slovakia	22.9	11	Macedonia	20.3
12	Poland	22.8	12	Iceland	20.2
13	Bosnia & Hercegovina	22.2		Lithuania	20.2
14	Malta	22.0	14	Malta	19.8
	Serbia	22.0	15	Czech Republic	18.8
16	Lithuania	21.9	16	Norway	18.5
17	Belarus	21.6	17	Belarus	18.4
18	Russia	21.0	18	Finland	18.3
19	Estonia	20.6	19	Sweden	18.1
	Latvia	20.6			

Most middle-aged populations
% aged 25–59
1995

1	Germany	51.7				
2	Switzerland	51.5	*2020*			
3	Luxembourg	51.1	1	Romania	50.1
4	Netherlands	50.9	2	Spain	50.0
5	Austria	50.2	3	Bosnia & Hercegovina	49.7
	Bosnia & Hercegovina	50.2	4	Azerbaijan	49.5
7	Denmark	49.6	5	Germany	49.2
	Finland	49.6	6	Russia	48.8
9	Italy	49.0	7	Slovenia	48.7
10	Slovenia	48.4	8	Bulgaria	48.6
11	Belgium	48.3	9	Portugal	48.5
12	Croatia	48.1	10	Albania	48.2
13	Russia	48.0	11	Belarus	48.1
14	Malta	47.7		Estonia	48.1
15	Latvia	47.3	13	Italy	47.9
16	Estonia	47.2	14	Turkey	47.7
17	Norway	47.1		Ukraine	47.7
18	Macedonia FYR	47.0	16	Greece	47.2
	United Kingdom	47.0	17	Austria	47.1
20	Greece	46.9	18	Armenia	47.0
	Ukraine	46.9		Macedonia FYR	47.0

Oldest populations
% aged 65 and over
1995

1	Sweden	17.3	*2020*			
2	Italy	16.0	1	Italy	23.2
3	Greece	15.9	2	Greece	22.2
	Norway	15.9	3	Germany	20.9
5	Belgium	15.8	4	Sweden	20.7
6	United Kingdom	15.5	5	Finland	20.5
7	Denmark	15.2	6	Belgium	20.3
	Germany	15.2		Spain	20.3
9	Austria	14.9	8	Switzerland	20.2
	France	14.9	9	Netherlands	20.0
	Spain	14.9	10	Denmark	19.9
12	Bulgaria	14.5	11	France	19.7
13	Switzerland	14.2	12	Austria	19.2
14	Finland	14.1		Luxembourg	19.2
	Portugal	14.1	14	Slovenia	18.8
			15	Bulgaria	18.3

Matters of breeding

Crude birth rate: countries compared
No. of live births per 1,000 population, 1995–2000

#	Country	Rate	#	Country	Rate
1	Turkey	24.6		Hungary	12.4
2	Albania	21.6	24	Bosnia & Hercegovina	12.3
3	Azerbaijan	19.3		Netherlands	12.3
4	Armenia	18.0		Switzerland	12.3
5	Iceland	16.8	27	Denmark	12.0
6	Cyprus	16.3	28	Belarus	11.8
7	Moldova	15.7		Belgium	11.8
8	Georgia	15.2		Portugal	11.8
9	Ireland	15.1	31	Romania	11.6
10	Macedonia FYR	15.0	32	Ukraine	11.5
11	Slovakia	14.8	33	Austria	11.4
12	Norway	14.2	34	Latvia	11.3
	Serbia	14.2	35	Croatia	11.1
14	Malta	13.9		Estonia	11.1
15	Czech Republic	13.8	37	Russia	10.8
16	Sweden	13.6	38	Bulgaria	10.6
17	Lithuania	13.5		Slovenia	10.6
	Poland	13.5	40	Greece	9.8
19	United Kingdom	12.9		Spain	9.8
20	Finland	12.5	42	Italy	9.6
	Luxembourg	12.5	43	Germany	9.2
22	France	12.4			

Fertility rate: countries compared
Average no. of children per woman, 1995–2000

#	Country	Rate	#	Country	Rate
1	Turkey	3.04	23	Belgium	1.71
2	Albania	2.66		Hungary	1.71
3	Armenia	2.40	25	Denmark	1.70
4	Cyprus	2.35	26	Switzerland	1.67
5	Azerbaijan	2.30	27	Belarus	1.65
6	Iceland	2.23		Croatia	1.65
7	Georgia	2.10	29	Latvia	1.64
	Ireland	2.10		Ukraine	1.64
	Moldova	2.10	31	Estonia	1.61
	Sweden	2.10		Netherlands	1.61
11	Malta	2.05	33	Austria	1.60
12	Serbia	2.03		Bosnia & Hercegovina	1.60
13	Norway	2.00	35	Portugal	1.55
14	Macedonia FYR	1.97	36	Russia	1.53
15	Finland	1.92	37	Bulgaria	1.50
	Slovakia	1.92		Romania	1.50
17	Poland	1.88	39	Slovenia	1.45
18	Czech Republic	1.83	40	Greece	1.40
	Lithuania	1.83	41	Germany	1.30
20	United Kingdom	1.81	42	Italy	1.27
21	France	1.74	43	Spain	1.23
22	Luxembourg	1.72			

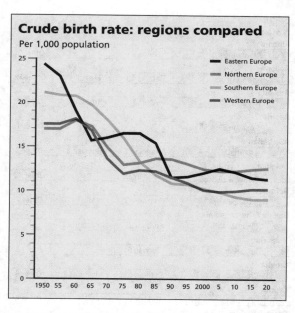

Crude birth rate: regions compared
Per 1,000 population

- Eastern Europe
- Northern Europe
- Southern Europe
- Western Europe

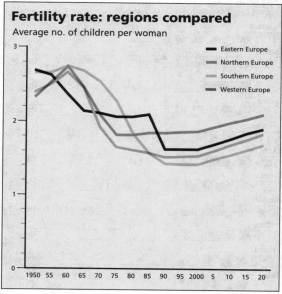

Fertility rate: regions compared
Average no. of children per woman

- Eastern Europe
- Northern Europe
- Southern Europe
- Western Europe

Who lives where

Ethnic breakdown
% of total population

Albania

Albanian 96	Greek 2		Other 3

Andorra

Andorran 30	Catalan 50	French 8	Other 12

Armenia

Aremian 93	Azeri 3	Russian 2	Other 2

Austria

Austrian 99			Other 1

Azerbaijan

Azeri 83	Armenian 6	Russian 6	Other 5

Belgium

Fleming 55	Walloon 33		Other 12

Belarus

Byelorussian 78	Russian 13	Polish 4	Other 4

Bosnia & Hercegovinia

Slovene 44	Serbian 31	Croatian 17	

Bulgaria

Bulgarian 85	Turkish 9		Other 6

Croatia

Croatian 78	Serbian 12	Slovenes 1	Other 9

Cyprus

Greek 78	Turkish 18		Other 4

Czech Republic

Czech 94	Slovakian 3		Other 3

Denmark

Danish 95			Other 5

Estonia

Estonian 62	Russian 30	Ukrainian 3	Other 4

Finland

Finnish 93	Russian 6		Other 1

France

French 91			Other 9

Georgia

Georgian 70	Armenian 8	Russian 6	Other 16

Germany

German 95	Turkish 2		Other 3

Greece

Greek 98			Other 2

Hungary

Hungarian 90	Gypsy 4	German 2	Other 4

Iceland

Icelandic 98			Other 2

Ireland

Celtic 94			Other 6

Italy

Italian 98			Other 2

Latvia

Latvian 52	Russian 34	Byelorussian 4	Other 10

Liechtenstein

Alemannic 95	Italian 3		Other 2

Lithuania

Lithuanian 80	Russian 9	Polish 8	Other 3

Luxembourg

Luxembourger 73	Portuguese 9	Italian 5	Other 13

Macedonia FYR

Macedonian 67	Albanian 21	Turkish 4	Other 8

Malta

Maltese 95	English 2		Other 3

Moldova

Moldovian 65	Ukrainian 13	Russian 13	Other 9

Monaco

French 47	Monegasque 16	Italian 16	Other 21

Netherlands

Dutch 96			Other 4

Norway

Germanic 97			Other 3

Poland

Polish 98	German 1		Other 1

Portugal

Portugese 98			Other 2

Romania

Romanian 89	Hungarian 9		Other 2

Russia

Russian 82	Tatar 3	Ukrainian 3	Other 12

San Marino

Sanmarinesi 87	Italian 12		Other 1

Serbia

Serbian 63	Albanians 14	Montenegrian 6	Other 17

Slovakia

Slovakian 86	Hungarian 11	Gypsy 1	Other 2

Slovenia

Slovene 91	Croatian 3	Serbian 2	Other 4

Spain

Spanish 73	Catalan 16	Galician 8	Other 3

Sweden

Swedish 91			Other 9

Switzerland

German 65	French 18	Italian 10	Other 7

Turkey

Turkish 85	Kurdish 12		Other 3

Ukraine

Ukrainian 73	Russian 22		Other 5

United Kingdom

English 82	Scottish 10	Welsh 2	Other 6

Migration

The recent picture
1990–95

	Migration rate per 1,000 pop.	Av. ann. net migration, '000s
Albania	-8.90	-27.77
Austria	6.18	49.35
Azerbaijan	-4.10	-3.70
Belarus	-1.80	-1.86
Belgium	1.58	1.58
Bosnia & Hercegovina	-50.30	-186.46
Bulgaria	-2.60	-22.03
Croatia	-0.40	-1.80
Czech Republic	0.50	5.18
Denmark	2.78	14.41
Estonia	-3.90	-6.05
Finland	1.60	8.11
France	1.20	69.01
Georgia	-5.50	-29.68
Germany	6.64	539.03
Greece	5.06	52.51
Hungary	-2.00	-20.58
Iceland	-1.68	-0.44
Ireland	-1.42	-5.06
Italy	1.84	104.98

Looking back

	1960–69	
	Migration rate per 1,000 pop.	Av. ann. net migration, '000s
Austria	0.75	5.45
Belgium	1.65	15.62
Denmark	0.20	0.10
Finland	-3.30	-15.06
France	4.20	204.78
Germany	2.55	193.88
Greece	-4.50	-38.48
Iceland	-1.50	-0.29
Ireland	-6.25	-17.98
Italy	-1.80	-93.80
Liechtenstein	12.30	0.23
Luxembourg	4.55	1.51
Malta	-14.18	-4.51
Netherlands	0.55	6.76
Norway	0.00	0.00
Portugal	-13.90	-126.89
Spain	-2.20	-70.59
Sweden	2.25	17.40
Switzerland	2.85	16.69
United Kingdom	0.55	29.98

	Migration rate per 1,000 pop.	Av. ann. net migration, '000s	1970–79 Migration rate per 1,000 pop.	1970–79 Av. ann. net migration, '000s	1980–89 Migration rate per 1,000 pop.	1980–89 Av. ann. net migration, '000s
Latvia	-6.90	-18.02	1.05	7.96	1.75	13.23
Liechtenstein	7.50	0.23	0.80	7.84	0.05	0.49
Lithuania	-2.70	-10.01	0.85	4.30	0.70	3.58
Luxembourg	10.64	4.21	-0.60	-2.83	0.65	3.19
Macedonia FYR	2.90	6.15	1.40	73.78	0.95	52.41
Malta	2.18	0.78	1.20	94.41	2.10	163.10
Moldova	-2.30	-1.00	1.65	14.93	2.10	20.86
Netherlands	2.36	36.10	-2.70	-0.59	0.20	0.05
Norway	1.82	7.85	3.25	10.33	-5.70	-20.25
Poland	-1.30	50.00	-0.35	-19.40	-0.25	-14.15
Portugal	-1.06	-10.43	13.00	0.31	2.15	0.06
Romania	-3.50	79.64	7.50	2.72	3.50	1.28
Russia	0.30	44.44	-3.46	-1.07	0.29	0.10
Serbia	8.60	93.30	2.30	31.40	1.45	21.01
Slovenia	3.10	5.86	0.90	3.61	1.40	5.81
Spain	0.66	25.80	2.25	20.46	-2.00	-19.81
Sweden	3.22	28.03	-0.05	-1.78	-0.30	-11.52
Switzerland	6.14	43.35	1.45	11.88	1.75	14.61
Ukraine	0.80	41.54	-2.00	-12.68	3.20	20.92
United Kingdom	1.34	78.27	-0.40	-22.57	0.40	22.75

Who speaks what

First language most spoken in Europe

		No. of people	% of pop. of Europe			No. of people	% of pop. of Europe
1	Russian	159.40	19.8	19	Swedish	8.90	1.1
2	German	94.41	11.7	20	Bulgarian	7.37	0.9
3	French	62.76	7.8	21	Catalan	6.11	0.8
4	English	61.91	7.7	22	Azerbaijani	5.96	0.7
5	Italian	55.09	6.8	23	Tartar	5.62	0.7
6	Turkish	50.92	6.3	24	Danish	5.18	0.6
7	Ukrainian	41.32	5.1	25	Albanian	5.10	0.6
8	Polish	38.81	4.8	26	Finnish	4.82	0.6
9	Spanish	34.08	4.2	27	Norwegian	4.30	0.5
10	Romanian	23.81	3.0	28	Armenian	4.32	0.5
11	Dutch	21.10	2.6	29	Georgian	3.82	0.5
12	Serbo-Croat	17.94	2.2	30	Lithuanian	3.07	0.4
13	Czecho-Slovak	15.14	1.9	31	Slovenian	2.03	0.3
14	Hungarian	12.43	1.5	32	Basque	1.52	0.2
15	Kurdish	12.00	1.5	33	Macedonian	1.48	0.2
16	Greek	10.88	1.3	34	Latvian	1.40	0.2
17	Portuguese	10.51	1.3	35	Estonian	0.98	0.1
18	Belorussian	9.69	1.2	36	Galician	0.90	0.1

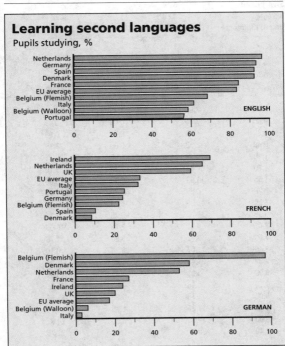

Learning second languages
Pupils studying, %

ENGLISH
Netherlands, Germany, Spain, Denmark, France, EU average, Italy, Belgium (Flemish), Belgium (Walloon), Portugal

FRENCH
Ireland, Netherlands, UK, EU average, Italy, Portugal, Germany, Belgium (Flemish), Spain, Denmark

GERMAN
Belgium (Flemish), Denmark, Netherlands, France, Ireland, UK, EU average, Belgium (Walloon), Italy

Part III
THE ECONOMY

Economic strength

Largest economies
GDP, $bn

1995

1	Germany	2,414	22	Czech Republic	33
2	France	1,535	23	Romania	28
3	United Kingdom	1,102	24	Belarus	22
4	Italy	1,088	25	Luxembourg	17
5	Spain	559	26	Slovenia	14
6	Netherlands	396	27	Croatia	12
7	Russia	392		Slovakia	12
8	Switzerland	304	29	Bulgaria	10
9	Belgium	269	30	Iceland	7
10	Austria	233	31	Latvia	6
11	Sweden	229	32	Lithuania	5
12	Denmark	173	33	Estonia	4
13	Turkey	165		Moldova	4
14	Norway	147		Azerbaijan	4
15	Finland	126	36	Armenia	3
16	Greece	112	37	Macedonia FYR	2
17	Portugal	104	38	Albania	1
18	Poland	95		**OECD total**	**22,318**
19	Ukraine	81		**EU15**	**8,418**
20	Ireland	61		**OECD Europe**	**9,040**
21	Hungary	39			

1980

1	Western Germany	758.5	13	Ex-Yugoslavia	56.7
2	France	601.6	14	Norway	52.4
3	United Kingdom	476.9	15	Romania	50.9
4	Italy	359.2	16	Finland	46.4
5	Spain	195.7	17	Greece	39.9
6	Netherlands	155.7	18	Portugal	22.4
7	Sweden	114.2	19	Hungary	20.7
8	Belgium	109.6	20	Ireland	16.3
9	Switzerland	101.4	21	Luxembourg	5.4
10	Austria	70.6	22	Iceland	2.7
11	Turkey	61.6	23	Cyprus	2.1
12	Denmark	61.5			

1970

1	Western Germany	180.3	11	Switzerland	20.9
2	France	157.4	12	Romania	18.9
3	United Kingdom	126.7	13	Hungary	16.5
4	Italy	94.6	14	Denmark	15.7
5	Poland	46.0	15	Austria	14.8
6	Eastern Germany	43.0	16	Ex-Yugoslavia	13.3
7	Spain	34.4	17	Finland	11.2
8	Sweden	32.5	18	Norway	11.1
9	Netherlands	31.7	19	Turkey	10.9
10	Belgium	26.3			

a 1993–95. b 1992–95. c 1990–92. d 1990–94.

Strongest growth
Average annual growth in GDP
1990–95

1	Slovakia^a	6.14	15	Belgium^d	1.15
2	Slovenia^b	5.09	16	France	1.12
3	Cyprus	4.55	17	Greece^d	1.10
4	Ireland	3.98	18	Portugal^d	1.08
5	Malta^c	3.50	19	Iceland	0.89
5	Norway	3.50	20	Italy^c	0.72
7	Turkey^c	2.10	21	Switzerland	0.16
8	Austria	2.02	22	Sweden	0.04
9	Denmark	2.01	23	Finland	-0.74
10	Netherlands	1.87	24	Hungary	-3.37
11	Germany^d	1.79	25	Latvia^b	-5.52
12	Luxembourg	1.63	26	Romania	-5.61
13	Spain	1.36	27	Estonia^b	-6.88
14	United Kingdom	1.18	28	Lithuania^b	-10.29

1980–89

1	Cyprus	6.13	8	Iceland	2.90
2	Malta	3.64	9	Norway	2.58
3	Luxembourg	3.61	10	Portugal	2.48
4	Ireland	3.49	11	Hungary	2.35
5	Finland	3.46	12	France	2.34
6	United Kingdom	2.92	13	Italy	2.22
	Spain	2.92	14	Sweden	2.14

1970–79

1	Malta	10.84	11	Austria	3.72
2	Iceland	6.54	12	Cyprus	3.34
3	Hungary	5.50	13	Finland	3.24
4	Greece	5.04	14	Belgium	3.19
5	Portugal	4.87	15	Netherlands	3.15
6	Norway	4.81	16	Germany	2.88
7	Ireland	4.69	17	Denmark	2.56
8	France	4.14	18	United Kingdom	2.40
9	Spain	3.78	19	Sweden	1.99
10	Italy	3.73	20	Switzerland	1.05

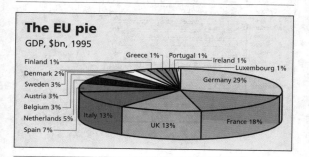

The EU pie
GDP, $bn, 1995

Finland 1%
Denmark 2%
Sweden 3%
Austria 3%
Belgium 3%
Netherlands 5%
Spain 7%
Italy 13%
UK 13%
France 18%
Germany 29%
Greece 1%
Portugal 1%
Ireland 1%
Luxembourg 1%

Living standards

GDP per head
$

1995

1	Luxembourg	44,042		14	Ireland	16,992
2	Switzerland	43,817		15	Spain	14,435
3	Norway	33,540		16	Greece	10,717
4	Denmark	33,391		17	Portugal	9,949
5	Germany	29,583		18	Czech Republic	4,350
6	Austria	27,763		19	Hungary	4,304
7	France	26,506		20	Poland	3,197
8	Belgium	26,324		21	Slovakia	2,949
9	Sweden	25,792		22	Turkey	2,828
10	Netherlands	25,316		23	Russia	2,458
11	Finland	24,070		24	Bulgaria	1,522
12	Italy	19,056		25	Romania	1,490
13	United Kingdom	18,940				

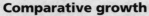

1980

1	Switzerland	15,980		13	United Kingdom	8,520
2	Luxembourg	15,100		14	Italy	6,400
3	Sweden	13,730		15	Spain	5,230
4	Norway	12,830		16	Ireland	4,930
5	Germany	12,320		17	Greece	4,160
6	Denmark	12,010		18	Cyprus	3,430
7	Iceland	11,680		19	Yugoslavia	2,540
8	France	11,200		20	Portugal	2,300
9	Belgium	11,120		21	Romania	2,290
10	Netherlands	11,010		22	Hungary	1,930
11	Finland	9,700		23	Turkey	1,390
12	Austria	9,360				

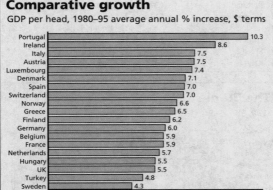

Comparative growth
GDP per head, 1980–95 average annual % increase, $ terms

Portugal	10.3
Ireland	8.6
Italy	7.5
Austria	7.5
Luxembourg	7.4
Denmark	7.1
Spain	7.0
Switzerland	7.0
Norway	6.6
Greece	6.5
Finland	6.2
Germany	6.0
Belgium	5.9
France	5.9
Netherlands	5.7
Hungary	5.5
UK	5.5
Turkey	4.8
Sweden	4.3

GDP per head in PPP
$

	1970	1980	1990	1994
Austria	3,048	8,850	16,623	20,210
Belgium	3,188	8,827	16,333	20,166
Denmark	3,551	8,746	16,548	20,546
Finland	2,885	8,004	16,193	16,208
France	3,539	9,414	17,347	19,201
Germany	3,096	8,249	15,779	19,675
Greece	1,459	4,325	7,424	11,315
Iceland	2,785	9,496	17,267	19,271
Ireland	1,829	5,172	11,206	15,212
Italy	2,987	8,464	16,274	18,681
Luxembourg	4,474	11,074	23,398	29,454
Netherlands	3,525	8,881	15,950	18,589
Norway	2,711	8,391	16,006	21,968
Portugal	1,563	4,550	9,363	12,335
Spain	2,230	5,868	11,755	13,581
Sweden	3,837	9,250	17,004	17,422
Switzerland	5,139	11,720	21,283	23,942
Turkey	938	2,284	4,660	5,271
UK	3,268	8,011	15,888	17,650
OECD Europe	2,872	7,455	14,035	16,321
EU	3,016	7,969	15,248	17,914

Comparative growth
GDP per head at PPP rates, annual average growth rates

	1970–94	1980–94	1990–94
Austria	8.2	6.1	5.0
Belgium	8.0	6.1	5.4
Denmark	7.6	6.3	5.6
Finland	7.5	5.2	0.0
France	7.3	5.2	2.6
Germany	8.0	6.4	5.7
Greece	8.9	7.1	11.1
Iceland	8.4	5.2	2.8
Ireland	9.2	8.0	7.9
Italy	7.9	5.8	3.5
Luxembourg	8.2	7.2	5.9
Netherlands	7.2	5.4	3.9
Norway	9.1	7.1	8.2
Portugal	9.0	7.4	7.1
Spain	7.8	6.2	3.7
Sweden	6.5	4.6	0.6
Switzerland	6.6	5.2	3.0
Turkey	7.5	6.2	3.1
UK	7.3	5.8	2.7
OECD Europe	7.5	5.8	3.8
EU average	7.7	6.0	4.1

Agriculture's contribution

Agricultural output
As % of GDP

1960

1	Turkey	41
2	Hungary	28
3	Portugal	25
4	Greece	23
5	Ireland	22
6	Finland	17
7	Italy	12
8	Austria	11
	Denmark	11
	France	11
11	Netherlands	9
	Norway	9
13	Sweden	7
14	Belgium	6
	Germany*	6

1970

1	Turkey	30
2	Greece	18
	Hungary	18
	Ex-Yugoslavia	18
5	Ireland	17
6	Finland	12
7	Italy	8
8	Austria	7
	Denmark	7
10	Netherlands	6
	Norway	6
12	Germany*	3
	United Kingdom	3

1980

1	Armenia	44
2	Albania	28
3	Turkey	23
4	Azerbaijan	22
5	Greece	20
6	Lithuania	19
7	Belarus	18
8	Bulgaria	14
	Estonia	14
10	Finland	10
11	Russia	9
12	Ex-Czechoslovakia	7
13	Denmark	6
	Italy	6
15	Austria	4
	France	4
	Norway	4
	Sweden	4
19	Belgium	2
	United Kingdom	2

1990

1	Latvia	20
2	Bulgaria	18
	Romania	18
	Turkey	18
5	Greece	17
6	Russia	13
7	Hungary	12
	Ex-Yugoslavia	12
9	Poland	10
10	Ex-Czechoslovakia	8
11	Finland	6
12	Denmark	5
13	France	4
	Italy	4
	Netherlands	4

1994

1	Georgia	61	8	Ukraine	19
2	Albania	55	9	Belarus	17
3	Armenia	49	10	Greece	16
4	Moldova	48		Turkey	16
5	Azerbaijan	27	12	Bulgaria	13
6	Lithuania	21		Croatia	13
	Romania	21	14	Estonia	10

a Western Germany.

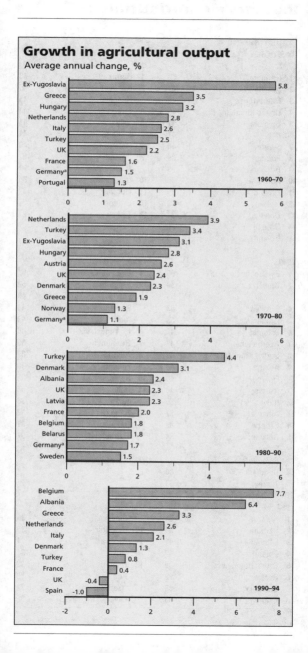

Growth in agricultural output

Average annual change, %

1960–70

Ex-Yugoslavia	5.8
Greece	3.5
Hungary	3.2
Netherlands	2.8
Italy	2.6
Turkey	2.5
UK	2.2
France	1.6
Germany[a]	1.5
Portugal	1.3

1970–80

Netherlands	3.9
Turkey	3.4
Ex-Yugoslavia	3.1
Hungary	2.8
Austria	2.6
UK	2.4
Denmark	2.3
Greece	1.9
Norway	1.3
Germany[a]	1.1

1980–90

Turkey	4.4
Denmark	3.1
Albania	2.4
UK	2.3
Latvia	2.3
France	2.0
Belgium	1.8
Belarus	1.8
Germany[a]	1.7
Sweden	1.5

1990–94

Belgium	7.7
Albania	6.4
Greece	3.3
Netherlands	2.6
Italy	2.1
Denmark	1.3
Turkey	0.8
France	0.4
UK	-0.4
Spain	-1.0

Industry's contribution

Industrial output
As % of GDP

1960

1	Germany[a]	53
2	Austria	47
3	Netherlands	46
4	United Kingdom	43
5	Belgium	41
	Italy	41
7	Sweden	40
8	France	39
	Hungary	39
10	Portugal	36
11	Finland	35
12	Norway	33
13	Denmark	31
14	Greece	26
	Ireland	26

1970

1	Germany[a]	49
2	Austria	45
	Hungary	45
4	United Kingdom	44
5	Italy	41
	Ex-Yugoslavia	41
7	Finland	40
8	Ireland	37
	Netherlands	37
10	Denmark	35
11	Norway	32
12	Greece	31
13	Turkey	27

1980

1	Ex-Czechoslovakia	63
2	Bulgaria	54
	Russia	54
4	Belarus	53
	Lithuania	53
6	Estonia	49
7	Azerbaijan	47
8	United Kingdom	43
9	Austria	40
	Finland	40
	Norway	40
12	Italy	39
13	Albania	37
14	Greece	35
15	Belgium	34
	France	34
	Sweden	34
18	Denmark	30
	Turkey	30

1990

1	Ex-Czechoslovakia	56
2	Bulgaria	52
3	Latvia	48
	Romania	48
	Russia	48
	Ex-Yugoslavia	48
7	Germany[a]	39
8	Austria	37
9	Finland	36
10	Sweden	35
11	Italy	33
	Turkey	33
13	Hungary	32
14	Belgium	31
	Netherlands	31

1994

1	Belarus	54		Slovakia	36
2	Ukraine	50	10	Bulgaria	35
3	Lithuania	41	11	Austria	34
4	Poland	40		Latvia	34
5	Czech Republic	39	13	Hungary	33
6	Russia	38		Romania	33
	Slovenia	38	15	Azerbaijan	32
8	Estonia	36		Finland	32

a Western Germany.

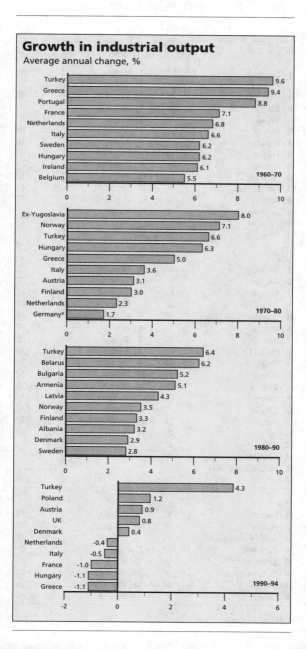

Growth in industrial output

Average annual change, %

1960–70

Turkey	9.6
Greece	9.4
Portugal	8.8
France	7.1
Netherlands	6.8
Italy	6.6
Sweden	6.2
Hungary	6.2
Ireland	6.1
Belgium	5.5

1970–80

Ex-Yugoslavia	8.0
Norway	7.1
Turkey	6.6
Hungary	6.3
Greece	5.0
Italy	3.6
Austria	3.1
Finland	3.0
Netherlands	2.3
Germany[a]	1.7

1980–90

Turkey	6.4
Belarus	6.2
Bulgaria	5.2
Armenia	5.1
Latvia	4.3
Norway	3.5
Finland	3.3
Albania	3.2
Denmark	2.9
Sweden	2.8

1990–94

Turkey	4.3
Poland	1.2
Austria	0.9
UK	0.8
Denmark	0.4
Netherlands	-0.4
Italy	-0.5
France	-1.0
Hungary	-1.1
Greece	-1.1

Services' contribution

Services' output
As % of GDP

1960

1	Denmark	58
	Norway	58
3	United Kingdom	54
4	Belgium	53
	Sweden	53
6	Ireland	52
7	Greece	51
8	France	50
9	Finland	48
10	Italy	47
11	Netherlands	45
12	Austria	42
13	Germany[a]	41
14	Portugal	39
15	Turkey	38

1970

1	Norway	62
2	Denmark	59
3	Netherlands	57
4	United Kingdom	53
5	Italy	51
6	Greece	50
7	Austria	48
	Finland	48
9	Germany[a]	47
10	Ireland	46
11	Turkey	43
12	Ex-Yugoslavia	41
13	Hungary	37

1980

1	Denmark	65
2	Belgium	64
3	France	62
	Sweden	62
5	Norway	57
6	Austria	56
7	Italy	55
	United Kingdom	55
9	Finland	51
10	Turkey	47
11	Belarus	45
12	Greece	44
13	Estonia	37
	Russia	37
15	Albania	35
16	Bulgaria	32
17	Azerbaijan	31
18	Ex-Czechoslovakia	30
19	Lithuania	29

1990

1	Poland	80
2	Belgium	67
	Denmark	67
	France	67
5	Netherlands	65
6	Italy	63
7	Sweden	62
8	Austria	60
9	Germany[a]	59
10	Finland	58
11	Greece	56
	Hungary	56
13	Turkey	49
14	Ex-Yugoslavia	40
15	Russia	39

1994

1	Ireland	83	9	Croatia	62
2	France	70	10	Hungary	60
	Netherlands	70		Italy	60
4	Denmark	69	12	Latvia	57
5	Sweden	68		Slovakia	57
6	United Kingdom	66		Slovenia	57
7	Austria	64	15	Czech Republic	55
8	Finland	63		Estonia	55

a Western Germany.

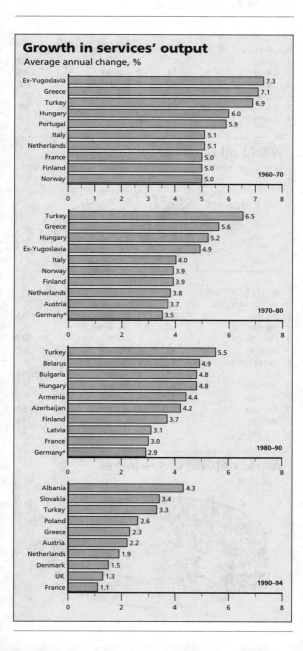

Growth in services' output
Average annual change, %

1960–70

Ex-Yugoslavia	7.3
Greece	7.1
Turkey	6.9
Hungary	6.0
Portugal	5.9
Italy	5.1
Netherlands	5.1
France	5.0
Finland	5.0
Norway	5.0

1970–80

Turkey	6.5
Greece	5.6
Hungary	5.2
Ex-Yugoslavia	4.9
Italy	4.0
Norway	3.9
Finland	3.9
Netherlands	3.8
Austria	3.7
Germany[a]	3.5

1980–90

Turkey	5.5
Belarus	4.9
Bulgaria	4.8
Hungary	4.8
Armenia	4.4
Azerbaijan	4.2
Finland	3.7
Latvia	3.1
France	3.0
Germany[a]	2.9

1990–94

Albania	4.3
Slovakia	3.4
Turkey	3.3
Poland	2.6
Greece	2.3
Austria	2.2
Netherlands	1.9
Denmark	1.5
UK	1.3
France	1.1

Mineral resources

Oil reserves
Proved reserves, 1995

1	Russia	6.7
2	Norway	1.1
3	United Kingdom	0.6
4	Romania	0.2
5	Azerbaijan	0.2
6	Denmark	0.1

Oil production
'000 barrels daily, 1995

1	Russia	6,200
2	Norway	2,995
3	United Kingdom	2,755
4	Denmark	190
5	Azerbaijan	185
6	Romania	140

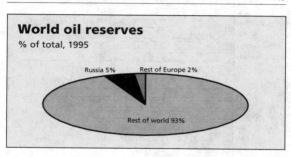

World oil reserves
% of total, 1995

Russia 5% Rest of Europe 2%

Rest of world 93%

Natural gas reserves
Proved reserves, 1995

1	Russia	48.1
2	Norway	2.0
3	Netherlands	1.9
4	Ukraine	1.1
5	United Kingdom	0.6
6	Italy	0.4
7	Germany	0.3
	Romania	0.3
9	Denmark	0.1
	Hungary	0.1
	Azerbaijan	0.1

Natural gas production
M tonnes of oil equivalent, 1995

1	Russia	499.9
2	United Kingdom	64.4
3	Netherlands	59.7
4	Norway	28.2
5	Italy	16.2
6	Romania	15.3
7	Ukraine	15.2
8	Germany	14.5
9	Azerbaijan	5.5
10	Denmark	4.5
11	Hungary	4.1

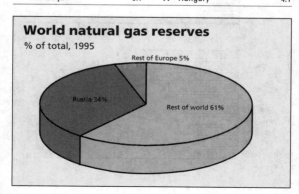

World natural gas reserves
% of total, 1995

Rest of Europe 5%

Russia 34%

Rest of world 61%

Bituminous coal
M tonnes, 1990

Proved reserves			Recoverable reserves		
1	United Kingdom	190,000	1	Ex Soviet Union	104,000
2	Ex Soviet Union	130,000	2	Poland	29,600
3	Poland	65,800	3	Germany	23,919
4	Germany	44,000	4	United Kingdom	3,300
5	Spain	1,750	5	Spain	850
6	Hungary	1,407	6	Hungary	596
7	Netherlands	1,406	7	Netherlands	497
8	France	745	8	Belgium	410
9	Belgium	715	9	France	178
10	Turkey	590	10	Turkey	162
11	Bulgaria	36	11	Bulgaria	30
12	Portugal	8	12	Portugal	3

Rough stone production
'000 tonnes, 1993

1	Italy	7,250	8	United Kingdom	715
2	Spain	3,100	9	Finland	414
3	Greece	1,900	10	Belgium	340
4	Ex-Comecon countries	1,787	11	Germany	210
5	Portugal	1,145	12	Norway	160
6	France	1,019	13	Sweden	100
7	Turkey	850	14	Austria	22

Natural wealth compared
$ '000 per person

	Estimated wealth	Human resources	Produced assets	Natural capital
Luxembourg	658	548.39	81.61	27.70
Switzerland	647	505.57	123.06	18.68
Sweden	496	276.45	77.03	142.66
Iceland	486	110.54	77.43	298.26
Denmark	463	351.43	78.98	32.22
Norway	424	203.09	94.97	125.94
France	413	317.65	68.32	27.36
Germany	399	313.24	66.13	19.51
Austria	394	295.42	71.26	27.59
Belgium	384	317.39	59.62	7.24
Netherlands	379	303.57	68.33	7.14
Italy	373	305.61	54.72	13.01
Finland	347	116.62	97.99	132.15
United Kingdom	324	267.57	45.99	10.04
Ireland	212	161.11	30.99	19.86
Greece	142	106.33	20.31	14.92
Portugal	141	114.79	16.67	9.92
Malta	134	111.15	21.90	0.59

Energy

Who produces most
M tonnes of coal equivalent, 1993

1	Russia	1,486.0
2	United Kingdom	329.7
3	Norway	217.2
4	Germany	210.8
5	France	161.9
6	Ukraine	153.6
7	Poland	132.3
8	Netherlands	106.2
9	Czech Republic	49.1
10	Romania	45.9
11	Italy	41.8
12	Spain	41.1
13	Sweden	32.4
14	Hungary	18.2
15	Denmark	17.9
16	Belgium	16.0
17	Switzerland	13.2
18	Bulgaria	12.8
19	Greece	12.0
20	Serbia	11.8
21	Finland	11.1
22	Austria	9.0
23	Slovakia	6.3
24	Croatia	6.1
25	Ireland	5.2
26	Lithuania	4.7
27	Belarus	4.2
28	Estonia	4.1
29	Slovenia	2.9
	Macedonia FYR	2.9
31	Albania	1.5

Who uses most
M tonnes of coal equivalent,, 1993

1	Russia	1,025.0
2	Germany	382.8
3	United Kingdom	324.8
4	France	312.3
5	Ukraine	274.9
6	Italy	230.3
7	Poland	138.4
8	Spain	114.6
9	Netherlands	112.8
10	Belgium	67.4
11	Romania	60.1
12	Sweden	56.6
13	Czech Republic	56.6
14	Belarus	42.6
15	Finland	34.6
16	Hungary	33.8
17	Greece	33.7
18	Switzerland	33.6
19	Austria	33.0
20	Bulgaria	32.9
21	Norway	30.9
22	Denmark	26.0
23	Slovakia	22.9
24	Portugal	20.6
25	Ireland	14.6
26	Serbia	13.0
27	Lithuania	12.6
28	Croatia	9.0
29	Moldova	8.0
30	Estonia	7.3
31	Slovenia	6.6

Highest consumption per head
Kg of coal equivalent,, 1993

1	Luxembourg	13,848	16	Estonia	4,698
2	Netherlands	7,381	17	Slovakia	4,313
3	Norway	7,172	18	Austria	4,191
4	Iceland	7,053	19	Belarus	4,182
5	Russia	6,937	20	Ireland	4,149
6	Finland	6,838	21	Italy	4,029
7	Belgium	6,711	22	Bulgaria	3,711
8	Sweden	6,516	23	Poland	3,613
9	Germany	6,241	24	Slovenia	3,424
10	United Kingdom	5,586	25	Lithuania	3,383
11	Czech Republic	5,499	26	Hungary	3,309
12	France	5,428	27	Greece	3,252
13	Ukraine	5,333	28	Spain	2,901
14	Denmark	5,032	29	Romania	2,611
15	Switzerland	4,745	30	Latvia	2,445

Biggest importers
M tonnes of coal equivalent,, 1993

1	Germany	231.0
2	Italy	201.7
3	France	194.7
4	Ukraine	133.8
5	Netherlands	132.1
6	United Kingdom	124.2
7	Spain	103.9
8	Belgium	87.5
9	Russia	57.6
10	Belarus	40.6
	Sweden	40.6
12	Greece	29.8
13	Poland	28.9
14	Finland	26.7
	Austria	26.7
16	Portugal	26.2
17	Bulgaria	24.0
18	Denmark	23.8
19	Switzerland	23.2
20	Romania	21.9
21	Czech Republic	21.4
22	Hungary	19.8
23	Slovakia	19.3
24	Lithuania	14.0
25	Ireland	10.9
26	Moldova	8.2
27	Croatia	7.5
28	Latvia	6.7
29	Norway	6.4
30	Luxembourg	5.4

Biggest exporters
M tonnes of coal equivalent,, 1993

1	Russia	471.5
2	Norway	187.7
3	United Kingdom	121.6
4	Netherlands	117.2
5	Italy	31.6
6	France	30.5
7	Belgium	26.9
8	Germany	23.8
9	Poland	23.4
10	Denmark	15.8
11	Sweden	14.5
12	Spain	14.0
13	Czech Republic	11.5
14	Ukraine	6.8
15	Lithuania	6.2
16	Greece	4.9
17	Finland	4.8
18	Portugal	4.4
19	Switzerland	4.2
20	Romania	4.0
21	Croatia	3.6
22	Slovakia	2.2
23	Austria	1.8
	Belarus	1.8
	Hungary	1.8
26	Latvia	1.3
27	Ireland	1.1
28	Bulgaria	0.9
29	Estonia	0.3
	Slovenia	0.3

Leading electricity generators
M kilowatts, 1993

1	Russia	213.4	17	Belgium	14.1
2	France	143.6	18	Bulgaria	12.1
3	Germany	114.3	19	Serbia	10.4
4	United Kingdom	68.5		Denmark	10.4
5	Italy	63.5	21	Greece	8.8
6	Ukraine	54.3	22	Portugal	8.7
7	Spain	43.9	23	Belarus	7.2
8	Sweden	37.2	24	Slovakia	7.1
9	Austria	33.0	25	Hungary	6.7
10	Poland	29.2	26	Lithuania	5.4
11	Norway	27.3	27	Ireland	3.9
12	Romania	22.3	28	Croatia	3.5
13	Netherlands	17.6	29	Bosnia & Hercegovina	3.4
14	Switzerland	15.6	30	Estonia	3.3
15	Czech Republic	14.2	31	Moldova	3.0
16	Finland	14.1	32	Slovenia	2.5

Current account balances

Recent picture
Current account balance, 1995

As % of GDP			$m		
1	Ireland	6.56	1	Italy	25,682
2	Switzerland	6.55	2	Switzerland	19,900
3	Belgium & Luxembourg	5.60	3	France	17,479
4	Latvia[a]	4.50	4	Netherlands	16,269
5	Netherlands	4.12	5	Russia	12,261
6	Slovakia	3.64	6	Norway	5,100
7	Norway	3.49	7	Sweden	4,633
8	Finland	3.49	8	Finland	4,394
9	Russia	3.37	9	Ireland	4,000
10	Italy	2.36	10	Spain	1,280
11	Sweden	2.02	11	Slovakia	635
12	France	1.14	12	Denmark	503
13	Iceland	0.87	13	Latvia[a]	201
14	Denmark	0.29	14	Iceland	61
15	Slovenia	0.23	15	Slovenia	42
16	Spain	0.23	16	Belgium & Luxembourg	15
17	Portugal	-0.31	17	Armenia[a]	-15
18	Germany	-0.82	18	Lithuania	-114
19	United Kingdom	-0.96	19	Albania[a]	-146
20	Turkey	-1.40	20	Macedonia FYR	-170
21	Lithuania	-1.87	21	Azerbaijan[a]	-179
22	Poland	-1.90	22	Moldova[a]	-180
23	Austria	-2.19	23	Estonia	-200
24	Armenia[a]	-2.30	24	Cyprus	-212
25	Bulgaria[a]	-2.31	25	Bulgaria[a]	-300
26	Cyprus	-2.48	26	Portugal	-300
27	Greece	-2.51	27	Malta	-366
28	Romania	-3.60	28	Georgia[a]	-500
29	Ukraine	-3.72	29	Ukraine	-1,152
30	Czech Republic	-4.17	30	Romania	-1,300
31	Azerbaijan[a]	-4.80	31	Croatia	-1,712
32	Estonia	-5.46	32	Czech Republic	-1,906
33	Hungary	-7.16	33	Poland	-2,180
34	Albania[a]	-8.31	34	Turkey	-2,340
35	Belarus[a]	-8.40	35	Greece	-2,864
36	Moldova[a]	-9.04	36	Hungary	-3,200
37	Croatia	-9.65	37	Austria	-5,113
38	Macedonia FYR	-10.28	38	United Kingdom	-10,569
39	Malta	-10.88	39	Germany	-19,770
40	Georgia[a]	-15.96			

a 1994.

Looking back
Current account balance as % GDP

Top 5, 1960			Bottom 5, 1960		
1	Malta	8.69	1	Iceland	-4.10
2	Spain	3.78	2	Norway	-2.47
3	Netherlands	3.13	3	Greece	-1.57
4	Western Germany	1.53	4	Austria	-1.42
5	Switzerland	1.09	5	United Kingdom	-1.00

Top 10, 1970			Bottom 10, 1970		
1	Belgium & Luxembourg	2.78	1	Ireland	-5.00
2	Switzerland	1.71	2	Greece	-4.24
3	United Kingdom	1.60	3	Denmark	-3.44
4	Italy	0.80	4	Finland	-2.20
5	Hungary	0.63	5	Norway	-2.17
6	Western Germany	0.46	6	Malta	-2.11
7	Iceland	0.42	7	Netherlands	-1.75
8	Spain	0.21	8	Sweden	-0.80
9	Cyprus	0.00	9	Austria	-0.52
10	France	-0.14	10	Turkey	-0.34

Top 10, 1980			Bottom 10, 1980		
1	Malta	3.42	1	Ireland	-11.07
2	Norway	1.87	2	Romania	-7.06
3	United Kingdom	1.27	3	Poland	-6.02
4	Cyprus	-0.01	4	Greece	-5.50
5	Switzerland	-0.20	5	Austria	-5.03
6	Netherlands	-0.58	6	Portugal	-4.24
7	France	-0.63	7	Belgium & Luxembourg	-4.18
8	Western Germany	-1.64	8	Denmark	-3.70
9	Italy	-2.34	9	Sweden	-3.47
10	Iceland	-2.35	10	Finland	-2.73

Top 10, 1990			Bottom 10, 1990		
1	Poland	5.20	1	Romania	-8.51
2	Norway	3.46	2	Russia[b]	-7.10
3	Netherlands	3.25	3	Slovakia	-7.00
4	Switzerland	3.07	4	Bulgaria	-6.30
5	Germany[a]	2.58	5	Finland	-5.15
6	Belgium & Luxembourg	1.89	6	Greece	-4.32
7	Hungary	1.15	7	Spain	-3.66
8	Denmark	1.06	8	Cyprus	-3.42
9	Austria	0.74	9	United Kingdom	-3.40
10	Portugal	-0.27	10	Sweden	-3.00

a Includes Eastern Germany from July 1990.
b Convertible currencies only.

Biggest visible traders

Recent picture
Exports plus imports, 1995

		% of GDP			$m
1	Macedonia FYR	83.18	1	Germany	956,335
2	Armenia	81.21	2	France	561,666
3	Malta	72.30	3	United Kingdom	505,550
4	Estonia	62.87	4	Italy	435,398
5	Ireland	62.29	5	Netherlands	371,639
6	Belgium & Luxembourg	59.93	6	Belgium	322,680
7	Czech Republic	52.66	7	Spain	206,740
8	Slovenia	49.05	8	Switzerland	154,634
9	Slovakia	48.88	9	Sweden	144,346
10	Lithuania	47.48	10	Russia	137,010
11	Netherlands	47.01	11	Austria	120,700
12	Moldova	38.02	12	Denmark	92,259
13	Bulgaria	37.69	13	Ireland	75,995
14	Ukraine	37.05	14	Norway	74,448
15	Latvia	35.77	15	Finland	67,687
16	Croatia	34.40	16	Turkey	57,310
17	Sweden	31.49	17	Portugal	54,659
18	Hungary	30.89	18	Poland	51,942
19	Cyprus	28.83	19	Czech Republic	48,091
20	Portugal	28.00	20	Greece	36,981
21	Finland	26.87	21	Hungary	27,613
22	Denmark	26.67	22	Ukraine	22,946
23	Austria	25.86	23	Slovenia	17,738
24	Norway	25.47	24	Slovakia	17,044
25	Switzerland	25.44	25	Romania	16,972
26	Iceland	25.26	26	Croatia	12,215
27	Albania[a]	25.20	27	Bulgaria	9,800
28	Romania	23.90	28	Belarus	9,410
29	United Kingdom	22.89	29	Lithuania	5,790
30	Poland	22.07	30	Cyprus	4,923
31	Georgia	20.75	31	Malta	4,864
32	Italy	19.97	32	Estonia	4,610
33	Germany	19.81	33	Iceland	3,560
34	Azerbaijan	19.10	34	Latvia	3,199
35	Russia	18.83	35	Macedonia FYR	2,750
36	Spain	18.49	36	Moldova	1,514
37	France	18.26	40	Azerbaijan	1,425
38	Turkey	17.16	38	Georgia	1,300
39	Greece	16.17	39	Armenia	1,059
40	Belarus[a]	12.71	40	Albania[a]	885

a 1994.

Looking back

Exports and imports, $m

1960

1	United Kingdom	23,637	6	Belgium & Luxembourg	7,640
2	Western Germany	21,588	7	Sweden	5,467
3	France	13,149	8	Switzerland	4,066
4	Netherlands	8,559	9	Denmark	3,301
5	Italy	8,391	10	Austria	2,536

1970

1	Western Germany	64,175	11	Spain	7,135
2	United Kingdom	41,294	12	Austria	6,406
3	France	36,998	13	Norway	6,157
4	Netherlands	28,917	14	Finland	4,944
5	Italy	28,179	15	Ex-Yugoslavia	4,553
6	Belgium & Luxembourg	22,854	16	Romania	3,968
7	Sweden	13,802	17	Hungary	3,603
8	Switzerland	11,441	18	Ireland	2,742
9	Denmark	7,763	19	Greece	2,601
10	Poland	7,156	20	Portugal	2,502

1980

1	Western Germany	380,862	11	Denmark	36,089
2	France	250,896	12	Norway	35,488
3	United Kingdom	225,679	13	Poland	30,881
4	Italy	178,845	14	Finland	29,785
5	Netherlands	173,438	15	Romania	25,052
6	Belgium & Luxembourg	136,400	16	Ex-Yugoslavia	24,054
7	Switzerland	65,973	17	Ireland	19,551
8	Sweden	64,344	18	Hungary	17,857
9	Spain	54,798	19	Greece	15,701
10	Austria	41,933	20	Portugal	13,949

1990

1	France	451,024	11	Austria	90,411
2	Germany	410,104	12	Denmark	67,361
3	United Kingdom	408,149	13	Norway	61,278
4	Italy	352,454	14	Finland	53,572
5	Germany	346,153	15	Ireland	44,412
6	Netherlands	257,873	16	Portugal	41,680
7	Belgium & Luxembourg	237,405	17	Turkey	35,261
8	Spain	143,357	18	Ex-Yugoslavia	33,179
9	Switzerland	133,465	19	Greece	27,882
10	Sweden	111,804	20	Poland	22,040

Visible trade balances

Recent picture
Visible trade balance, 1995

	As % of GDP				$m	
1	Malta	31.22		1	Germany	66,010
2	Ireland	17.87		2	Italy	44,046
3	Sweden	6.97		3	Russia	22,754
4	Belarus	6.90		4	Netherlands	19,138
5	Russia	6.25		5	Sweden	15,973
6	Norway	5.75		6	France	12,045
7	Netherlands	4.84		7	Ireland	10,900
8	Italy	4.04		8	Belgium & Luxembourg	8,800
9	Denmark	3.86		9	Norway	8,400
10	Finland	3.49		10	Denmark	6,685
11	Belgium & Luxembourg	3.27		11	Finland	4,394
12	Bulgaria	3.08		12	Malta	1,050
13	Iceland	2.93		13	Switzerland	700
14	Germany	2.73		14	Bulgaria	400
15	France	0.78		15	Iceland	207
16	Switzerland	0.23		16	Slovakia	23
17	Slovakia	0.13		17	Moldova	-100
18	United Kingdom	-1.65		18	Azerbaijan	-177
19	Poland	-2.22		19	Armenia	-179
20	Austria	-2.33		20	Georgia	-300
21	Spain	-3.17		21	Lithuania	-313
22	Romania	-3.38		22	Estonia	-400
23	Slovenia	-4.32		23	Latvia	-400
24	Azerbaijan	-4.75		24	Albania	-460
25	Moldova	-5.02		25	Slovenia	-782
26	Lithuania	-5.13		26	Romania	-1,200
27	Hungary	-7.38		27	Croatia	-2,126
28	Portugal	-7.89		28	Cyprus	-2,323
29	Turkey	-7.91		29	Poland	-2,610
30	Czech Republic	-8.65		30	Ukraine	-2,702
31	Ukraine	-8.72		31	Hungary	-3,300
32	Latvia	-8.95		32	Czech Republic	-3,951
33	Georgia	-9.58		33	Austria	-5,446
34	Estonia	-10.91		34	Portugal	-7,700
35	Croatia	-11.98		35	Turkey	-13,210
36	Greece	-12.62		36	Greece	-14,425
37	Albania	-26.20		37	Spain	-17,721
38	Cyprus	-27.21		38	United Kingdom	-18,266
39	Armenia	-27.45				

Looking back
Visible trade balance as % of GDP

Top 5, 1960

1	Western Germany	2.91
2	Spain	0.40
3	Belgium & Luxembourg	0.12
4	Finland	-0.04
5	Sweden	-0.81

Bottom 5, 1960

1	Malta	-47.82
2	Cyprus	-17.23
3	Norway	-10.18
4	Ireland	-10.05
5	Greece	-7.13

Top 10, 1970

1	Western Germany	3.07
2	Belgium & Luxembourg	1.80
3	Sweden	0.91
4	Iceland	0.54
5	France	0.18
6	United Kingdom	0.00
7	Cyprus	-0.02
8	Italy	-0.38
9	Finland	-1.62
10	Hungary	-1.84

Bottom 10, 1970

1	Malta	-41.40
2	Ireland	-10.91
3	Norway	-10.32
4	Greece	-9.00
5	Switzerland	-5.09
6	Spain	-5.07
7	Denmark	-4.80
8	Austria	-4.67
9	Netherlands	-2.70
10	Turkey	-1.89

Top 10, 1980

1	Norway	3.29
2	Western Germany	0.98
3	United Kingdom	0.62
4	Iceland	0.61
5	Cyprus	-0.03
6	Netherlands	-0.06
7	Hungary	-0.65
8	Finland	-1.33
9	Sweden	-1.76
10	France	-2.12

Bottom 10, 1980

1	Malta	-30.57
2	Portugal	-15.72
3	Greece	-13.80
4	Ireland	-11.53
5	Austria	-8.44
6	Spain	-5.54
7	Switzerland	-5.17
8	Romania	-4.85
9	Italy	-3.51
10	Belgium & Luxembourg	-3.27

Top 10, 1990

1	Ireland	8.80
2	Norway	6.73
3	Poland	6.09
4	Netherlands	4.25
5	Germany	3.83
6	Denmark	3.78
7	Hungary	1.62
8	Sweden	1.61
9	Iceland	1.27
10	Belgium & Luxembourg	0.87

Bottom 10, 1990

1	Cyprus	-27.98
2	Malta	-24.22
3	Greece	-12.35
4	Portugal	-9.94
5	Romania	-8.74
6	Turkey	-6.35
7	Spain	-5.93
8	Austria	-4.40
9	Bulgaria	-4.17
10	United Kingdom	-3.33

Biggest invisible traders

Recent picture
Invisibles trade, total credits and debits, 1995

As % of GDP			$m		
1	Belgium & Luxembourg	105.7	1	France	436,290
2	Malta[a]	61.7	2	United Kingdom	402,260
3	Denmark	53.3	3	Germany	389,580
4	Ireland	52.0	4	Belgium & Luxembourg	284,500
5	Cyprus[a]	46.2	5	Italy	219,859
6	Netherlands	38.5	6	Netherlands	152,127
7	United Kingdom	36.4	7	Switzerland	93,200
8	Croatia	32.2	8	Denmark	92,291
9	Switzerland	30.7	9	Sweden	68,110
10	Czech Republic	30.4	10	Austria	66,894
11	Sweden	29.7	11	Spain	56,933
12	Austria	28.7	12	Russia	44,354
13	France	28.4	13	Norway	41,400
14	Norway	28.3	14	Ireland	31,700
15	Estonia[a]	28.1	15	Finland	27,656
16	Slovakia	27.2	16	Turkey	25,810
17	Latvia[a]	23.4	17	Portugal	22,351
18	Hungary	23.3	18	Greece	18,281
19	Portugal	22.9	19	Czech Republic	13,887
20	Finland	22.0	20	Poland	12,390
21	Slovenia	21.6	21	Hungary	10,400
22	Iceland[a]	21.5	22	Croatia	5,717
23	Italy	20.2	23	Ukraine	5,108
24	Ukraine	16.5	24	Slovakia	4,736
25	Germany	16.1	25	Cyprus[a]	3,946
26	Greece	16.0	26	Slovenia	3,905
27	Turkey	15.5	27	Romania	3,500
28	Russia	12.2	28	Malta[a]	2,074
29	Lithuania[a]	12.0	29	Iceland[a]	1,515
30	Poland	10.5	30	Latvia[a]	1,047
31	Spain	10.2	31	Estonia[a]	1,029
32	Romania	9.9	32	Lithuania[a]	733

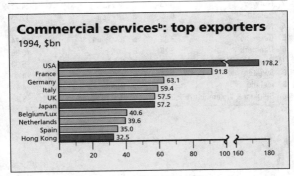

Commercial services[b]: top exporters
1994, $bn

USA	178.2
France	91.8
Germany	63.1
Italy	59.4
UK	57.5
Japan	57.2
Belgium/Lux	40.6
Netherlands	39.6
Spain	35.0
Hong Kong	32.5

0   20   40   60   80   100 160   180

a 1994.   b Transportation, travel and other private services.

Looking back
Invisible trade, total credits and debits, $m

	1990			*1980*	
1	United Kingdom	387,040	1	United Kingdom	176,733
2	France	367,691	2	France	114,816
3	Germany[a]	248,320	3	Germany[a]	102,430
4	Belgium & Luxembourg	183,770	4	Belgium & Luxembourg	62,545
5	Italy	153,636	5	Netherlands	59,289
6	Netherlands	114,273	6	Italy	49,524
7	Switzerland	78,711	7	Switzerland	29,321
8	Spain	63,158	8	Spain	22,133
9	Austria	56,708	9	Austria	21,159
10	Sweden	54,635	10	Norway	19,508
11	Denmark	40,778	11	Sweden	18,362
12	Norway	35,615	12	Denmark	15,199
13	Finland	23,091	13	Finland	7,131
14	Ireland	18,458	14	Poland	6,676
15	Turkey	15,429	15	Greece	6,152
16	Portugal	11,918	16	Ireland	5,492
17	Greece	11,899	17	Portugal	4,485
18	Poland	10,639	18	Hungary	3,688
19	Hungary	7,271	19	Romania	3,031
20	Cyprus	3,116	20	Turkey	2,500
21	Malta	1,636	21	Cyprus	1,821
22	Romania	1,586	22	Malta	935
23	Iceland	1,492	23	Iceland	683

	1970			*1960*	
1	United Kingdom	20,961	1	United Kingdom	11,034
2	France	14,267	2	Germany[a]	6,000
3	Italy	13,588	3	Italy	3,043
4	Netherlands	8,188	4	Netherlands	2,131
5	Belgium & Luxembourg	6,185	5	Belgium & Luxembourg	1,764
6	Poland	5,417	6	Sweden	1,539
7	Switzerland	5,179	7	Norway	1,486
8	Norway	3,698	8	Switzerland	1,438
9	Sweden	3,427	9	Denmark	805
10	Austria	2,393	10	Spain	614
11	Denmark	2,205	11	Austria	576
12	Germany[a]	1,951	12	Finland	402
13	Spain	1,782	13	Greece	387
14	Ireland	1,277	14	Ireland	286
15	Finland	1,016	15	Turkey	237
16	Greece	847	16	Malta	101
17	Hungary	608	17	Cyprus	86
18	Turkey	508	18	Iceland	58
19	Cyprus	188			
20	Iceland	177			
21	Malta	151			

a Western only up to June 1990.

Invisible trade balances

The recent picture
Invisible trade balance
1995

	As % of GDP			$m	
1	Cyprus	24.70	1	Switzerland	23,500
2	Switzerland	7.73	2	United Kingdom	19,472
3	Slovenia	4.40	3	Spain	13,899
4	Turkey	3.82	4	France	12,176
5	Belgium & Luxembourg	3.53	5	Belgium & Luxembourg	9,500
6	Finland	3.49	6	Turkey	6,380
7	Ukraine	3.48	7	Finland	4,394
8	Czech Republic	3.18	8	Greece	3,553
9	Greece	3.11	9	Netherlands	3,471
10	Slovakia	3.02	10	Cyprus	2,109
11	Spain	2.49	11	Austria	1,836
12	United Kingdom	1.76	12	Czech Republic	1,453
13	Netherlands	0.88	13	Ukraine	1,078
14	France	0.79	14	Slovenia	796
15	Austria	0.79	15	Slovakia	526
16	Portugal	0.41	16	Portugal	400
17	Poland	-0.44	17	Iceland	-149
18	Romania	-0.85	18	Bulgaria	-200
19	Italy	-1.26	19	Croatia	-232
20	Norway	-1.37	20	Romania	-300
21	Bulgaria	-1.54	21	Poland	-520
22	Germany	-1.87	22	Hungary	-1,200
23	Iceland	-2.11	23	Norway	-2,000
24	Hungary	-2.68	24	Denmark	-5,221
25	Russia	-3.01	25	Sweden	-8,348
26	Denmark	-3.02	26	Ireland	-9,800
27	Sweden	-3.64	27	Russia	-10,944
28	Croatia	-6.82	28	Italy	-13,746
29	Ireland	-16.07	29	Germany	-45,240

Current transfers
$m, 1995

Biggest net inflows			Biggest net outflows		
1	Greece	8,008	1	Germany	-40,540
2	Portugal	7,131	2	United Kingdom	-11,776
3	Spain	5,102	3	France	-6,742
4	Turkey	4,500	4	Netherlands	-6,340
5	Ireland	1,800	5	Italy	-4,625
6	Hungary	1,100	6	Switzerland	-3,400
7	Poland	950	7	Sweden	-2,991
8	Croatia	646	8	Belgium	-2,958
9	Czech Republic	600	9	Austria	-1,503
10	Albania	477	10	Norway	-1,300
11	Ukraine	472	11	Denmark	-862
12	Russia	451	12	Finland	-411
13	Romania	300	13	Iceland[a]	-9

a 1994.

Looking back
Invisible trade balance as % of GDP

Top 5, 1960
1	Malta	43.44
2	Cyprus	8.38
3	Norway	8.02
4	Ireland	6.60
5	Netherlands	4.14

Bottom 5, 1960
1	Finland	-0.87
2	Turkey	-0.59
3	Western Germany	-0.25
4	Sweden	0.28
5	Belgium	0.74

Top 10, 1970
1	Malta	22.23
2	Switzerland	8.38
3	Norway	8.25
4	Austria	4.09
5	Spain	3.50
6	Ireland	3.26
7	United Kingdom	1.96
8	Denmark	1.64
9	Belgium	1.58
10	Greece	1.29

Bottom 10, 1970
1	Sweden	-1.25
2	Western Germany	-1.19
3	Turkey	-1.03
4	Finland	-0.53
5	Iceland	-0.04
6	Cyprus	0.01
7	France	0.29
8	Hungary	0.76
9	Italy	0.97
10	Netherlands	1.06

Top 10, 1980
1	Malta	29.39
2	Switzerland	6.09
3	Greece	5.59
4	Austria	3.50
5	Spain	2.13
6	France	2.11
7	United Kingdom	1.50
8	Italy	0.93
9	Netherlands	0.24
10	Belgium & Luxembourg	0.13

Bottom 10, 1980
1	Ireland	-5.78
2	Poland	-4.16
3	Iceland	-2.92
4	Romania	-2.21
5	Hungary	-2.17
6	Finland	-1.18
7	Western Germany	-1.03
8	Sweden	-0.73
9	Denmark	-0.70
10	Norway	-0.52

Top 10, 1990
1	Cyprus	24.09
2	Malta	18.05
3	Switzerland	7.28
4	Austria	5.14
5	Greece	2.26
6	Belgium & Luxembourg	2.16
7	Spain	1.70
8	Turkey	1.62
9	Portugal	1.48
10	France	0.96

Bottom 10, 1990
1	Ireland	-14.50
2	Poland	-5.14
3	Finland	-4.97
4	Russia	-4.87
5	Sweden	-3.70
6	Iceland	-3.42
7	Hungary	-2.85
8	Bulgaria	-2.60
9	Denmark	-2.40
10	Norway	-1.99

Who exports to whom

Most important export destinations

Exports to main partners and to EU 15 countries as % of total exports

1995	Main ptnrs	EU 15		Main ptnrs	EU 15
Armenia		17.7	**Estonia**		60.7
Russia	32.5		Finland	16.5	
Turkmenistan	25.5		Russia	12.9	
Austria		59.3	**Finland**		56.7
Germany	32.2		Germany	13.5	
Italy	9.4		United Kingdom	10.4	
Azerbaijan		17.3	**France**		62.9
Iran	30.0		Germany	17.5	
Russia	18.2		Italy	9.6	
Belarus		32.7	**Georgia**		18.2
Germany	15.7		Armenia	27.6	
Poland	12.0		Russia	26.1	
Belgium & Lux		71.6	**Germany**		57.0
Germany	20.3		France	11.6	
France	16.8		United Kingdom	8.0	
Bulgaria		49.4	**Greece**		55.5
Germany	11.9		Germany	18.6	
Italy	10.7		Italy	13.7	
Croatia		55.6	**Hungary**		64.4
Italy	22.5		Germany	29.4	
Germany	20.9		Austria	10.4	
Cyprus		34.8	**Iceland**		63.1
United Kingdom	14.0		United Kingdom	19.3	
Russia	9.1		Germany	13.9	
Czech Republic		46.4	**Ireland**		72.2
Germany	28.2		United Kingdom	25.5	
Slovakia	13.0		Germany	14.4	
Denmark		49.4	**Italy**		56.9
Germany	15.1		Germany	18.7	
Sweden	9.9		France	13.0	

1970	Main ptnrs	EU 15		Main ptnrs	EU 15
Austria		56.3	**Germany, Western**[a]		59.4
Western Germany	23.7		France	12.4	
Switzerland	10.4		Netherlands	10.6	
Belgium & Lux		78.1	**Greece**		56.6
Western Germany	24.1		Western Germany	20.2	
France	19.9		Italy	10.0	
Denmark		63.3	**Iceland**		40.3
United Kingdom	18.6		United States	30.0	
Sweden	16.6		United Kingdom	13.2	
Finland		63.7	**Ireland**		73.1
United Kingdom	17.4		United Kingdom	60.8	
Sweden	15.1		United States	9.2	
France		59.6	**Italy**		55.3
Western Germany	20.4		Western Germany	21.6	
Italy	11.0		France	12.8	

	Main ptnrs	EU 15		Main ptnrs	EU 15
Latvia		44.3	**Russia**		33.0
Russia	24.9		Ukraine	8.7	
Germany	13.9		Germany	7.7	
Lithuania		44.4	**Serbia**		89.7
Germany	14.4		Italy	76.9	
Russia	13.0		Germany	10.3	
Macedonia FYR		64.6	**Slovakia**		42.1
Germany	29.5		Czech Republic	32.9	
Italy	19.2		Germany	23.4	
Malta		71.1	**Slovenia**		67.2
Italy	30.4		Germany	30.2	
Germany	14.8		Italy	14.6	
Moldova		11.5	**Spain**		72.2
Russia	48.3		France	20.5	
Romania	14.0		Germany	15.4	
Netherlands		61.7	**Sweden**		48.3
Germany	22.3		Germany	10.2	
Belgium & Lux	9.9		United States	7.4	
Norway		76.6	**Switzerland**		65.0
United Kingdom	20.0		Germany	24.5	
Germany	12.0		United States	9.1	
Poland		70.1	**Turkey**		51.3
Germany	38.3		Germany	23.3	
Netherlands	5.6		United States	7.0	
Portugal		80.8	**Ukraine**		14.9
Germany	21.8		Russia	52.0	
Spain	15.1		Italy	6.3	
Romania		53.0	**United Kingdom**		53.4
Germany	17.8		United States	12.1	
Italy	15.6		Germany	12.0	

	Main ptnrs	EU 15		Main ptnrs	EU 15
Netherlands		76.9	**Sweden**		71.6
Western Germany	32.6		United Kingdom	12.5	
Belgium & Lux	13.9		Western Germany	11.7	
Norway		78.6	**Switzerland**		60.4
United Kingdom	17.9		Western Germany	14.8	
Western Germany	17.9		Italy	9.4	
Portugal		52.6	**Turkey**		52.6
United Kingdom	20.3		Western Germany	19.9	
Angola	12.5		United States	9.5	
Spain		52.3	**United Kingdom**		44.7
United States	14.2		United States	11.7	
Western Germany	11.8		Western Germany	6.2	

a Trade between Western and Eastern Germany is excluded.

Who imports from where

Most important sources of imports

Imports from main partners and to EU 15 countries as % of total imports

1995	Main ptnrs	EU 15		Main ptnrs	EU 15
Armenia		13.2	**Estonia**		63.8
Russia	20.0		Finland	33.5	
Turkmenistan	19.1		Russia	14.5	
Austria		73.8	**Finland**		58.2
Germany	44.8		Germany	15.6	
Italy	9.0		Sweden	11.7	
Azerbaijan		12.6	**France**		63.5
Turkey	21.2		Germany	18.2	
Russia	13.2		Italy	10.0	
Belarus		49.8	**Georgia**		23.9
Germany	26.5		Russia	10.6	
Poland	12.5		Turkey	10.0	
Belgium & Lux		70.6	**Germany**		54.4
Germany	21.7		France	10.7	
France	15.6		Netherlands	8.4	
Bulgaria		54.1	**Greece**		67.2
Germany	18.3		Italy	17.8	
Russia	13.2		Germany	15.2	
Croatia		63.5	**Hungary**		63.1
Italy	20.8		Germany	24.1	
Germany	20.6		Russia	12.2	
Cyprus		51.7	**Iceland**		59.0
United States	13.0		Germany	11.2	
United Kingdom	11.8		Norway	10.1	
Czech Republic		53.9	**Ireland**		55.9
Germany	28.4		United Kingdom	35.5	
Slovakia	11.1		United States	17.7	
Denmark		72.4	**Italy**		60.5
Germany	24.5		Germany	19.1	
Sweden	10.7		France	13.9	

1970	Main ptnrs	EU 15		Main ptnrs	EU 15
Austria		68.5	**Germany, Western**[a]		57.4
Western Germany	41.3		France	12.7	
Switzerland	7.4		Netherlands	12.2	
Belgium & Lux		69.2	**Greece**		56.9
Western Germany	23.4		Western Germany	18.6	
France	17.1		Japan	12.7	
Denmark		53.4	**Iceland**		63.6
Western Germany	18.8		Western Germany	15.1	
Sweden	15.9		United Kingdom	14.2	
Finland		61.9	**Ireland**		72.9
Western Germany	16.5		United Kingdom	51.7	
Sweden	16.1		Western Germany	6.8	
France		58.9	**Italy**		51.0
Western Germany	22.1		Western Germany	19.8	
Belgium & Lux	11.2		France	13.2	

	Main ptnrs	EU 15		Main ptnrs	EU 15
Latvia		52.0	**Russia**		31.1
Russia	20.4		Ukraine	11.4	
Germany	14.6		Germany	11.3	
Lithuania		46.0	**Serbia**		82.7
Russia	37.4		Germany	38.6	
Germany	19.6		Italy	15.7	
Macedonia FYR		67.7	**Slovakia**		44.2
Germany	24.2		Czech Republic	30.9	
Italy	22.7		Germany	23.6	
Malta		45.1	**Slovenia**		68.9
Italy	27.1		Germany	23.2	
United Kingdom	16.0		Italy	17.0	
Moldova		13.7	**Spain**		65.3
Russia	33.1		France	17.1	
Ukraine	27.2		Germany	15.3	
Netherlands		47.4	**Sweden**		69.3
Germany	16.6		Germany	21.0	
Belgium & Lux	8.4		United Kingdom	10.1	
Norway		71.3	**Switzerland**		82.9
Sweden	15.4		Germany	35.1	
Germany	14.0		France	11.8	
Poland		64.7	**Turkey**		47.0
Germany	26.6		Germany	15.5	
Italy	8.5		United States	10.4	
Portugal		74.9	**Ukraine**		23.8
Spain	21.1		Russia	66.9	
Germany	14.6		Germany	12.2	
Romania		48.8	**United Kingdom**		51.0
Germany	16.9		Germany	13.7	
Italy	13.0		United States	12.2	

	Main ptnrs	EU 15		Main ptnrs	EU 15
Netherlands		66.8	**Sweden**		64.3
Western Germany	27.1		Western Germany	18.9	
Belgium & Lux	16.8		United Kingdom	13.8	
Norway		68.4	**Switzerland**		78.7
Sweden	20.1		Western Germany	30.5	
Western Germany	14.3		France	12.3	
Portugal		57.1	**Turkey**		45.3
Western Germany	15.1		United States	18.2	
United Kingdom	13.9		Western Germany	17.3	
Spain		44.7	**United Kingdom**		36.7
United States	18.9		United States	13.0	
Western Germany	12.6		Canada	7.6	

a Trade between Western and Eastern Germany is excluded.

Top traders by sector

Food

		Value, bn	As % of world exports	
		1994	1980	1994
Exporters				
1	United States	50.03	17.8	13.2
2	**France**	34.45	8.0	9.1
3	**Netherlands**	30.79	6.6	8.1
4	**Germany**	22.36	4.5	5.9
5	**United Kingdom**	15.19	3.5	4.0
6	**Belgium & Luxembourg**	14.36	2.7	3.8
7	Canada	12.84	3.5	3.4
8	**Italy**	12.81	2.4	3.4
	EU 12	162.44	34.0	42.8
	Intra-exports	114.54	22.2	30.2
	Extra-exports	47.90	11.8	12.6
Importers				
1	Japan	49.43	7.2	12.3
2	**Germany**	37.44	9.6	9.3
3	United States	34.66	8.7	8.6
4	**France**	25.47	5.9	6.3
5	**United Kingdom**	22.80	6.6	5.7
6	**Italy**	20.84	5.5	5.2
7	Netherlands	19.71	4.9	4.9
8	**Belgium & Luxembourg**	14.02	3.4	3.5

Textiles

		Value, bn	As % of world exports	
		1994	1980	1994
Exporters				
1	**Germany**	12.56	11.4	9.7
2	China[b]	11.82	4.6	9.2
3	**Italy**	10.86	7.6	8.4
4	South Korea	10.69	4.0	8.3
5	Taiwan	10.20	3.2	7.9
6	**Belgium & Luxembourg**	6.80	6.5	5.3
7	Japan	6.78	9.3	5.3
	EU 12	48.31	46.3	37.5
	Intra-exports	28.81	29.1	22.4
	Extra-exports	19.50	17.1	15.1
Importers				
1	**Germany**	10.72	11.9	7.9
2	United States	9.66	4.4	7.1
3	China[b]	9.35	1.9	6.9
4	**United Kingdom**	6.68	6.2	4.9
5	**France**	6.59	7.1	4.9
6	**Italy**	5.62	4.5	4.2
7	Japan	5.15	2.9	3.8

Clothing

	Value, bn 1994	As % of world exports 1980	As % of world exports 1994
Exporters			
1 China[b]	23.73	4.0	17.0
2 **Italy**	12.53	11.3	9.0
3 Hong Kong[c]	9.46	11.5	6.8
4 **Germany**	6.64	7.1	4.8
5 South Korea	5.65	7.3	4.0
6 United States	5.62	3.1	4.0
7 **France**	4.97	5.7	3.6
8 Thailand	4.66	0.7	3.3
EU 12	39.50	38.0	28.3
Intra-exports	24.73	25.9	17.7
Extra-exports	14.77	12.1	10.6
Importers			
1 United States	38.64	16.3	26.3
2 **Germany**	22.45	19.5	15.3
3 Japan	15.27	3.6	10.4
4 **France**	9.12	6.2	6.2
5 **United Kingdom**	7.27	6.7	5.0
6 Netherlands	5.03	6.7	3.4
7 **Italy**	3.97	1.9	2.7
8 **Belgium & Luxembourg**	3.85	4.3	2.6

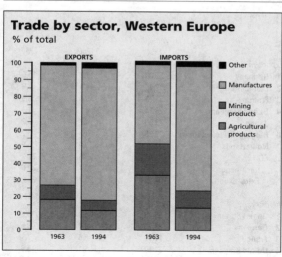

Trade by sector, Western Europe
% of total

EXPORTS · IMPORTS

1963 · 1994 · 1963 · 1994

■ Other
■ Manufactures
■ Mining products
■ Agricultural products

a Russia is not included in tables due to lack of data.
b Includes signifcant shipments through processing zones.
c Domestic exports ie, excluding re-exports.

Automotive products

		Value, bn 1994	As % of world exports	
			1980	1994
Exporters				
1	Japan	82.43	19.8	20.9
2	**Germany**	70.46	21.0	17.9
3	United States	49.61	12.7	12.6
4	Canada	40.92	6.9	10.4
5	France	28.35	9.9	7.2
6	**Belgium & Luxembourg**	21.70	4.9	5.5
7	Spain	17.81	1.8	4.5
8	**United Kingdom**	15.51	5.8	3.9
	EU 12	173.96	49.4	44.1
	Intra-exports	114.43	28.5	29.0
	Extra-exports	59.53	20.9	15.1
Importers				
1	United States	102.76	20.4	25.9
2	**Germany**	35.27	6.2	8.9
3	Canada	32.04	8.7	8.1
4	**United Kingdom**	24.73	5.7	6.2
5	France	22.15	5.5	5.6
6	Italy	14.83	5.6	3.7
7	**Belgium & Luxembourg**	13.60	5.4	3.4
8	Spain	13.41	0.9	3.4

Chemicals

		Value, bn 1994	As % of world exports	
			1980	1994
Exporters				
1	**Germany**	57.00	17.2	15.0
2	United States	52.45	14.9	13.8
3	France	33.72	9.4	8.9
4	**United Kingdom**	28.14	8.7	7.4
5	Japan	23.59	4.7	6.2
6	**Belgium & Luxembourg**	23.33	5.3	6.2
7	**Netherlands**	22.25	8.0	5.9
	EU 12	198.04	55.6	52.2
	Intra-exports	113.80	30.4	30.0
	Extra-exports	84.24	25.2	22.2
Importers				
1	United States	35.48	6.3	9.2
2	**Germany**	33.25	9.4	8.6
3	France	27.32	8.6	7.1
4	**United Kingdom**	21.57	5.1	5.6
5	Italy	21.47	5.6	5.5
6	Japan	19.77	4.2	5.1
7	**Belgium & Luxembourg**	16.62	4.2	4.3

Machinery and transport equipment

	Value, bn 1994	As % of world exports	
		1980	1994
Exporters			
1 Japan	284.64	14.5	17.9
2 United States	252.34	17.0	15.9
3 Germany	208.09	16.3	13.1
4 France	91.90	7.0	5.8
5 United Kingdom	83.04	7.6	5.2
6 Italy	69.86	4.8	4.4
7 Canada	66.39	3.2	4.2
EU 12	583.97	43.0	36.8
Intra-exports	310.59	20.9	19.6
Extra-exports	273.38	22.1	17.2
Importers			
1 United States	314.62	12.2	19.7
2 Germany	127.32	6.7	8.0
3 United Kingdom	90.60	5.8	5.7
4 France	80.50	5.5	5.0
5 Canada	76.25	5.1	4.8
6 Japan	52.66	1.6	3.3
7 China	51.47	1.0	3.2

Office machines and telecoms equipment

	Value, bn 1994	As % of world exports	
		1980	1994
Exporters			
1 Japan	94.52	21.1	20.1
2 United States	78.98	20.2	16.8
3 Singapore^c	32.30	2.5	6.9
4 United Kingdom	27.73	6.4	5.9
5 Germany	24.84	9.9	5.3
6 Malaysia	24.50	1.4	5.2
7 South Korea	23.69	2.0	5.0
EU 12	109.54	32.6	23.3
Intra-exports	64.99	19.3	13.8
Extra-exports	44.55	13.3	9.5
Importers			
1 United States	113.71	15.9	24.1
2 Germany	35.80	9.7	7.6
3 United Kingdom	29.21	7.0	6.2
4 Japan	22.88	2.6	4.8
5 France	19.84	6.5	4.2
6 Singapore^c	18.99	1.9	4.0
7 Canada	16.55	4.1	3.5

See page 73 for footnotes.

Exchange rates

Currency units per dollar

	1960	1965	1970	1975
Austria	26.04	25.89	25.88	18.51
Belgium-Luxembourg	49.70	49.64	49.68	39.53
Cyprus	0.36	0.36	0.42	0.39
Czech Republic				
Denmark	6.91	6.89	7.49	6.18
Estonia				
Finland	3.21	3.22	4.18	3.85
France	4.90	4.90	5.55	4.49
Germany	4.17	4.01	3.65	2.62
Greece	30.00	30.00	30.00	35.65
Hungary			60.00	43.51
Iceland	0.38	0.43	0.88	1.71
Ireland	0.36	0.36	0.42	0.49
Italy	620.60	624.70	623.00	683.60
Latvia				
Lithuania				
Malta	0.36	0.36	0.42	0.40
Netherlands	3.77	3.61	3.60	2.69
Norway	7.15	7.15	7.14	5.59
Poland			0.00	0.00
Portugal	28.83	28.83	28.75	27.47
Romania			6.00	20.00
Russia				
Slovakia				
Slovenia				
Spain	60.15	59.99	69.72	59.77
Sweden	5.18	5.18	5.17	4.39
Switzerland	4.31	4.32	4.32	2.62
Turkey	9.02	9.04	9.00	15.20
United Kingdom	0.36	0.36	0.42	0.49

Changing values
Currencies change against the dollar, %
1990–95

1	Latvia	55.5	13	Cyprus	-5.7
2	Estonia	12.7	14	Norway	-6.5
3	Czech Republic	12.6	15	Ireland	-10.0
	Switzerland	12.6	16	Portugal	-10.6
5	Slovakia	12.3	17	Sweden	-14.4
6	Austria	5.8	18	Malta	-14.7
7	Netherlands	5.3	19	Iceland	-15.1
8	Belgium-Luxembourg	5.3	20	Finland	-16.6
9	France	4.7	21	United Kingdom	-19.7
10	Germany	4.2	22	Spain	-20.4
11	Denmark	4.1	23	Italy	-28.7
12	Lithuania	-5.3			

1980	1985	1990	1995	Oct 4 1996
13.81	17.28	10.68	10.09	10.76
31.52	50.36	30.98	29.42	31.52
0.36	0.54	0.43	0.46	0.47
		29.96	26.60	27.26
6.02	8.97	5.78	5.55	5.86
		12.91	11.46	12.23
3.84	5.42	3.63	4.36	4.57
4.52	7.56	5.13	4.90	5.18
1.96	2.46	1.49	1.43	1.53
46.54	147.76	157.63	237.04	240.99
32.21	47.35	61.45	139.47	155.43
6.24	42.06	55.39	65.23	67.22
0.53	0.80	0.56	0.62	0.63
930.50	1678.50	1130.20	1584.70	1521.95
		0.84	0.54	0.55
		3.79	4.00	4.00
0.35	0.42	0.30	0.35	0.36
2.13	2.77	1.69	1.60	1.72
5.18	7.58	5.91	6.32	6.51
0.00	0.01	0.95	2.47	2.82
53.04	157.49	133.60	149.41	154.89
18.00	15.73	34.71	2578.00	3260.00
		415.00	4640.00	5424.00
		33.20	29.57	31.25
		56.69	125.99	139.05
79.25	154.15	96.61	121.41	128.75
4.37	7.62	5.70	6.66	6.62
1.76	2.08	1.30	1.15	1.26
90.10	576.90	2930.10	59650.00	92930.00
0.42	0.69	0.52	0.65	0.64

1960–95

1	Switzerland	274.2	**11**	Sweden	-22.2
2	Germany	191.0	**12**	Finland	-26.5
3	Austria	158.1	**13**	Ireland	-42.7
4	Netherlands	135.0	**14**	United Kingdom	-44.7
5	Belgium-Luxembourg	69.0	**15**	Spain	-50.5
6	Denmark	24.5	**16**	Italy	-60.8
7	Norway	13.1	**17**	Portugal	-80.7
8	Malta	1.3	**18**	Greece	-87.3
9	France	0.1	**19**	Iceland	-99.4
10	Cyprus	-21.1	**20**	Turkey	-100.0

Inflation

Snapshots
Consumer price inflation, %
1995

1	Ukraine	376.7	18	Malta	4.0
2	Russia	197.4	19	United Kingdom	3.4
3	Turkey	93.6	20	Cyprus	2.6
4	Lithuania	39.7	21	Ireland	2.5
5	Romania	32.2		Norway	2.5
6	Estonia	28.9		Sweden	2.5
7	Hungary	28.3	24	Austria	2.3
8	Poland	26.8	25	Denmark	2.1
9	Latvia	25.0	26	Luxembourg	1.9
10	Slovenia	12.6		Netherlands	1.9
11	Slovakia	9.9	28	France	1.8
12	Greece	9.3		Germany	1.8
13	Czech Republic	9.1		Switzerland	1.8
14	Italy	5.2	31	Iceland	1.7
15	Spain	4.7	32	Belgium	1.5
16	Croatia	4.1	33	Finland	1.0
	Portugal	4.1			

1980			*1970*		
1	Turkey	110.2	1	Iceland	13.1
2	Iceland	58.5	2	Norway	10.6
3	Ex-Yugoslavia	30.9	3	Ex-Yugoslavia	9.5
4	Greece	24.9	4	Ireland	8.2
5	Italy	21.3	5	Sweden	7.0
6	Ireland	18.2	6	Turkey	6.9
7	United Kingdom	18.0	7	Denmark	6.5
8	Portugal	16.6	8	United Kingdom	6.4
9	Malta	15.7	9	France	5.8
10	Spain	15.6	10	Spain	5.7
11	Sweden	13.7	11	Italy	4.8
12	Cyprus	13.5	12	Luxembourg	4.6
	France	13.5	13	Portugal	4.5
14	Denmark	12.3	14	Austria	4.4
15	Finland	11.6	15	Belgium	3.9
16	Norway	10.9	16	Malta	3.7
17	Poland	9.7	17	Netherlands	3.7
18	Hungary	9.3	18	Switzerland	3.6
19	Belgium	6.7	19	Germany	3.4
20	Netherlands	6.5	20	Greece	2.9
21	Austria	6.3	21	Finland	2.7
	Luxembourg	6.3		Cyprus	2.4
23	Germany	5.4	23	Poland[a]	1.1
24	Switzerland	4.0	24	Romania[a]	0.6
25	Czechoslovakia	2.9			
26	Romania	1.5			

a 1971.

Highest averages
Average annual consumer price inflation, %

1990–95

1	Russia[a]	435.4	14	Portugal	7.2
2	Croatia	254.9	15	Spain	5.2
3	Romania	148.6	16	Italy	5.0
4	Turkey	79.7	17	Cyprus	4.7
5	Slovenia	63.6	18	Sweden	4.2
6	Lithuania	62.3	19	Iceland	3.6
7	Estonia[a]	53.4	20	United Kingdom	3.4
8	Latvia[a]	52.5	21	Malta	3.3
9	Poland	42.8	22	Germany	3.3
10	Hungary	25.2	23	Austria	3.2
11	Slovakia	22.2	24	Switzerland	3.2
12	Czech Republic	20.4	25	Luxembourg	2.8
13	Greece	13.9	26	Netherlands	2.7

1980–90

1	Poland	69.9	10	Norway	7.6
2	Turkey	45.8		Sweden	7.6
3	Iceland	33.4	12	Finland	6.7
4	Greece	19.0	13	United Kingdom	6.6
5	Portugal	17.1	14	France	6.3
6	Hungary	10.7	15	Denmark	5.9
7	Italy	9.6	16	Cyprus	4.9
8	Spain	9.3	17	Belgium	4.5
9	Ireland	7.7	18	Luxembourg	4.4

1970–80

1	Iceland	34.0	10	Denmark	9.9
2	Turkey	27.7	11	France	9.7
3	Portugal	18.1	12	Sweden	9.1
4	Spain	15.3	13	Norway	8.4
5	Greece	14.4	14	Cyprus	7.9
6	Italy	13.9	15	Belgium	7.4
7	Ireland	13.7	16	Netherlands	7.3
	United Kingdom	13.7	17	Malta	6.7
9	Finland	11.2	18	Luxembourg	6.6

1960–70

1	Iceland	11.6	10	France	4.0
2	Spain	6.2		Sweden	4.0
3	Denmark	5.9		Turkey	4.0
4	Finland	5.0	13	Italy	3.6
5	Ireland	4.7		Austria	3.6
6	Norway	4.5	15	Switzerland	3.3
7	Netherlands	4.3	16	Belgium	3.0
8	Portugal	4.2	17	Germany	2.6
9	United Kingdom	4.1		Luxembourg	2.6

a 1992–95.

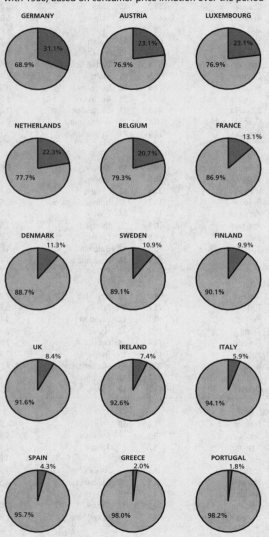

The currency in your pocket

Purchasing power of national currencies in 1995 compared with 1960, based on consumer price inflation over the period

GERMANY
31.1%
68.9%

AUSTRIA
23.1%
76.9%

LUXEMBOURG
23.1%
76.9%

NETHERLANDS
22.3%
77.7%

BELGIUM
20.7%
79.3%

FRANCE
13.1%
86.9%

DENMARK
11.3%
88.7%

SWEDEN
10.9%
89.1%

FINLAND
9.9%
90.1%

UK
8.4%
91.6%

IRELAND
7.4%
92.6%

ITALY
5.9%
94.1%

SPAIN
4.3%
95.7%

GREECE
2.0%
98.0%

PORTUGAL
1.8%
98.2%

General government revenue

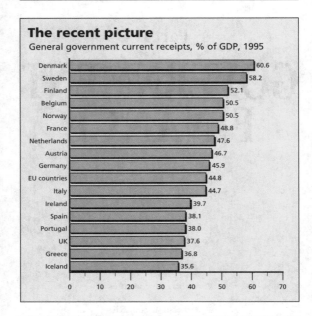

The recent picture

General government current receipts, % of GDP, 1995

Country	%
Denmark	60.6
Sweden	58.2
Finland	52.1
Belgium	50.5
Norway	50.5
France	48.8
Netherlands	47.6
Austria	46.7
Germany	45.9
EU countries	44.8
Italy	44.7
Ireland	39.7
Spain	38.1
Portugal	38.0
UK	37.6
Greece	36.8
Iceland	35.6

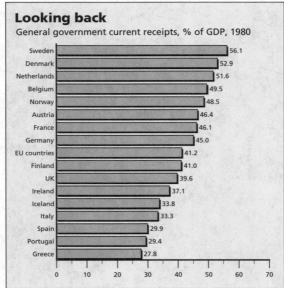

Looking back

General government current receipts, % of GDP, 1980

Country	%
Sweden	56.1
Denmark	52.9
Netherlands	51.6
Belgium	49.5
Norway	48.5
Austria	46.4
France	46.1
Germany	45.0
EU countries	41.2
Finland	41.0
UK	39.6
Ireland	37.1
Iceland	33.8
Italy	33.3
Spain	29.9
Portugal	29.4
Greece	27.8

General government spending

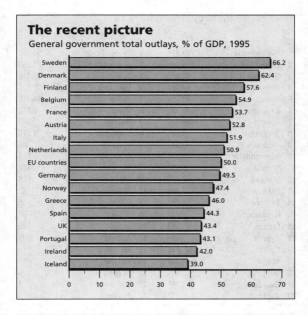

The recent picture
General government total outlays, % of GDP, 1995

Country	%
Sweden	66.2
Denmark	62.4
Finland	57.6
Belgium	54.9
France	53.7
Austria	52.8
Italy	51.9
Netherlands	50.9
EU countries	50.0
Germany	49.5
Norway	47.4
Greece	46.0
Spain	44.3
UK	43.4
Portugal	43.1
Ireland	42.0
Iceland	39.0

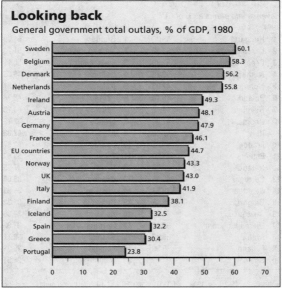

Looking back
General government total outlays, % of GDP, 1980

Country	%
Sweden	60.1
Belgium	58.3
Denmark	56.2
Netherlands	55.8
Ireland	49.3
Austria	48.1
Germany	47.9
France	46.1
EU countries	44.7
Norway	43.3
UK	43.0
Italy	41.9
Finland	38.1
Iceland	32.5
Spain	32.2
Greece	30.4
Portugal	23.8

Central government revenue

How much central governments raise
$bn

1994			1984		
1	Netherlands	182,276	1	United Kingdom	90,298
2	United Kingdom[a]	139,441	2	Netherlands	64,260
3	Denmark	63,524	3	Norway	23,725
4	Norway[b]	50,267	4	Denmark	21,127
5	Russia	49,588	5	Finland	14,515
6	Finland[a]	36,695	6	Switzerland	8,632
7	Poland	36,112	7	Ireland	5,647
8	Switzerland	27,231	8	Luxembourg	1,673
9	Ireland	7,281	9	Iceland	746
10	Luxembourg[a]	6,714	10	France	208
11	Croatia	5,331	11	Germany	184
12	Iceland	1,991	12	Malta	86
13	Lithuania	1,008	13	Sweden	37
14	Estonia	922	14	Belgium	35
15	Germany[a]	698	15	Poland	33
16	France	598	16	Spain	26
17	Cyprus	516	17	Austria	23
18	Spain	119	18	Romania	14
19	Malta[a]	115	19	Hungary	11
20	Belgium	111	20	Greece	8
21	Sweden	80	21	Turkey	7
22	Austria[b]	77	22	Portugal	6

...and relative revenue
Revenue and grants as % of GDP

1994			1984		
1	Hungary[f]	53.30	1	Hungary	54.70
2	Luxembourg[b]	53.08	2	Netherlands	51.76
3	Czech Republic[f]	51.20	3	Luxembourg	50.12
4	Netherlands[a]	50.76	4	Belgium	46.09
5	Norway[c]	47.35	5	Ireland	43.81
6	Poland[f]	46.70	6	Poland	43.74
7	Belgium[b]	44.15	7	Norway	43.13
8	Denmark	41.60	8	France	42.13
	Italy[b]	41.60	9	Malta	42.03
10	France[b]	41.35	10	Sweden	40.97
11	Estonia[f]	41.20	11	Denmark	39.57
12	Ireland[b]	39.70	12	United Kingdom	37.35
13	Portugal[c]	39.36	13	Greece	36.06
14	Sweden[a]	39.31	14	Austria	35.83
15	Bulgaria[f]	38.00	15	Romania	35.39
16	Austria[b]	36.85	16	Italy	34.88
17	United Kingdom[a]	36.20	17	Portugal	33.93
18	Malta[b]	35.47	18	Germany	30.11
19	Finland[b]	33.99	19	Finland	29.23
20	Spain[a]	31.59	20	Iceland	26.51

a 1993. b 1992. c 1990. d 1991. e 1988. f General government expenditure.

Central government spending

How much central governments spend

$bn

1994			*1984*		
1	Netherlands	198,624	1	United Kingdom	97,821
2	United Kingdom[a]	169,707	2	Netherlands	72,335
3	Denmark	73,728	3	Denmark	23,549
4	Russia	60,922	4	Norway	20,600
5	Norway[b]	53,498	5	Finland	15,028
6	Finland[a]	50,063	6	Switzerland	8,580
7	Poland	38,251	7	Ireland	7,323
8	Switzerland	31,691	8	Luxembourg	1,594
9	Ireland	7,482	9	Iceland	718
10	Luxembourg[a]	6,440	10	France	226
11	Croatia	5,445	11	Germany	193
12	Iceland	2,093	12	Malta	86
13	Lithuania	1,073	13	Belgium	43
14	Estonia	836	14	Sweden	42
15	Germany[a]	741	15	Spain	37
16	France	687	16	Poland	34
17	Cyprus	539	17	Austria	25
18	Spain	149	18	Turkey	12
19	Malta[a]	130	19	Greece	11
20	Belgium[a]	125		Hungary	11
21	Sweden	104		Romania	11
22	Austria[a]	87	22	Portugal	8

...and relative spending

Expenditure as % of GDP

1994			*1984*		
1	Hungary[c]	62.00	1	Belgium	59.54
2	Italy[b]	52.51	2	Netherlands	59.10
3	Luxembourg[a]	51.97	3	Ireland	54.51
	Netherlands[a]	51.97	4	Hungary	53.09
5	Belgium[b]	51.21	5	Greece	50.09
6	Sweden[a]	51.16	6	Sweden	49.29
7	Czech Republic	50.70	7	Italy	48.01
8	Finland[b]	48.75	8	Luxembourg	47.60
9	Poland	48.70	9	France	45.20
10	Norway[c]	46.65	10	Poland	44.20
11	France[b]	45.07	11	Portugal	43.60
12	Bulgaria	45.00	12	Denmark	43.51
13	Portugal[c]	44.61	13	Malta	41.58
14	Armenia	44.00	14	Norway	41.15
15	Denmark[a]	43.93	15	United Kingdom	40.50
16	Greece[a]	43.12	16	Austria	40.39
17	Ireland[b]	41.72	17	Spain	34.65
18	United Kingdom[b]	41.22	18	Germany	31.82
19	Austria[b]	40.76	19	Cyprus	31.21
20	Estonia	39.90	20	Finland	30.25

a 1993. b 1992. c 1990.

Spending on what?

General public services
Central government spending, % of total

1984			1994		
1	Hungary	18	**1**	Turkey[b]	35
2	Luxembourg	10	**2**	Hungary[f]	14
3	Malta	9	**3**	Germany[g]	9
4	Cyprus	8		Luxembourg[j]	9
5	Finland	7	**5**	Cyprus[j]	8
	Ireland	7		Estonia	8
	Italy[a]	7		Ireland[h]	8
	Portugal	7		Italy[d]	8
	Spain	7		Malta[j]	8
10	Denmark[a]	6	**10**	Denmark[h]	7
	France[a]	6		Portugal[d]	7
12	Austria	5	**12**	Czech Republic	6
	Netherlands[a]	5		Greece[j]	6
	Norway	5		Netherlands	6
	Switzerland[b]	5	**15**	Austria[j]	5
16	Bulgaria[c]	4		France[h]	5
	Germany[a]	4		Iceland[j]	5
	Iceland[a]	4		Latvia	5
	Sweden[a]	4		Lithuania	5
	United Kingdom	4		Norway[h]	5
21	Belgium	3		Russia	5
22	Romania[a]	1	**22**	Bulgaria	4
				Croatia	4
				United Kingdom[h]	4

Public order
Central government spending, % of total

1984			1994		
1	Switzerland[b]	12	**1**	Estonia	8
2	Cyprus	8		Latvia	8
3	Spain	4		Lithuania	8
4	Austria	3	**4**	Croatia	7
	Malta	3	**5**	Cyprus[j]	6
	Sweden[a]	3		Russia	6
7	Denmark[a]	2	**7**	Bulgaria	4
	Netherlands[a]	2		Romania	4
	Norway	2		United Kingdom[h]	4
10	Belgium	1	**10**	Hungary[f]	3
	Bulgaria[c]	1		Malta[j]	3
	France	1		Netherlands	3
	United Kingdom	1		Spain[h]	3

Note: These figures are for central government spending. In countries such as
Germany a lot of government spending is done at the regional level.

Education
Central government spending, % of total

1984			1994		
1	Finland	14	**1**	Belarus[i]	18
2	Switzerland[b]	13	**2**	Latvia	15
3	Belgium	12	**3**	Iceland[i]	14
	Iceland[a]	12		Turkey[b]	14
	Ireland	12	**5**	Ireland[h]	13
6	Cyprus	11	**6**	Belgium[d]	12
	Netherlands[a]	11		Malta[i]	12
8	Austria	10	**8**	Cyprus[i]	11
	Portugal	10		Czech Republic	11
	Turkey[ab]	10		Finland[i]	11
11	Denmark[a]	9		Portugal[d]	11

Health
Central government spending, % of total

1984			1994		
1	Switzerland[b]	50	**1**	Czech Republic	17
2	France[a]	21		Estonia	17
3	Germany[a]	18		Germany[g]	17
4	Ireland	13	**4**	France[h]	15
	Spain	13	**5**	Ireland[h]	14
	United Kingdom	13		Netherlands	14
7	Austria	12		United Kingdom[h]	14
	Italy[a]	12	**8**	Austria[i]	13
9	Netherlands[a]	11		Croatia	13
	Norway	11	**10**	Malta[i]	12
11	Finland	10	**11**	Italy[d]	11

Social security
Central government spending, % of total

1984			1994		
1	Germany[a]	49	**1**	Luxembourg[i]	51
	Luxembourg	49	**2**	Sweden	48
3	Spain	48	**3**	Austria[i]	46
4	Austria	45		Finland[i]	46
5	Sweden[a]	42	**5**	France[h]	45
6	Denmark[a]	39		Germany[g]	45
7	Belgium	38	**7**	Belgium[d]	42
8	France[a]	37	**8**	Denmark[h]	40
	Malta	37	**9**	Norway[h]	39
10	Netherlands[a]	36		Spain[h]	39
11	Norway	35	**11**	Italy[d]	38
12	Finland	33		Lithuania	38
13	Italy[a]	32	**13**	Latvia	37
14	United Kingdom	29		Netherlands	37
15	Ireland	25	**15**	Belarus[i]	36

a 1985.	d 1988.	h 1992.
b Including public order.	f 1990.	i 1993.
c 1987.	g 1991.	

Debt: rich countries

Total debt
General government gross financial liabilities as % of GDP

		1980	1990	1995
1	Belgium	78.7	130.9	133.5
2	Italy	57.7	106.4	123.0
3	Greece	22.9	81.6	111.5
4	Ireland	71.8	97.1	85.8
5	Sweden	44.3	44.3	81.8
6	Denmark	44.7	68.0	80.1
7	Netherlands	46.9	78.8	79.1
8	Spain	18.3	50.3	71.1
9	Portugal	33.0	68.6	70.7
10	Austria	37.3	58.3	69.4
11	Finland	14.1	16.9	63.0
12	Germany	32.8	45.5	61.6
13	France	30.9	40.2	57.9
14	United Kingdom	54.0	39.3	57.6

Net debt
General government net financial liabilities as % of GDP

		1980	1990	1995
1	Belgium	69.6	119.3	127.6
2	Italy	52.7	84.3	109.0
3	Spain	6.1	31.7	50.3
4	Austria	20.0	38.6	49.7
5	Denmark	14.2	34.0	45.8
6	Germany	11.8	20.6	44.1
7	Netherlands	24.6	36.9	43.3
8	United Kingdom	36.2	18.8	39.6
9	France	-3.3	16.3	34.8
10	Iceland	3.3	17.6	34.7
11	Sweden	-13.9	-8.1	27.8
12	Finland	-30.7	-36.1	-7.1

Interest payments
General government net interest payments as % of GDP

		1980	1990	1995
1	Greece	2.3	10.2	12.9
2	Italy	4.7	9.1	10.5
3	Belgium	5.4	9.9	8.8
4	Portugal	2.8	8.7	5.7
5	Spain	0.3	3.3	5.1
6	Netherlands	2.4	4.4	4.7
7	Ireland	3.6	6.1	4.2
8	Denmark	0.5	3.4	3.7
9	Austria	1.7	3.2	3.5
10	France	0.8	2.4	3.4
11	United Kingdom	3.1	2.3	3.0
12	Germany	1.3	2.0	2.9
	Sweden	-0.4	0.1	2.9
14	Iceland	-0.3	2.0	2.4

Debt: poor countries

External debt
$bn, 1995

1	Russia	94,232	8	Romania	5,492
2	Turkey	66,332	9	Ukraine	5,430
3	Poland	42,160	10	Slovakia	4,067
4	Hungary	28,016	11	Croatia	2,304
5	Ex-Yugoslavia	13,557	12	Slovenia	2,290
6	Czech Republic	10,694	13	Belarus	1,272
7	Bulgaria	10,468	14	Georgia	1,227

As % of GDP, 1994

1	Bulgaria	105.7	8	Slovakia	33.2
2	Hungary	70.1	9	Czech Republic	29.7
3	Georgia	58.6	10	Malta[a]	29.2
4	Macedonia FYR	56.9	11	Russia	25.4
5	Turkey	51.4	12	Romania	18.3
6	Poland	46.8	13	Croatia	17.3
7	Albania	44.3	14	Slovenia	16.4

As % of exports, 1994

1	Hungary	256.8	8	Moldova	79.5
2	Poland	215.7	9	Macedonia FYR	75.3
3	Turkey	202.8	10	Romania	74.0
4	Bulgaria	189.9	11	Czech Republic	54.6
5	Albania	171.2	12	Belarus	45.9
6	Russia	159.7	13	Slovakia	44.5
7	Armenia	83.2	14	Ukraine	37.6

Interest payments
$bn, 1994

1	Turkey	3,987	8	Bulgaria	197
2	Hungary	1,731	9	Slovenia	121
3	Russia	1,383	10	Croatia	112
4	Poland	1,197	11	Ukraine	79
5	Czech Republic	502	12	Macedonia FYR	35
6	Slovakia	290	13	Malta	34
7	Romania	276	14	Belarus	31

As % of GDP, 1994

1	Hungary	15.9	8	Czech Republic	2.6
2	Turkey	12.2	9	Russia	2.3
3	Poland	6.1	10	Croatia	1.6
4	Romania	3.7	11	Lithuania	1.4
5	Bulgaria	3.6		Moldova	1.4
6	Slovakia	3.2		Slovenia	1.4
7	Macedonia FYR	2.9	14	Latvia	1.2

a 1993.

Aid

Givers
Official Development Assistance (ODA) from
Development Assistance Committee (DAC) countries to developing countries
$bn

1985–86			1995		
1	France	7.50	1	France	8.44
2	Germany	5.87	2	Germany	7.48
3	Italy	3.10	3	Netherlands	3.32
4	United Kingdom	2.86	4	United Kingdom	3.19
5	Netherlands	2.30	5	Sweden	1.98
6	Sweden	1.74	6	Denmark	1.63
7	Norway	1.05	7	Italy	1.52
8	Denmark	0.99	8	Spain	1.31
9	Belgium	0.86	9	Norway	1.24
10	Switzerland	0.64	10	Switzerland	1.08
11	Finland	0.48	11	Belgium	1.03
12	Austria	0.41	12	Austria	0.75
13	Spain	0.23	13	Finland	0.39
14	Ireland	0.08	14	Portugal	0.27
15	Portugal	0.03	15	Ireland	0.14
	Total DAC	49.62	16	Luxembourg	0.07
	Total EU	23.81		Total EU	31.52

% of GDP

1985–86			1995		
1	Norway	1.10	1	Denmark	0.97
2	Netherlands	0.97	2	Sweden	0.89
3	Denmark	0.85	3	Norway	0.87
	Sweden	0.85	4	Netherlands	0.80
5	France	0.59	5	France	0.55
6	Belgium	0.51	6	Belgium	0.38
7	Germany	0.44		Luxembourg	0.38
8	Finland	0.43	8	Switzerland	0.34
9	Italy	0.34	9	Austria	0.32
10	United Kingdom	0.32		Finland	0.32
11	Switzerland	0.30	11	Germany	0.31
12	Austria	0.28	12	United Kingdom	0.29
13	Ireland	0.27	13	Ireland	0.27
14	Spain	0.09		Portugal	0.27
15	Portugal	0.06	15	Spain	0.23
	DAC average	0.34	16	Italy	0.14
	EU average	0.48		EU average	0.38

Per head, $, 1995

1	Denmark	315	9	Austria	94
2	Norway	286	10	Germany	92
3	Sweden	226	11	Finland	76
4	Netherlands	214	12	United Kingdom	55
5	Luxembourg	172	13	Ireland	39
6	Switzerland	150	14	Spain	33
7	France	146	15	Italy	27
8	Belgium	102		Portugal	27

Receivers

Aid (ODA) received, $m, 1994

1	Russia	1,962	11	Czech Republic	132
2	Poland	1,892		Belarus	132
3	Ukraine	324	13	Albania	96
4	Georgia	263	14	Greece	80
5	Hungary	195	15	Slovakia	71
6	Armenia	175	16	Lithuania	70
7	Bulgaria	164	17	Moldova	54
8	Azerbaijan	150	18	Latvia	53
9	Turkey	149	19	Estonia	39
10	Romania	140			

Aid (ODA) as % of GDP, 1994

1	Georgia	8.4	11	Belarus	0.6
2	Albania	7.8		Slovakia	0.6
3	Armenia	6.9	13	Hungary	0.5
4	Azerbaijan	4.0		Romania	0.5
5	Poland	2.0		Russia	0.5
6	Bulgaria	1.6	16	Czech Republic	0.4
7	Lithuania	1.4		Ukraine	0.4
	Moldova	1.4	18	Greece	0.1
9	Estonia	0.9		Turkey	0.1
	Latvia	0.9			

Aid (ODA) per head, $, 1994

1	Poland	49	11	Belarus	13
2	Georgia	48		Czech Republic	13
3	Armenia	46		Russia	13
4	Albania	28		Slovakia	13
5	Estonia	25	15	Moldova	12
6	Latvia	21	16	Greece	8
7	Azerbaijan	20	17	Romania	6
8	Bulgaria	19		Ukraine	6
	Hungary	19	19	Turkey	3
	Lithuania	19			

Money supply

Narrow money
Average annual % growth

1980–90			1990–95		
1	Poland	60	**1**	Romania	95
2	Turkey	45	**2**	Turkey	66
3	Iceland	38	**3**	Poland	32
4	Greece	20	**4**	Hungary[a]	17
	Norway	20	**5**	Greece	13
6	Portugal	17	**6**	Portugal	12
7	Spain	14	**7**	Ireland	10
8	Denmark	12		Iceland	10
9	Cyprus	11	**9**	Austria	9
	Finland	11	**10**	Finland[b]	8
	Italy	11	**11**	Cyprus	7
12	Germany, Western	9		Germany	7
13	France	8		Netherlands	7
	Romania	8	**13**	Italy	5
15	Ireland	7		Malta	5
	Luxembourg	7		Norway	5
	Netherlands	7		United Kingdom	5
18	Austria	5	**16**	Spain	4
19	Belgium	4		Denmark	4
	Malta	4		Switzerland	4
21	Switzerland	2	**21**	Belgium	3
			22	France	1

1994–95					
1	Ukraine	151	**17**	Iceland	11
2	Russia	121		Portugal	11
3	Moldova	76	**19**	France	9
4	Turkey	68	**20**	Malta	8
5	Romania	58	**21**	Czech Republic	7
6	Lithuania	42		Germany	7
7	Poland	36	**23**	Cyprus	6
8	Estonia	29		Switzerland	6
9	Greece	28	**25**	Denmark	5
10	Slovenia	26		Belgium	5
11	Croatia	24		United Kingdom	5
12	Slovakia	21	**27**	Spain	3
13	Ireland	19	**27**	Norway	1
14	Austria	16		Italy	1
15	Finland	14		Latvia	1
	Netherlands	14			

a 1990–1994.
b 1991–1995.

Broad money
Average growth

1980–90

1	Poland	62
2	Turkey	58
3	Iceland	42
4	Greece	22
5	United Kingdom	21
6	Portugal	19
7	Cyprus	15
8	Finland	13
9	Spain	12
10	Denmark	11
	Luxembourg	11
	Norway	11
13	Italy	10
	Romania	10
15	Ireland	9
16	Austria	8
	Malta	8
	Sweden	8
19	Belgium	7
	France	7
	Germany, Western	7
	Switzerland	7
23	Netherlands	6

1990–95

1	Romania	102
2	Turkey	93
3	Poland	40
4	Hungary[a]	22
5	Portugal	15
6	Cyprus	14
7	Ireland	13
8	Malta	11
9	Greece	9
	Spain	9
11	Germany	7
	United Kingdom	7
13	Austria	6
	Iceland	6
15	France	4
	Italy	4
	Netherlands	4
	Norway	4
	Switzerland	4
20	Denmark	3
	Sweden	3
22	Belgium	2
	Finland	2

1994–95

1	Ukraine	115	17	Malta	12
2	Croatia	112	18	Cyprus	11
3	Russia	108		France	11
4	Turkey	104	20	Portugal	10
5	Romania	70	21	Spain	7
6	Moldova	65	22	Denmark	6
7	Poland	36		Finland	6
8	Lithuania	30		Netherlands	6
9	Czech Republic	29	25	Austria	5
	Slovenia	29		Belgium	5
11	Estonia	27		Germany	5
12	Greece	25		Switzerland	5
13	Albania	24	29	Iceland	4
14	Slovakia	18		Norway	4
15	Ireland	15	31	Sweden	3
16	United Kingdom	13	32	Latvia	-21

Reserves

Recent picture
Total reserves minus gold, $m, 1995

1	Germany	85,005	19	Denmark	11,016
2	United Kingdom	42,020	20	Finland	10,038
3	Switzerland	36,413	21	Ireland	8,630
4	Italy	34,905	22	Slovakia	3,364
5	Spain	34,485	23	Croatia	2,036
6	Netherlands	33,714	24	Slovenia	1,821
7	France	26,853	25	Malta	1,605
8	Sweden	24,051	26	Romania	1,579
9	Norway	22,518	27	Cyprus	1,117
10	Austria	18,730	28	Ukraine	1,051
11	Belgium	16,177	29	Lithuania	757
12	Portugal	15,850	30	Estonia	580
13	Greece	14,780	31	Latvia	506
14	Poland	14,774	32	Iceland	308
15	Russia	14,383	33	Albania	241
16	Czech Republic	13,843	34	Moldova	240
17	Turkey	12,442	35	Luxembourg	75
18	Hungary	12,052			

Gold
Fine troy ounces, m, 1995

1	Germany	95.18	17	Czech Republic	1.99
2	Switzerland	83.28	18	Finland	1.60
3	France	81.85	19	Slovakia	1.29
4	Italy	66.67	20	Norway	1.18
5	Netherlands	34.77	21	Poland	0.47
6	Belgium	20.54	22	Cyprus	0.46
7	United Kingdom	18.43	23	Ireland	0.36
8	Portugal	16.07	24	Luxembourg	0.31
9	Spain	15.63	25	Latvia	0.25
10	Austria	11.99	26	Lithuania	0.19
11	Russia	9.41	27	Hungary	0.11
12	Sweden	4.80	28	Albania	0.06
13	Turkey	3.75	29	Iceland	0.05
14	Greece	3.46		Ukraine	0.05
15	Romania	2.70	31	Malta	0.04
16	Denmark	2.00	32	Estonia	0.01

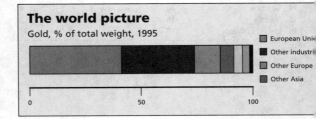

The world picture

Gold, % of total weight, 1995

- European Union
- Other industrial
- Other Europe
- Other Asia

0   50   100

Looking back
Total reserves minus gold, $m

1970

1	Germany	9,630	11	Ireland		681
2	Italy	2,465	12	Portugal		602
3	Switzerland	2,401	13	Sweden		561
4	United Kingdom	1,480	14	Finland		425
5	Netherlands	1,454	15	Denmark		419
6	France	1,428	16	Turkey		304
7	Belgium	1,377	17	Cyprus		194
8	Spain	1,319		Greece		194
9	Austria	1,044	19	Malta		148
10	Norway	787.9	20	Iceland		53

1980

1	Germany	48,592	12	Denmark	3,387
2	France	27,340	13	Ireland	2,860
3	Italy	23,126	14	Finland	1,870
4	United Kingdom	20,650	15	Greece	1,346
5	Switzerland	15,656	16	Turkey	1,077
6	Spain	11,863	17	Malta	990
7	Netherlands	11,645	18	Portugal	795
8	Belgium	7,823	19	Cyprus	368
9	Norway	6,048	20	Romania	323
10	Austria	5,280	21	Iceland	174
11	Sweden	3,418	22	Poland	128

1990

1	Germany	67,902	13	Finland	9,644
2	Italy	62,927	14	Austria	9,376
3	Spain	51,228	15	Turkey	6,050
4	France	36,778	16	Ireland	5,223
5	United Kingdom	35,850	17	Poland	4,492
6	Switzerland	29,223	18	Greece	3,412
7	Sweden	17,988	19	Cyprus	1,507
8	Netherlands	17,484	20	Malta	1,432
9	Norway	15,332	21	Hungary	1,070
10	Portugal	14,485	22	Romania	524
11	Belgium	12,151	23	Iceland	436
12	Denmark	10,591	24	Luxembourg	81

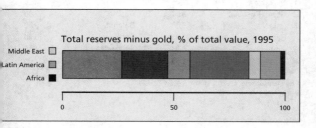

Total reserves minus gold, % of total value, 1995

Middle East ☐
Latin America ☐
Africa ■

0   50   100

Interest rates

Central bank discount rates

%

1980

1	Iceland	28.00	11	Spain	10.90
2	Turkey	26.00	12	Sweden	10.00
3	Greece	20.50	13	Finland	9.25
4	Portugal	18.00	14	Norway	9.00
5	Italy	16.50	15	Netherlands	8.00
6	United Kingdom	15.11	16	Germany	7.50
7	Ireland	14.00	17	Austria	6.75
8	Belgium	12.00	18	Cyprus	6.00
9	France	11.90	19	Malta	5.50
10	Denmark	11.00	20	Switzerland	3.00

1990

1	Poland	48.00	13	Belgium	10.50
2	Turkey	45.00		Norway	10.50
3	Ex-Yugoslavia	30.00	15	France	9.55
4	Hungary	22.00	16	Denmark	8.50
5	Iceland	21.00		Finland	8.50
6	Greece	19.00	18	Netherlands	7.25
7	Spain	14.71	19	Austria	6.50
8	Portugal	14.50		Cyprus	6.50
9	United Kingdom	14.09	21	Germany	6.00
10	Italy	12.50		Switzerland	6.00
11	Sweden	11.50	23	Malta	5.50
12	Ireland	11.25			

1995

1	Russia[a]	190.40	17	Sweden	7.00
2	Ukraine[a]	110.00	18	Norway	6.75
3	Turkey	45.00	19	Cyprus	6.50
4	Romania[b]	41.30		Ireland	6.50
5	Hungary	28.00	21	United Kingdom[c]	6.33
6	Lithuania[b]	26.80	22	Iceland	5.93
7	Poland[a]	25.00	23	Malta	5.50
8	Latvia	24.00	24	Netherlands[d]	5.00
9	Greece	18.00	25	France[e]	4.96
10	Slovenia	10.00	26	Finland	4.88
11	Slovakia	9.75	27	Denmark	4.25
12	Czech Republic	9.50	28	Austria	3.00
13	Italy	9.00		Belgium	3.00
	Spain	9.00		Germany	3.00
15	Portugal	8.93	31	Switzerland	1.50
16	Croatia	8.50			

a Refinancing rate.
b Interbank rate.
c Treasury bill.
d 1993.
e Repurchase agreements.

Central bank deposit rates
%

1980

1	Iceland	38.80	12	Turkey	8.00
2	Portugal	19.00	13	Germany	7.95
3	Greece	14.50	14	Belgium	7.69
4	United Kingdom	14.13	15	France	7.25
5	Spain	13.05	16	Luxembourg	6.50
6	Italy	12.70	17	Netherlands	5.96
7	Ireland	12.00	18	Cyprus	5.75
8	Sweden	11.25	19	Austria	5.00
9	Denmark	10.80		Malta	5.00
10	Finland	9.00		Norway	5.00
11	Switzerland	8.80	22	Hungary	3.00

1990

1	Turkey	47.60	13	Finland	7.50
2	Poland	41.70	14	Germany	7.07
3	Hungary	24.70	15	Italy	6.80
4	Greece	19.52	16	Ireland	6.29
5	Portugal	13.99	17	Belgium	6.13
6	United Kingdom	12.54	18	Luxembourg	6.00
7	Iceland	12.30	19	Cyprus	5.75
8	Spain	10.65	20	France	4.50
9	Sweden	9.93		Malta	4.50
10	Norway	9.68	22	Austria	3.41
11	Switzerland	8.28	23	Netherlands	3.31
12	Denmark	7.90			

1995

1	Russia	102.00	17	Cyprus	5.75
2	Turkey	76.13	18	Croatia	5.00
3	Ukraine	70.30		Luxembourg	5.00
4	Poland	26.80	20	Norway	4.95
5	Hungary	26.10	21	France	4.50
6	Greece	15.75		Malta	4.50
7	Slovenia	15.32	23	United Kingdom	4.11
8	Latvia	14.79	24	Belgium	4.04
9	Slovakia	9.01	25	Germany	3.85
10	Estonia	8.70	26	Denmark[f]	3.80
11	Lithuania	8.40	27	Iceland	3.40
12	Portugal	8.38	28	Finland	3.19
13	Spain	7.68	29	Netherlands	2.63
14	Czech Republic	6.96	30	Austria	2.19
15	Italy	6.45	31	Switzerland	1.28
16	Sweden	6.16	32	Ireland	0.44

f 1994.

Taxation

Total tax revenue
As % of GDP

1980

1	Sweden	48.8	11	United Kingdom	35.3
2	Norway	47.1	12	Ireland	33.8
3	Luxembourg	46.3	13	Switzerland	30.8
4	Denmark	45.5	14	Italy	30.2
5	Netherlands	45.0	15	Greece	29.4
6	Belgium	44.4	16	Iceland	29.2
7	France	41.7	17	Portugal	25.2
8	Austria	41.2	18	Spain	24.1
9	Germany	38.2	19	Turkey	17.9
10	Finland	36.9			

1990

1	Sweden	55.6	11	Greece	37.5
2	Denmark	48.7	12	Germany	36.7
3	Finland	45.4	13	United Kingdom	36.4
4	Belgium	44.8	14	Ireland	35.2
5	Netherlands	44.6	15	Spain	34.4
6	France	43.7	16	Switzerland	31.5
7	Luxembourg	43.6	17	Iceland	31.4
8	Norway	41.8	18	Portugal	31.0
9	Austria	41.3	19	Turkey	20.0
10	Italy	39.1			

1995

1	Denmark	51.7	12	Italy	41.8
2	Sweden	50.2	13	Norway	41.7
3	Belgium	45.9	14	Hungary[a]	41.0
4	Czech Republic	45.8	15	Germany	39.1
5	Finland	45.8	16	Ireland	35.4
6	France	44.5	17	United Kingdom	35.2
7	Netherlands	44.4	18	Switzerland	34.4
8	Luxembourg	43.7	19	Spain	34.2
9	Poland	43.6	20	Portugal	33.9
10	Greece[a]	42.5	21	Iceland	30.9
11	Austria	42.0	22	Turkey	21.1

EU15 tax revenue by type

% of total, 1994

Social security 29%
Other 6%
Income and profits 34%
Goods and services 31%

a 1994.

The changing workforce

Force in numbers
Total no. in workforce, 1994, m

1	Russia	77		Greece	4
2	Germany	40		Switzerland	4
3	United Kingdom	29	22	Azerbaijan	3
4	France	26		Denmark	3
	Ukraine	26		Finland	3
6	Italy	25		Georgia	3
7	Poland	19		Slovakia	3
	Turkey	19	27	Albania	2
9	Spain	17		Armenia	2
10	Romania	11		Croatia	2
11	Netherlands	7		Lithuania	2
12	Czech Republic	6		Norway	2
13	Belarus	5	32	Estonia	1
	Hungary	5		Iceland	1
	Portugal	5		Ireland	1
	Sweden	5		Latvia	1
17	Austria	4		Macedonia FYR	1
	Belgium	4		Moldova	1
	Bulgaria	4		Slovenia	1

Most male workforce
Male % of workforce, 1994

1	Malta[b]	0.73	11	Austria	0.60
2	Ireland	0.67		Belgium	0.60
3	Turkey	0.65		Switzerland	0.60
	Luxembourg[a]	0.65	14	Croatia	0.59
5	Greece	0.64		Germany	0.59
	Spain	0.64		Macedonia FYR	0.59
7	Italy	0.63	17	Albania	0.57
8	Netherlands	0.61		Portugal	0.57
	Cyprus[b]	0.61		United Kingdom	0.57
	San Marino[b]	0.61	20	Azerbaijan	0.56

Most female workforce
Female % of workforce, 1994

1	Estonia	0.51		Finland	0.47
	Latvia	0.51		Georgia	0.47
3	Bulgaria	0.50		Sweden	0.47
4	Moldova	0.49		Iceland[c]	0.47
5	Belarus	0.48	15	Denmark	0.46
	Lithuania	0.48		Poland	0.46
	Russia	0.48	17	Armenia	0.45
	Slovakia	0.48		Norway	0.45
	Ukraine	0.48		Romania	0.45
10	Czech Republic	0.47		Slovenia	0.45

Total no. in workforce, 1980, m

1	Russia	76	20	Austria	3
2	Germany	37		Azerbaijan	3
3	Turkey	28		Denmark	3
4	United Kingdom	27		Georgia	3
5	Ukraine	26		Switzerland	3
6	France	24	25	Croatia	2
7	Italy	23		Finland	2
8	Poland	19		Lithuania	2
9	Spain	14		Norway	2
10	Romania	11		Slovakia	2
11	Netherlands	6	30	Albania	1
12	Belarus	5		Armenia	1
	Bulgaria	5		Estonia	1
	Czech Republic	5		Ireland	1
	Hungary	5		Latvia	1
	Portugal	5		Macedonia FYR	1
17	Belgium	4		Moldova	1
	Greece	4		Slovenia	1
	Sweden	4			

Male % of workforce, 1980

1	Malta[d]	0.75	11	Switzerland	0.63
2	Greece	0.72		Cyprus[d]	0.63
	Ireland	0.72	13	Croatia	0.62
	Spain	0.72		San Marino[d]	0.62
5	Netherlands	0.69	15	Albania	0.61
6	Luxembourg[d]	0.67		Portugal	0.61
	Italy	0.67		United Kingdom	0.61
8	Belgium	0.66	18	Austria	0.60
	Macedonia FYR	0.66		France	0.60
10	Turkey	0.65		Germany	0.60

Female % of workforce, 1980

1	Estonia	0.51		Czech Republic	0.47
	Latvia	0.51	12	Finland	0.46
3	Belarus	0.50		Romania	0.46
	Lithuania	0.50		Iceland[a]	0.46
	Moldova	0.50	15	Bulgaria	0.45
	Ukraine	0.50		Poland	0.45
7	Georgia	0.49		Slovakia	0.45
	Russia	0.49	18	Denmark	0.44
9	Armenia	0.48		Slovenia	0.44
10	Azerbaijan	0.47		Sweden	0.44

a 1991.   b 1993.   c 1994.   d 1985.

What people do – and did

Agriculture
% of workforce employed in agriculture, 1995

1	Turkey[a]	45	11	Russia[c]		15
2	Moldova[b]	40	12	Cyprus[c]		13
3	Romania[c]	36		Hungary[c]		13
4	Poland[b]	25		Ireland[c]		13
5	Albania	24	15	Slovakia[c]		12
6	Lithuania[a]	23	16	Portugal		11
7	Bulgaria[a]	22	17	Estonia[a]		9
8	Belarus[c]	21		Iceland[a]		9
	Greece[a]	21		Slovenia[c]		9
10	Latvia[b]	20		Spain		9

Industry
% of workforce employed in industry, 1995

1	Latvia[b]	75	15	Belarus[c]	55
2	Croatia[c]	71	16	Romania[c]	54
3	Macedonia FYR	70	17	Lithuania[a]	53
4	Slovenia[c]	68	18	Moldova[b]	39
5	Cyprus[c]	66	19	Germany	38
6	San Marino[c]	65	20	Austria[a]	33
7	Estonia[a]	63		Italy[a]	33
8	Slovakia[c]	61	22	Portugal	32
9	Albania	60	23	Luxembourg[e]	30
10	Russia[b]	59		Spain	30
11	Hungary[b]	58	25	Switzerland	29
12	Bulgaria[a]	57	26	Belgium[e]	28
13	Malta[d]	56		Finland	28
	Poland[b]	56		Ireland[c]	28

Services
% of workforce employed in services, 1995

1	Netherlands[a]	73		Italy[a]	60
2	United Kingdom	72	16	Germany	59
3	Norway	71	17	Greece[a]	56
	Sweden	71		Portugal	56
5	Belgium[e]	69	19	Malta[d]	42
	France	69	20	San Marino[c]	33
7	Denmark[a]	68		Turkey[a]	33
8	Switzerland	67	22	Estonia[a]	28
9	Luxembourg[e]	66		Hungary[b]	28
10	Iceland[a]	65	24	Russia[b]	26
11	Finland	64		Slovakia[a]	26
12	Spain	61	26	Croatia[c]	24
13	Austria[a]	60		Lithuania[a]	24
	Ireland[c]	60	28	Belarus[c]	23

a 1994.
b 1992.
c 1993.
d 1991.
e 1990.

% of workforce employed in agriculture, 1973

1	Turkey	60	11	Bulgaria[a]	21
2	Greece	37		Hungary[a]	21
	Moldova[a]	37	13	Lithuania[a]	20
4	Romania[a]	29	14	Italy	18
5	Poland[a]	28	15	Latvia[b]	17
6	Portugal	27		Finland	17
7	Belarus[a]	25	17	Austria	16
8	Ireland	24		Cyprus[a]	16
	Spain	24		Iceland	16
10	Albania[a]	22	20	Slovakia[a]	15

% of workforce employed in industry, 1973

1	Latvia[b]	77		Lithuania[a]	58
2	Croatia[a]	75	16	Romania[a]	57
	Macedonia FYR[a]	75	17	Belarus[a]	55
4	Slovenia[a]	73	18	Germany	47
5	Cyprus[a]	65	19	Switzerland	45
	San Marino[a]	65	20	Luxembourg	44
	Slovakia[a]	65	21	Moldova[a]	43
8	Estonia[a]	63	22	United Kingdom	42
9	Bulgaria[a]	62	23	Austria	41
10	Russia[b]	60		Belgium	41
11	Albania[a]	59	25	France	40
	Hungary[a]	59	26	Italy	39
13	Malta[a]	58	27	Netherlands	37
	Poland[a]	58		Spain	37

% of workforce employed in services, 1973

1	Netherlands	58	15	Italy	42
2	Denmark	57	16	Portugal	39
3	Sweden	56		Spain	39
4	Belgium	55	18	Malta[a]	37
	United Kingdom	55	19	Greece	36
6	Norway	54	20	San Marino[a]	32
7	France	49	21	Russia[b]	26
	Iceland	49	22	Estonia[a]	24
9	Luxembourg	48	23	Lithuania[a]	23
	Switzerland	48	24	Turkey	21
11	Finland	47	25	Belarus[a]	20
12	Germany	45		Croatia[a]	20
13	Ireland	44		Hungary[a]	20
14	Austria	43	28	Moldova[a]	19

a 1985.
b 1990.

Unemployment

The size of the problem
Total no. unemployed, '000s, 1995

1	Spain	3,586	17	Czech Republic	189
2	Germany	3,249	18	Ireland	187
3	France	2,990	19	Denmark	186
4	Italy	2,877	19	Macedonia FYR	186
5	Poland	2,838	21	Austria	142
6	United Kingdom	2,254	22	Slovenia	127
7	Turkey	1,633	22	Switzerland	127
8	Belgium	629	24	Norway	107
9	Bulgaria	488	25	Belarus	101
10	Netherlands	474	26	Latvia	84
11	Hungary	451	27	Lithuania	78
12	Finland	430	28	Moldova	21
13	Greece	414	29	Estonia	15
14	Portugal	345	30	Cyprus	8
15	Slovakia	337		Iceland	8
16	Sweden	332	32	Luxembourg	4

The burden on the economy
Public expenditure on unemployment benefit as % of GDP, 1995

Finland	3.62	United Kingdom	1.41
Netherlands	3.06	Austria	1.31
Denmark	3.00	Switzerland	1.25
Spain	2.60	Norway	1.10
Sweden	2.52	Portugal	0.99
Belgium	2.25	Greece	0.51
Germany	2.08	Luxembourg	0.47
France	1.57	Czech Republic	0.15

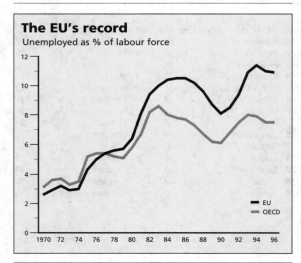

The EU's record
Unemployed as % of labour force

— EU
— OECD

The problem in proportion
% of workforce unemployed, 1995

1	Macedonia FYR	32.0		18	Denmark	8.0
2	Spain	22.7		19	Greece	7.2
3	Finland	17.1		20	Portugal	7.1
4	Albania	17.0		21	Austria	6.5
5	Poland	16.9			Netherlands	6.5
6	Slovakia	14.4		23	Latvia	6.2
7	Slovenia	14.3		24	Iceland	5.3
8	Bulgaria	13.3		25	Norway	4.9
9	Ireland	12.9		26	Lithuania	3.8
10	Italy	12.2		27	Switzerland	3.3
11	France	11.6		28	Czech Republic	3.1
12	Hungary	11.0		29	Cyprus	2.7
13	Romania	10.8		30	Estonia	2.3
14	Belgium	9.4		31	Russia	2.0
15	Sweden	9.2		32	Belarus	1.8
16	United Kingdom	8.7		33	Moldova	1.1
17	Germany	8.2		34	Ukraine	0.4

Looking back

% of workforce unemployed, 1990

1	Macedonia FYR	23.6
2	Spain	15.9
3	Ireland	13.3
4	Italy	10.3
5	Denmark	9.7
6	Albania	9.5
7	France	8.9
8	Croatia	8.0
9	Netherlands	7.5
10	Turkey	7.4
11	Belgium	7.2
12	United Kingdom	6.9
13	Greece	6.4
14	San Marino	5.5
15	Austria	5.4
16	Norway	5.2
17	Germany	4.8
18	Slovenia	4.7
19	Portugal	4.6
20	Malta	3.9
21	Poland	3.5
22	Finland	3.4
23	Cyprus	1.8
	Iceland	1.8
	Sweden	1.8
26	Bulgaria	1.7
	Hungary	1.7
28	Slovakia	1.5
29	Luxembourg	1.3

% of workforce unemployed, 1983

1	Macedonia FYR	21.6
2	Spain	17.0
3	Ireland	14.0
4	United Kingdom	12.4
5	Belgium	12.1
6	Netherlands	12.0
7	Turkey	11.2
8	Denmark	9.1
9	Italy	8.8
10	France	8.3
11	Malta	8.1
12	Greece	7.8
	Portugal	7.8
14	Germany	7.7
15	Croatia	7.0
16	San Marino	6.9
17	Albania	6.7
18	Finland	5.4
19	Austria	4.8
20	Sweden	3.9
21	Norway	3.4
22	Cyprus	3.3
23	Luxembourg	1.7
24	Switzerland	1.0
25	Iceland	0.9

What people earn

Skilled industrial worker
$ '000s

	Gross income	Net income
Switzerland (Zurich)	44.4	35.8
Switzerland (Geneva)	43.3	34.9
Denmark	36.9	22.0
Germany (Frankfurt)	33.9	23.7
Norway	33.1	23.4
Luxembourg	32.9	30.6
Austria	29.9	20.9
Netherlands	29.9	22.0
Germany (Dusseldorf)	28.1	20.7
Finland	25.9	16.1
United Kingdom	25.3	17.2
Belgium	23.3	18.1
Italy	21.5	14.5
Sweden	21.4	15.3
France	19.1	14.9
Ireland	17.8	13.9
Spain	17.0	13.4
Cyprus	12.4	9.9
Greece	12.1	9.6
Portugal	11.2	8.6
Hungary	3.8	2.6
Czech Republic	3.3	2.6

School teacher
$ '000s

	Gross income	Net income
Switzerland (Zurich)	74.2	56.8
Switzerland (Geneva)	69.4	49.2
Luxembourg	61.5	50.8
Germany (Frankfurt)	41.3	49.2
Germany (Dusseldorf)	39.9	32.9
Denmark	33.8	20.5
Netherlands	31.5	23.8
United Kingdom	29.5	19.9
Norway	26.3	19.1
Ireland	26.1	19.8
Finland	25.6	17.1
Austria	25.3	18.8
Sweden	24.7	17.4
Belgium	24.6	16.0
Spain	21.7	16.6
Cyprus	21.0	16.2
France	20.3	16.2
Italy	18.8	13.0
Portugal	15.4	11.3
Greece	11.9	10.1
Hungary	2.9	2.1
Czech Republic	2.2	1.8

Department manager
$ '000s

	Gross income	Net income
Switzerland (Zurich)	120.7	82.5
Switzerland (Geneva)	90.4	61.2
Luxembourg	86.7	62.5
Germany (Dusseldorf)	85.2	57.8
Germany (Frankfurt)	78.9	52.4
France	78.1	55.8
Finland	58.1	30.9
Netherlands	57.8	33.6
Norway	57.5	36.0
Belgium	56.0	30.3
Austria	55.6	36.5
Denmark	53.6	30.8
Sweden	39.0	24.8
Ireland	37.3	25.8
United Kingdom	37.0	25.1
Italy	31.9	20.4
Spain	24.6	18.4
Cyprus	22.1	16.2
Greece	16.0	12.3
Portugal	15.1	11.0
Hungary	11.4	6.4
Czech Republic	7.4	5.5

Secretary
$ '000s

	Gross income	Net income
Switzerland (Geneva)	44.8	30.5
Switzerland (Zurich)	41.2	31.5
Luxembourg	38.3	27.1
Germany (Dusseldorf)	34.5	21.2
Germany (Frankfurt)	32.9	19.8
Denmark	32.8	19.9
Norway	28.1	18.9
Netherlands	25.9	17.0
Belgium	24.4	14.9
Austria	24.2	17.6
France	22.6	16.3
Sweden	22.6	16.1
Spain	21.0	16.0
Finland	20.7	13.7
Ireland	19.7	13.6
United Kingdom	18.4	12.6
Italy	18.1	12.5
Cyprus	10.4	8.1
Greece	10.2	8.9
Portugal	10.0	7.8
Hungary	3.5	2.4
Czech Republic	2.8	2.2

Taxing matters

The taxman's take
Marginal rates of personal income taxes, 1995

| | | Top rates, % | | Bottom rate, % |
		Central and local government	Central government	Central government
1	Finland	69	39	7
2	Italy	67	51	10
3	Denmark	63	35	13
4	Sweden	61	25	25
5	Netherlands	60	60	6
6	France	57	57	12
7	Spain	56	56	20
8	Belgium	55	55	25
	Turkey	55	55	25
10	Germany	53	53	a
11	Austria	50	50	10
12	Ireland	48	48	27
13	Iceland	47	38	33
14	Switzerland	44	12	1
15	Norway	42	14	10
16	Greece	40	40	5
	Portugal	40	40	15
	United Kingdom	40	40	20

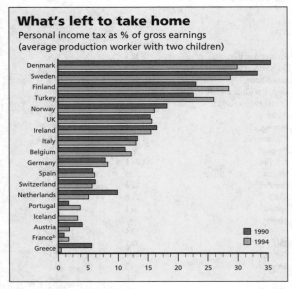

What's left to take home
Personal income tax as % of gross earnings
(average production worker with two children)

■ 1990
■ 1994

a Not applicable; tax calculated by formula.
b 1991.

Strikes

Time out
Working days not worked per 1,000 employees, all industries

1994			1985		
1	Spain	760	1	Denmark	1,056
2	Greece	329	2	Greece	618
3	Finland	327	3	Ireland	521
4	Italy	246	4	Spain	444
5	Belgium	145	5	United Kingdom	299
6	Norway	55	6	Italy	266
7	Denmark	34	7	Sweden	126
8	Switzerland	32	8	Portugal	100
9	Portugal	30	9	Finland	84
10	Ireland	28	10	France	50
11	France	26	11	Belgium	45
12	United Kingdom	13	12	Norway	38
13	Germany	9	13	Netherlands	20
14	Netherlands	8	14	Austria	8
15	Sweden	5	15	Germany	1
16	Iceland	1		Iceland	1
17	Austria	0	17	Switzerland	0

Average working days lost
All industries

1990–94			1985–89		
1	Greece	3,500	1	Greece	3,976
2	Spain	492	2	Spain	647
3	Turkey	253	3	Turkey	343
4	Italy	240	4	Finland	337
5	Finland	218	5	Italy	300
6	Ireland	135	6	Ireland	292
7	OECD average	100	7	Denmark	235
8	Norway	72	8	United Kingdom	180
9	Belgium	57	9	Norway	135
	Sweden	57	10	Sweden	121
11	Portugal	39	11	Portugal	94
12	Denmark	37	12	France	57
	United Kingdom	37	13	Belgium	52
14	France	30	14	Netherlands	9
15	Germany	23	15	Austria	2
16	Netherlands	16		Germany	2
17	Austria	7	17	Iceland	1
18	Switzerland	1	18	Switzerland	0
19	Iceland	0			

Work and play

Working hours
Average working hours, 1995

		Per week	Per year
1	Hungary	38.1	1,980
2	Czech Republic	38.0	1,978
3	Portugal	36.7	1,908
4	United Kingdom	36.2	1,880
5	Switzerland	36.1	1,879
6	Sweden	34.7	1,803
7	Netherlands	34.5	1,792
8	France	34.4	1,790
9	Italy	34.3	1,785
10	Luxembourg	34.2	1,780
11	Greece	34.1	1,775
12	Austria	33.5	1,744
13	Belgium	33.2	1,725
	Finland	33.2	1,726
	Ireland	33.2	1,727
	Norway	33.2	1,728
17	Spain	33.1	1,721
18	Germany	32.3	1,682
19	Denmark	32.1	1,669

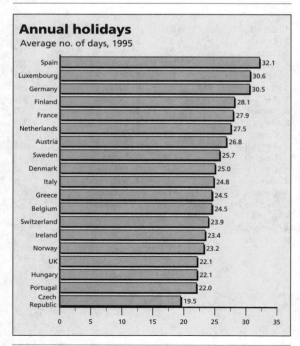

Annual holidays
Average no. of days, 1995

- Spain — 32.1
- Luxembourg — 30.6
- Germany — 30.5
- Finland — 28.1
- France — 27.9
- Netherlands — 27.5
- Austria — 26.8
- Sweden — 25.7
- Denmark — 25.0
- Italy — 24.8
- Greece — 24.5
- Belgium — 24.5
- Switzerland — 23.9
- Ireland — 23.4
- Norway — 23.2
- UK — 22.1
- Hungary — 22.1
- Portugal — 22.0
- Czech Republic — 19.5

Part VI

BUSINESS AND FINANCE

Agriculture: leading producers

Wheat

'000 tonnes

1980			1995		
1	Ex-USSR	92,500	1	France	30,878
2	France	23,781	2	Russia	30,118
3	Turkey	16,554	3	Turkey	18,015
4	Germany	11,254	4	Germany	17,816
5	Italy	9,156	5	Ukraine	16,273
6	United Kingdom	8,470	6	United Kingdom	14,400
7	Romania	6,264	7	Poland	8,668
8	Hungary	6,077	8	Italy	7,995
9	Spain	6,040	9	Romania	7,667
10	Czechoslovakia	5,386	10	Hungary	4,600
11	Ex-Yugoslavia	5,091	11	Denmark	4,420
12	Poland	4,175	12	Czech Republic	3,823
13	Bulgaria	3,847	13	Bulgaria	3,523
14	Greece	2,970	14	Serbia	3,002
15	Austria	1,201	15	Spain	2,958
16	Sweden	1,193	16	Greece	2,000
17	Belgium & Luxembourg	906	17	Slovakia	1,938
18	Netherlands	882	18	Sweden	1,554
19	Denmark	652	19	Belgium & Luxembourg	1,536
20	Albania	496	20	Austria	1,301

Potatoes

'000 tonnes

1980			1995		
1	Ex-USSR	67,023	1	Russia	37,300
2	Poland	26,391	2	Poland	24,891
3	Germany	17,146	3	Ukraine	14,729
4	United Kingdom	7,105	4	Germany	10,382
5	France	6,618	5	Belarus	8,570
6	Netherlands	6,266	6	Netherlands	7,363
7	Spain	5,737	7	United Kingdom	6,445
8	Romania	3,942	8	France	5,754
9	Turkey	3,000	9	Turkey	4,750
10	Italy	2,923	10	Spain	4,195
11	Czechoslovakia	2,695	11	Romania	3,020
12	Ex-Yugoslavia	2,440	12	Belgium & Luxembourg	2,100
13	Belgium & Luxembourg	1,450	13	Italy	2,061
14	Hungary	1,392	14	Lithuania	1,594
15	Austria	1,264	15	Denmark	1,480
16	Portugal	1,200	16	Portugal	1,454
17	Sweden	1,084	17	Czech Republic	1,330
18	Greece	1,084	18	Hungary	1,150
19	Ireland	880	19	Sweden	1,074
20	Switzerland	853	20	Serbia	931

Sugar
'000 tonnes

1980			1995		
1	Ex-USSR	80,987	1	France	30,360
2	France	28,442	2	Ukraine	29,650
3	Germany	26,156	3	Germany	26,077
4	Italy	13,478	4	Russia	19,072
5	Poland	10,139	5	Poland	13,309
6	United Kingdom	7,380	6	Italy	12,933
7	Spain	7,259	7	Turkey	11,680
8	Czechoslovakia	7,258	8	United Kingdom	8,125
9	Turkey	6,766	9	Spain	7,795
10	Netherlands	5,931	10	Netherlands	7,600
11	Belgium & Luxembourg	5,868	11	Belgium & Luxembourg	5,729
12	Romania	5,298	12	Hungary	4,192
13	Yugoslavia	5,213	13	Denmark	2,942
14	Hungary	3,941	14	Austria	2,886
15	Denmark	3,010	15	Romania	2,764
16	Austria	2,587	16	Greece	2,690
17	Sweden	2,257	17	Sweden	2,508
18	Greece	1,664	18	Serbia	2,100
19	Bulgaria	1,449	19	Moldova	2,100
20	Ireland	1,156	20	Ireland	1,370

Meat
'000 tonnes

1980			1995		
1	Ex-USSR	15,072	1	France	6,497
2	Germany	6,960	2	Russia	5,946
3	France	5,449	3	Germany	5,748
4	Italy	3,564	4	Italy	3,974
5	United Kingdom	3,070	5	Spain	3,844
6	Poland	2,893	6	United Kingdom	3,453
7	Spain	2,644	7	Netherlands	2,916
8	Netherlands	1,901	8	Poland	2,582
9	Romania	1,611	9	Ukraine	2,294
10	Hungary	1,448	10	Denmark	1,906
11	Ex-Yugoslavia	1,446	11	Belgium & Luxembourg	1,691
12	Czechoslovakia	1,416	12	Romania	1,245
13	Denmark	1,319	13	Turkey	1,181
14	Belgium & Luxembourg	1,136	14	Hungary	968
15	Austria	714	15	Czech Republic	936
16	Ireland	694	16	Ireland	893
17	Turkey	688	17	Serbia	891
18	Bulgaria	651	18	Austria	872
19	Sweden	545	19	Belarus	854
20	Greece	531	20	Portugal	637

Industry: who makes what

Cars
Production, '000s, 1995

1	Germany	4,362	8	Belgium	351
2	France	3,031	9	Poland	348
3	Spain	1,950	10	Turkey	243
4	United Kingdom	1,532	11	Czech Republic	230
5	Italy	1,422	12	Netherlands	100
6	Russia & Ukraine	898	13	Romania	42
7	Sweden	388	14	Hungary	40

Commercial vehicles
Production, '000s, 1995

1	Germany	358.8	7	Belgium	84.0
2	France	312.9	8	Portugal	64.6
3	United Kingdom	213.8	9	Netherlands	16.6
4	Spain	247.4	10	Austria	10.4
5	Italy	236.8	11	Finland	0.5
6	Sweden	87.8			

Steel
Production, '000 tonnes, 1995

1	Russia	51,425	18	Bulgaria	2,728
2	Germany	41,845	19	Luxembourg	2,613
3	Italy	27,675	20	Hungary	1,866
4	Ukraine	21,842	21	Greece	938
5	France	18,104	22	Portugal	817
6	United Kingdom	17,680	23	Belarus	724
7	Spain	13,937	24	Moldova	662
8	Turkey	12,716	25	Denmark	651
9	Poland	11,921	26	Norway	505
10	Belgium	11,592	27	Slovenia	394
11	Czech Republic	7,184	28	Ireland	310
12	Romania	6,520	29	Serbia	180
13	Netherlands	6,415	30	Georgia	86
14	Austria	4,981	31	Croatia	45
15	Sweden	4,926	32	Macedonia FYR	27
16	Slovakia	3,709	33	Azerbaijan	12
17	Finland	3,182			

Pharmaceuticals
Value added, m ecus, 1993

1	Germany	6,419	6	Denmark	1,173
2	United Kingdom	5,927	7	Belgium	884
3	France	5,102	8	Netherlands	631
4	Italy	3,500	9	Portugal	193
5	Spain	2,231	10	Greece	93

Inventiveness and investment

Patents granted
Per '000 of the labour force, 1993

1	Switzerland	32.8		Poland	7.7
2	Germany	22.9	**13**	Norway	7.0
3	Sweden	20.8	**14**	Italy	6.9
4	Finland	18.8		Netherlands	6.9
5	France	15.2	**16**	Ireland	3.1
6	Austria	14.9	**17**	Russia	3.0
7	Czech Republic	9.2	**18**	Spain	2.5
8	United Kingdom	7.9	**19**	Greece	1.6
9	Denmark	7.8	**20**	Iceland	0.8
10	Belgium	7.7	**21**	Portugal	0.1
	Hungary	7.7		Turkey	0.1

Spending on research and development
As % of GDP, 1994

1	Sweden[a]	3.3		Iceland[b]	1.3
2	Switzerland[b]	2.7	**14**	Ireland[a]	1.2
3	France	2.4		Italy	1.2
	Germany	2.4	**16**	Slovakia	1.0
5	Finland[a]	2.2	**17**	Hungary	0.9
	United Kingdom	2.2	**18**	Poland	0.8
7	Netherlands[a]	1.9		Russia	0.8
	Norway	1.9		Spain	0.8
9	Denmark[a]	1.8	**21**	Greece[a]	0.6
10	Belgium[c]	1.7		Portugal[b]	0.6
11	Austria	1.6	**23**	Turkey	0.5
12	Czech Republic	1.3		EU15	2.0

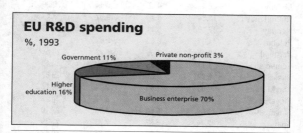

EU R&D spending
%, 1993

Government 11%
Private non-profit 3%
Higher education 16%
Business enterprise 70%

Spending on IT
As % of GDP, 1994

1	Sweden	2.4	**8**	France	1.8
	Switzerland	2.4		Belgium	1.8
3	United Kingdom	2.2	**10**	Germany	1.6
4	Netherlands	2.1	**11**	Austria	1.5
	Norway	2.1	**12**	Italy	1.2
6	Denmark	1.9	**13**	Spain	1.0
	Finland	1.9			

a 1993. b 1992. c 1991.

Service sectors

Working at it
% of labour force in different sub sectors, 1994 or latest year available

	Trade, restaurants and hotels	Transport, storage, communi- cation	Finance, insurance, property, business services	Community, social and personal services
Albania[a]	7.22	4.70	3.35	0.00
Austria	18.86	6.50	7.42	24.68
Belarus	8.99	6.77	0.87	23.42
Belgium	17.42	7.13	8.63	32.64
Bulgaria[a]	12.32	7.31	2.15	20.87
Croatia[a]	15.76	8.88	3.69	23.93
Denmark	15.56	7.12	9.96	36.08
Estonia[a]	12.28	9.36	5.87	28.09
Finland	14.37	7.87	8.55	34.36
France	16.81	6.32	10.59	34.98
Germany	15.12	5.75	9.20	29.38
Greece	18.65	6.79	5.44	20.08
Hungary	14.31	8.66	–	–
Iceland	14.53	6.74	8.03	30.66
Ireland	17.74	5.80	8.40	25.41
Italy	21.10	5.40	7.57	25.67
Latvia[a]	13.90	7.81	5.58	5.35
Lithuania	14.03	5.50	3.71	23.59
Luxembourg	21.20	6.80	8.86	29.48
Macedonia FYR[a]	9.60	5.30	3.03	21.46
Malta	10.44	7.37	3.84	41.90
Moldova	5.41	4.98	0.44	20.59
Netherlands	18.34	6.26	10.52	35.43
Norway	17.10	8.11	7.86	38.53
Poland	11.82	6.62	2.62	18.73
Portugal	19.45	4.66	6.73	24.84
Romania	7.11	5.88	4.79	10.40
Russia	6.82	7.81	0.69	25.87
San Marino	17.53	1.95	2.74	34.11
Slovakia	6.01	8.99	5.77	26.43
Slovenia[a]	11.09	5.60	4.38	23.10
Spain	22.74	5.87	7.83	22.79
Sweden	14.47	6.90	9.65	40.47
Switzerland	19.78	6.23	12.75	28.58
Turkey	12.81	4.93	2.44	13.96
United Kingdom	22.39	6.08	16.18	30.60

a % of total employees.

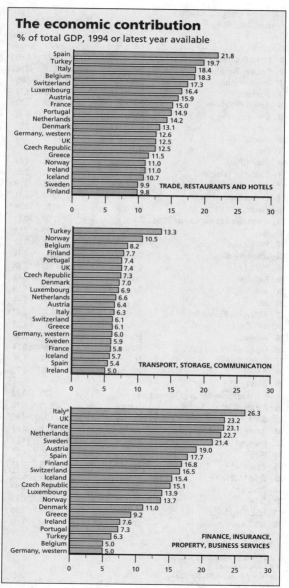

The economic contribution
% of total GDP, 1994 or latest year available

TRADE, RESTAURANTS AND HOTELS

Spain	21.8
Turkey	19.7
Italy	18.4
Belgium	18.3
Switzerland	17.3
Luxembourg	16.4
Austria	15.9
France	15.0
Portugal	14.9
Netherlands	14.2
Denmark	13.1
Germany, western	12.6
UK	12.5
Czech Republic	12.5
Greece	11.5
Norway	11.0
Ireland	11.0
Iceland	10.7
Sweden	9.9
Finland	9.8

TRANSPORT, STORAGE, COMMUNICATION

Turkey	13.3
Norway	10.5
Belgium	8.2
Finland	7.7
Portugal	7.4
UK	7.4
Czech Republic	7.3
Denmark	7.0
Luxembourg	6.9
Netherlands	6.6
Austria	6.4
Italy	6.3
Switzerland	6.1
Greece	6.1
Germany, western	6.0
Sweden	5.9
France	5.8
Iceland	5.7
Spain	5.4
Ireland	5.0

FINANCE, INSURANCE, PROPERTY, BUSINESS SERVICES

Italy[a]	26.3
UK	23.2
France	23.1
Netherlands	22.7
Sweden	21.4
Austria	19.0
Spain	17.7
Finland	16.8
Switzerland	16.5
Iceland	15.4
Czech Republic	15.1
Luxembourg	13.9
Norway	13.7
Denmark	11.0
Greece	9.2
Ireland	7.6
Portugal	7.3
Turkey	6.3
Belgium	5.0
Germany, western	5.0

a Includes community, social and personal services.

Big business

Europe's biggest companies
By sales, 1995, $bn

	Company	Country	Sales	Profits/ losses
1	Royal Dutch/Shell Group	Britain/Netherlands	109.83	6.90
2	Daimler-Benz	Germany	72.26	-3.60
3	Volkswagen	Germany	61.49	0.25
4	Siemens[a]	Germany	60.67	1.27
5	British Petroleum	Britain	56.98	1.77
6	Metro Holding	Switzerland	56.46	0.40
7	Unilever	Britain/Netherlands	49.74	2.32
8	Nestlé	Switzerland	47.78	2.47
9	Fiat	Italy	46.47	1.32
10	Veba Group	Germany	46.28	1.34
11	Deutsche Telekom[b]	Germany	46.15	3.68
12	Allianz Holding[c]	Germany	46.05	0.59
13	Elf Aquitaine	France	43.62	1.01
14	Électricité de France[b]	France	43.51	0.25
15	Union des Assurances de Paris	France	42.00	-0.41
16	IRI[b]	Italy	41.90	0.39
17	Philips Electronics	Netherlands	40.15	1.57
18	Deutsche Bank[d]	Germany	38.42	1.44
19	RWE Group[e]	Germany	37.23	0.73
20	Renault[b]	France	36.89	0.43
21	Hoechst	Germany	36.41	1.19
22	ENI[b]	Italy	36.39	2.66
23	ABB Asea Brown Boveri	Switzerland	33.74	1.32
24	ING Group	Netherlands	33.42	1.65
25	Peugeot	France	33.07	0.34
26	Cie Générale des Eaux	France	32.66	-0.74
27	Crédit Agricole	France	32.34	1.30
28	BASF	Germany	32.26	1.72
29	BMW (Bayerische Motoren Werke)	Germany	32.20	0.48
30	Alcatel Alsthom	France	32.15	-5.13
31	GAN	France	31.22	-0.36
32	Bayer	Germany	31.11	1.67
33	France Télécom	France	30.06	1.84
34	Viag	Germany	29.26	0.81
35	Carrefour	France	28.99	0.71
36	Crédit Lyonnais[b]	France	28.50	0.00
37	Thyssen[a]	Germany	28.03	0.51
38	Total	France	27.23	0.45
39	HSBC Holdings	Britain	26.68	3.89
40	ABN Amro Holding	Netherlands	26.53	1.63

a Year ended September 30th 1995.
b Goverment owned.
c Year ended December 31st 1994.
d Figures in accordance with International Accounting Standards.
e Year ended June 30th 1995.

Europe's biggest employers
1995, '000s

	Company	Country	No. of employees
1	Siemens	Germany	373.0
2	Deutsche Post	Germany	342.4
3	Deutsche Bahn	Germany	312.6
4	Daimler-Benz	Germany	311.0
5	Unilever	Britain/Netherlands	308.0
6	La Poste	France	290.8
7	Philips Electronics	Netherlands	265.1
8	IRI	Italy	263.1
9	Volkswagen	Germany	242.4
10	Fiat	Italy	237.4
11	Cie Générale des Eaux	France	221.2
12	Nestlé	Switzerland	220.2
13	Deutsche Telekom	Germany	220.0
14	SNCF	France	215.8
15	ABB Asea Brown Boveri	Switzerland	209.6
16	Alcatel Alsthom	France	191.8
17	Post Office	Britain	191.3
18	Metro Holding	Switzerland	178.6
19	BAT Industries	Britain	170.4
20	France Télécom	France	167.7

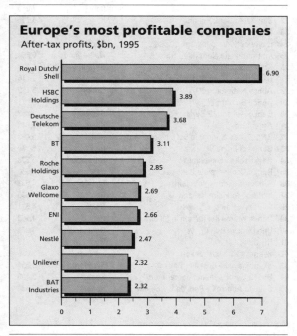

Europe's most profitable companies
After-tax profits, $bn, 1995

Royal Dutch/Shell	6.90
HSBC Holdings	3.89
Deutsche Telekom	3.68
BT	3.11
Roche Holdings	2.85
Glaxo Wellcome	2.69
ENI	2.66
Nestlé	2.47
Unilever	2.32
BAT Industries	2.32

Banking

Europe's biggest banks
By capital, $m, 1995

	Bank	Country	Capital
1	HSBC Holdings	Britain	21,445
2	Crédit Agricole	France	20,386
3	Union Bank of Switzerland	Switzerland	19,903
4	Deutsche Bank	Germany	18,937
5	CS Holding	Switzerland	13,751
6	ABN-Amro Bank	Netherlands	13,372
7	Groupe Caisse d'Epargne	France	12,667
8	Swiss Bank Corporation	Switzerland	11,733
9	National Westminster Bank	Britain	11,501
10	Banque Nationale de Paris	France	11,453
11	Rabobank Nederland	Netherlands	11,310
12	Barclays Bank	Britain	11,068
13	Compagnie Financière de Paribas	France	10,980
14	Société Génerale	France	10,474
15	Dresdner Bank	Germany	9,203
16	Westdeutsche Landesbank Girozent	Germany	8,717
17	Commerzbank	Germany	8,210
18	Crédit Lyonnais	France	7,835
19	Crédit Mutuel Confédération Nationale	France	7,775
20	Lloyds TSB Group	Britain	7,171
21	Cariplo	Italy	7,015
22	San Paolo Bank Holding	Italy	6,796
23	Banco Bilbao Viizcaya	Spain	6,439
24	Bayerische Vereinsbank	Germany	6,278
25	Internationale Nederland Bank	Netherlands	6,254
26	Kreditanstalt für Wiederaufbau	Germany	6,228
27	Bayerische Hypo & Wechsel-Bank	Germany	6,116
28	Abbey National	Britain	6,109
29	Banco Santander	Spain	6,021
30	Bankgesellschaft Berlin	Germany	5,853
31	Argentaria	Spain	5,645
32	BNL-Banca Nationale del Lavoro	Italy	5,493
33	Banca di Roma	Italy	5,360
34	Bayerische Landesbank	Germany	5,208
35	Banca Commerciale Italiana	Italy	4,530
36	Groupe Banques Populaires	France	4,633
37	Istituto Mobiliare Italiano	Italy	4,530
38	Generale Bank	Belgium	4,521
39	Banca Monte dei Paschi di Siena	Italy	4,168
40	Den Danske Bank	Denmark	4,075
41	DG Bank	Germany	3,712
42	Svenska Handelsbanken	Sweden	3,665
43	Skandinaviska Enskilda Banken	Sweden	3,554
44	Banco Central Hispanoamericano	Spain	3,409
45	Caja de Ahorros y Pen. de Barcelona	Spain	3,326

Note: capital is essentially equity and reserves.

Central Europe's biggest banks
By capital, $m, 1995

	Bank	Country	Capital
1	Komercni banka	Czech Republic	988
2	Bank Handlowy w Warszawie	Poland	725
3	Ceská Sporitelna	Czech Republic	636
4	Bank Gospordarki Zywnoscoiwej	Poland	610
5	Ceskoslovenská obchodni banka	Czech Republic	537
6	Investicni a Postovni banka	Czech Republic	494
7	Privredna Banka Zagreb	Croatia	437
8	Vseobecná úverová banka	Slovakia	403
9	Bank Pekao	Poland	391
10	Bulbank (Bulgarian Foreign Trade Bank)	Bulgaria	349
11	Zagrebacka Banka	Croatia	314
12	Powszechna Kasa Oszczednosci BP	Poland	297
13	Beogradska Banka	Serbia	292
14	OTP Bank	Hungary	265
15	Bank Slaski S.A. W Katowicach	Poland	222
16	Powszechny Bank Kredytowy w Warszawie	Poland	212
17	Hungarian Foreign Trade Bank (MKB)	Hungary	193
18	bank Przemyslowo-Handlowy	Poland	189
19	Slovenská Sporitel'na	Slovakia	185
20	Nova Ljubljanska Banka	Slovenia	179

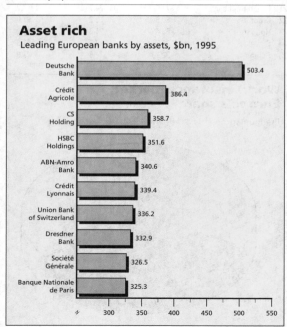

Asset rich
Leading European banks by assets, $bn, 1995

Deutsche Bank	503.4
Crédit Agricole	386.4
CS Holding	358.7
HSBC Holdings	351.6
ABN-Amro Bank	340.6
Crédit Lyonnais	339.4
Union Bank of Switzerland	336.2
Dresdner Bank	332.9
Société Générale	326.5
Banque Nationale de Paris	325.3

Insurance

Who buys most insurance?
Premiums per person, 1994, $

		Non-life	Life	Total
1	Switzerland	1,380.7	2,205.9	3,586.6
2	United Kingdom	721.6	1,280.6	2,002.2
3	Netherlands	931.7	981.3	1,913.0
4	France	703.5	1,204.7	1,908.2
5	Luxembourg	1,082.5	531.9	1,614.4
6	Germany	946.5	631.4	1,577.9
7	Denmark	723.9	709.3	1,433.2
8	Norway	792.8	630.5	1,423.3
9	Finland	458.3	889.4	1,347.7
10	Austria	863.7	439.8	1,303.5
11	Sweden	558.6	679.4	1,238.0
12	Ireland	556.2	611.5	1,167.7
13	Belgium	614.8	473.7	1,088.5
14	Iceland	726.6	25.4	752.0
15	Spain	354.9	274.7	629.6
16	Italy	399.0	202.0	601.0
17	Portugal	251.7	132.4	384.1
18	Cyprus	176.4	180.9	357.3
19	Slovenia	209.3	35.1	244.4
20	Greece	94.7	83.4	178.1
21	Czech Republic	73.5	24.7	98.2
22	Croatia	88.8	3.2	92.0
23	Hungary	63.4	21.8	85.2
24	Slovakia	39.7	12.2	51.9
25	Poland	32.7	14.6	47.3

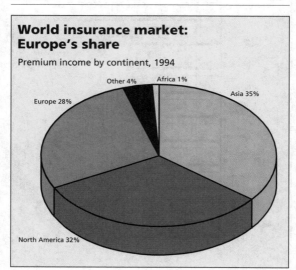

World insurance market: Europe's share

Premium income by continent, 1994

Other 4% Africa 1%
Asia 35%
Europe 28%
North America 32%

More premium comparisons
Insurance premiums as % of GDP, 1994

		Non-life	Life	Total
1	United Kingdom	4.12	7.31	11.43
2	Switzerland	3.75	5.99	9.74
3	Netherlands	4.29	4.51	8.80
4	Ireland	4.18	4.59	8.77
5	France	2.87	4.91	7.78
6	Finland	2.56	4.98	7.54
7	Germany	4.20	2.80	7.00
8	Sweden	2.89	3.51	6.40
9	Austria	4.12	2.10	6.22
10	Luxembourg	3.97	1.95	5.92
11	Denmark	2.77	2.71	5.48
12	Belgium	3.09	2.38	5.47
13	Norway	2.93	2.33	5.26
14	Spain	2.88	2.23	5.11
15	Portugal	3.31	1.65	4.96
16	Cyprus	2.11	2.17	4.28
17	Iceland	3.71	0.13	3.84
18	Slovenia	3.00	0.50	3.50
19	Italy	2.24	1.13	3.37
20	Croatia	3.04	0.11	3.15
21	Czech Republic	2.14	0.72	2.86
22	Greece	1.27	1.12	2.39
23	Hungary	1.67	0.58	2.25
	Slovakia	1.72	0.53	2.25
25	Bulgaria	1.38	0.67	2.05

Europe's largest insurance companies
Assets, $bn, 1995

1	Allianz	Germany	199.95
2	Axa	France	193.74
3	Compagnie UAP	France	183.58
4	Prudential	United Kingdom	116.30
5	Internationale Nederlanden Groep	Netherlands	97.12
6	Aegon	Netherlands	93.66
7	Commercial Union	United Kingdom	87.43
8	Zurich Insurance	Switzerland	83.04
9	Royal & Sun Alliance	United Kingdom	82.21
10	Assurances Generales de France	France	71.98
11	Winterthur Group	Switzerland	70.23
12	Standard Life Assurance	United Kingdom	68.19
13	Swiss Life Insurance & Pension	Switzerland	63.79
14	Norwich Union	United Kingdom	61.86
15	Legal & General	United Kingdom	59.09

Mergers and acquisitions

Activity in the EU
Mergers and acquisitions, 1990–95

Target	Targeter/Bidder		
	Own country	EU15	Outside EU
Belgium	60.2	31.9	7.9
Denmark	67.0	22.0	11.0
Germany	79.5	12.3	8.2
Greece	73.1	19.2	7.7
Spain	80.9	11.5	7.6
France	66.0	24.5	9.5
Ireland	36.9	49.0	14.1
Italy	77.8	14.9	7.3
Luxembourg	2.0	86.1	11.9
Netherlands	57.9	30.5	11.7
Austria	22.4	65.7	11.9
Portugal	64.9	35.1	0.0
Finland	78.8	14.4	6.8
Sweden	56.8	29.4	13.7
United Kingdom	73.8	12.9	13.3
EU 15	70.8	18.7	10.5

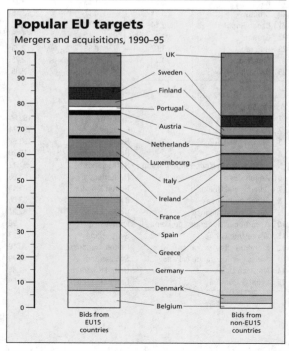

Popular EU targets
Mergers and acquisitions, 1990–95

UK
Sweden
Finland
Portugal
Austria
Netherlands
Luxembourg
Italy
Ireland
France
Spain
Greece
Germany
Denmark
Belgium

Bids from EU15 countries

Bids from non-EU15 countries

The big ones

Main EU mergers and acquisitions, 1995

	Target	Bidder	Amount, m ecus
1	Wellcome	Glaxo	11,572
2	Telecom Italia Mobile	(Telecom Italia divestment)	7,737
3	TSB Group	Lloyds Bank	7,022
4	Marion Merrell Dow	Hoechst	5,620
5	Pharmacia	Upjohn	4,963
6	ENI	Market purchase	3,035
7	Eastern Group	Hanson	2,888
8	BTR Nylex	BTR	2,446
9	S.G. Warburg (investment banking)	Schweizerischer Bankverein	2,361
10	Cheltenham & Gloucester Building Society	Lloyds Bank	2,344
11	Fisons	Rhône-Poulenc	2,206
12	Norweb	North West Water Group	2,197
13	ITT Commercial Finance Corp.	Deutsche Bank	2,155
14	PET	Grand Metropolitan	2,138
15	Vereinte Versicherung/ Magdeburger Versicherung	Allianz	2,082
16	Dr Pepper/Seven Up Companies	Cadbury Schweppes	2,021
17	Rothmans International	Financière Richemont	1,945
18	Credito Romagnolo	Credito Italiano	1,920
19	Leeds Permanent Building Society	Halifax Building Society	1,628
20	Banco Portugues do Atlantico	Banco Comercial Portugues/ Mello Group	1,571

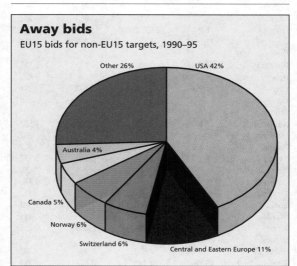

Away bids

EU15 bids for non-EU15 targets, 1990–95

Other 26%
USA 42%
Australia 4%
Canada 5%
Norway 6%
Switzerland 6%
Central and Eastern Europe 11%

Privatisation

How much has been sold
Privatisation proceeds (public offers and private sales), $m

	1988	1989	1990	1991
Austria	569	315	55	35
Denmark			700	
Finland	303	107		
France	360			376
Germany	1,333	237	1,340	11,995
Greece			42	232
Hungary		130	32	180
Ireland				489
Italy	840	987		
Netherlands		2,062		150
Norway			127	
Poland			32	350
Portugal		494	796	1,014
Spain	800	1,465	132	252
Sweden		3,820		
Turkey		105	267	
United Kingdom	4,770	8,699	10,850	19,348
Total	**8,975**	**18,421**	**14,373**	**34,421**

	1992	1993	1994	1995
Austria	162	101	1,150	801
Belgium		984	471	2,665
Bulgaria			84	18
Croatia			13	
Czech Republic	361	270	7	1,593
Denmark		110	3,453	
Finland		204	953	258
France	1,353	8,252	11,362	6,036
Germany	12,165	4,570	6,006	2,016
Greece	648	294		
Hungary	845	1,011	227	2,570
Ireland		100		675
Italy	1,566	1,295	7,892	7,697
Latvia			160	
Lithuania		29		
Netherlands	100	695	3,750	4,507
Norway		301		291
Poland	309	391	334	837
Portugal	1,023	404	990	2,177
Romania				60
Russia	50			1,165
Slovakia				113
Spain		3,004	1,460	2,986
Sweden	263	144	3,720	893
Turkey	304	364	333	211
Ukraine				25
United Kingdom	1,038	8,620	1,262	8,760
Total, incl. others	**19,826**	**31,143**	**43,627**	**46,354**

Big ones

Biggest European privatisations, $bn

1988	United Kingdom	British Steel	4.50
1989	Sweden	Procordia (39%)	3.82
	United Kingdom	Water industry	8.38
1990	United Kingdom	Regional electricity companies	10.20
1991	Germany	5,200 East German companies	11.75
	United Kingdom	Power companies	9.06
	United Kingdom	British Telecommunications (22%)	9.99
1992	Germany	5,550 companies	12.16
1993	France	Banque Nationale de Paris	4.81
	France	Rhône-Poulenc	2.20
	United Kingdom	British Telecommunications (20.7%)	8.06
1994	Denmark	TeleDanmark	3.33
	France	Elf Aquitaine	6.82
	France	UAP	2.83
	Germany	Treuhandanstalt	3.60
	Italy	INA	3.00
	Netherlands	Koninklijke PTT Nederland (30%)	3.75
1995	Belgium	Belgacom	2.45
	France	Usinor Sacilor	2.90
	Italy	ENI	3.96
	Netherlands	Koninklijke PTT Nederland 2	4.07
	United Kingdom	Power companies 2	4.68

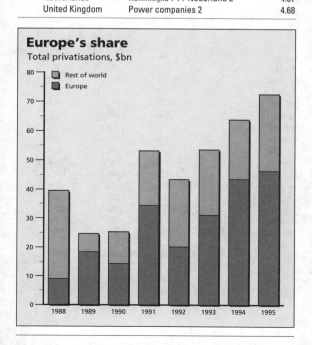

Europe's share
Total privatisations, $bn

Foreign direct investment

Inward

	Inflows, $m			Stock, $bn
	1984–89 av.	*1990*	*1995*	*1995*
Albania	...	...	70	0.2
Armenia	...	...	10	0.2
Austria	318	653	1,040	14.0
Azerbaijan	...	...	110	0.1
Belarus	...	...	20	0.1
Belgium	2,793	8,047	9,107	84.6
Bulgaria	...	...	135	0.4
Croatia	...	...	86	0.3
Cyprus	64	127	80	1.4
Czech Republic	...	...	2,500	6.1
Czechoslovakia	43	207	...	...
Denmark	323	1,132	3,360	21.8
Estonia	...	...	188	0.6
Finland	314	812	897	6.6
France	5,364	13,183	20,124	162.4
Germany	1,833	2,689	8,996	134.0
Greece	624	1,005	890	19.1
Hungary	...	...	3,500	9.9
Iceland	1	6	14	0.3
Ireland	85	99	90	5.4
Italy	2,560	6,411	4,347	64.7
Latvia	...	...	250	0.5
Lithuania	...	...	50	0.1
Malta	30	46	60	0.8
Moldova	...	...	32	0.1
Netherlands	3,787	12,349	9,850	102.6
Norway	408	1,003	1,313	15.6
Poland	16	89	2,510	7.4
Portugal	639	2,610	1,386	6.9
Romania	...	...	373	0.9
Russia	...	...	2,017	4.1
Slovakia	...	...	250	0.7
Slovenia	...	...	150	0.5
Spain	4,535	13,984	8,250	128.9
Sweden	982	1,982	13,672	32.8
Switzerland	1,620	4,961	2,292	43.1
Turkey	245	684	1,037	5.3
Ukraine	...	...	200	0.8
United Kingdom	13,545	32,430	29,910	244.1
EU total	62,641	132,959	132,285	1,028.1

Outward

	Outflows, $m			Stock, $bn
	1984–89 av.	1990	1995	1995
Albania	...	...	12	0.0
Austria	325	1,701	716	12.0
Belgium	2,561	6,314	5,633	57.8
Cyprus	1	5	12	0.1
Czech Republic	...	...	69	0.3
Czechoslovakia	...	20	...	...
Denmark	776	1,482	2,851	19.8
Estonia	...	...	6	0.0
Finland	1,424	3,313	1,512	15.3
France	8,828	34,823	17,554	200.9
Germany	9,599	24,214	35,302	235.0
Greece	...	...	-6	...
Hungary	...	...	29	0.1
Iceland	2	9	4	0.0
Ireland	297	499	540	5.1
Italy	2,775	7,585	3,210	86.7
Latvia	...	...	16	...
Lithuania	...	...	2	...
Malta	...	...	1	0.0
Netherlands	7,052	15,388	12,431	158.6
Norway	1,152	1,471	972	15.3
Poland	14		20	0.2
Portugal	31	163	762	2.8
Romania	...	18	4	0.0
Russia	...	...	129	0.5
Slovakia	...	...	12	0.1
Slovenia	...	...	7	...
Spain	722	3,522	3,574	34.3
Sweden	4,969	14,629	10,367	61.6
Switzerland	4,165	5,370	8,627	108.3
Turkey	2	-16	80	0.4
Ukraine	...	...	3	0.0
United Kingdom	23,283	19,327	37,839	319.0
EU total	62,641	132,959	132,285	1,208.8

Stockmarkets

Largest by market capitalisation

1980, $bn			1990, $bn		
1	United Kingdom	205.20	1	United Kingdom	848.87
2	Germany[a]	71.70	2	Germany[a]	355.07
3	France	54.60	3	France	314.38
4	Switzerland	37.60	4	Switzerland	160.04
5	Netherlands	29.30	5	Italy	148.77
6	Italy	25.30	6	Netherlands	119.83
7	Spain	16.60	7	Spain	111.40
8	Sweden	12.90	8	Sweden	92.10
9	Belgium	10.00	9	Belgium	65.45
10	Denmark	5.40	10	Denmark	39.06
11	Greece	3.02	11	Norway	26.13
12	Austria	2.00	12	Finland	22.72
13	Turkey	0.48	13	Turkey	19.07
			14	Greece	15.23
			15	Austria	11.48

Largest by annual value traded

1980, $m			1990, $m		
1	Switzerland	96,262	1	Germany[a]	501,805
2	United Kingdom	35,791	2	United Kingdom	278,740
3	Germany[a]	15,248	3	France	116,893
4	France	10,118	4	Italy	42,566
5	Italy	8,574	5	Spain	40,967
6	Netherlands	5,099	6	Netherlands	40,199
7	Sweden	1,796	7	Austria	18,609
8	Spain	981	8	Sweden	15,718
9	Belgium	838	9	Norway	13,996
10	Austria	105	10	Denmark	11,105
11	Greece	86	11	Belgium	6,425
12	Denmark	58	12	Turkey	5,841
			13	Finland	3,933
			14	Portugal	1,687

Largest by number of companies listed

1980			1990		
1	United Kingdom	2,655	1	United Kingdom	1,701
2	France	586	2	France	578
3	Spain	496	3	Spain	427
4	Germany[a]	459	4	Germany[a]	413
5	Belgium	225	5	Netherlands	260
6	Denmark	218	6	Denmark	258
7	Netherlands	214	7	Italy	220
8	Italy	134	8	Switzerland	182
9	Greece	116		Belgium	182
10	Sweden	103	10	Portugal	181

a Western Germany.

End 1995, $bn

1	United Kingdom	1,407.74	14	Luxembourg	30.44
2	Germany	577.37	15	Ireland	25.82
3	France	522.05	16	Turkey	20.77
4	Switzerland	433.62	17	Portugal	18.36
5	Netherlands	356.48	18	Greece	17.06
6	Italy	209.52	19	Russia	15.86
7	Spain	197.79	20	Czech Republic	15.66
8	Sweden	178.05	21	Poland	4.56
9	Belgium	104.96	22	Cyprus	2.53
10	Denmark	56.22	23	Hungary	2.40
11	Norway	44.59	24	Malta	1.24
12	Finland	44.14		Slovakia	1.24
13	Austria	32.51			

1995, $m

1	Germany	1,147,079	14	Italy	9,155
2	United Kingdom	1,020,262	15	Norway	8,407
3	France	729,099	16	Greece	6,091
4	Switzerland	310,928	17	Portugal	4,233
5	Netherlands	248,606	18	Czech Republic	3,630
6	Sweden	93,197	19	Poland	2,770
7	Spain	59,791	20	Slovakia	832
8	Turkey	51,392	21	Russia	465
9	Denmark	25,942	22	Hungary	355
10	Austria	25,759	23	Slovenia	345
11	Finland	19,006	24	Cyprus	302
12	Belgium	15,249	25	Luxembourg	205
13	Ireland	13,241			

End 1995

1	United Kingdom	2,078	11	Denmark	213
2	Czech Republic	1,635	12	Greece	212
3	Germany	678	13	Turkey	205
4	Italy	654	14	Russia	170
5	France	450	15	Portugal	169
6	Netherlands	387	16	Norway	151
7	Spain	362	17	Belgium	143
8	Lithuania	351	18	Austria	109
9	Switzerland	233	19	Ireland	80
10	Sweden	223	20	Finland	73

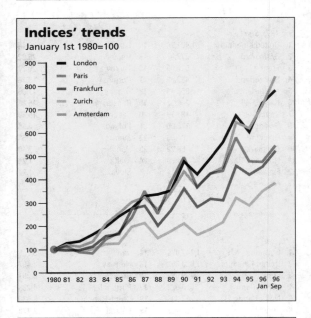

Indices' trends
January 1st 1980=100

Legend:
- London
- Paris
- Frankfurt
- Zurich
- Amsterdam

Y-axis: 0, 100, 200, 300, 400, 500, 600, 700, 800, 900

X-axis: 1980 81 82 83 84 85 86 87 88 89 90 91 92 93 94 95 96 96
Jan Sep

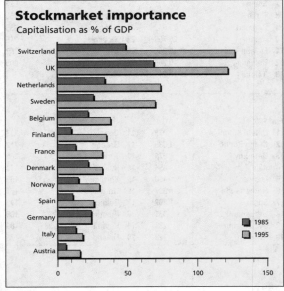

Stockmarket importance
Capitalisation as % of GDP

Categories (top to bottom): Switzerland, UK, Netherlands, Sweden, Belgium, Finland, France, Denmark, Norway, Spain, Germany, Italy, Austria

Legend:
- 1985
- 1995

X-axis: 0, 50, 100, 150

Part VII

TOURISM
AND
TRANSPORT

Tourism

Most popular destinations
Tourist arrivals, '000s

	1985	1990	1995
France	36,748	52,497	60,000
Spain	27,477	37,441	44,886
Italy	25,047	26,679	29,953
United Kingdom	14,449	18,013	23,746
Hungary	9,724	20,510	20,700
Poland	2,749	3,400	19,200
Austria	15,168	19,011	17,173
Czech Republic		7,278	15,500
Germany	12,686	17,045	14,847
Switzerland	11,900	13,200	11,500
Greece	6,574	8,873	10,130
Portugal	4,989	8,020	9,706
Turkey	2,230	4,799	7,083
Netherlands	3,329	5,795	6,574
Belgium	4,445	5,147	5,224
Russia			4,796
Ireland	2,536	3,666	4,231
Bulgaria	3,427	4,500	4,125
Norway	1,933	1,955	2,880
Romania	2,314	3,009	2,608
Cyprus	770	1,561	2,100
Denmark	1,281	1,275	1,614
Croatia		7,049	1,324
Malta	518	872	1,116
Finland	543	866	835
Slovakia		822	827
Ukraine			794
Luxembourg	622	820	767
Slovenia		650	732

Biggest spenders
Spending on tourism, $m

1	Germany	48,101	17	Greece	1,320
2	United Kingdom	24,625	18	Ireland	1,267
3	France	16,315	19	Hungary	965
4	Italy	12,411	20	Turkey	912
5	Austria	11,699	21	Croatia	771
6	Netherlands	11,455	22	Romania	695
7	Belgium	7,995	23	Slovakia	330
8	Switzerland	6,543	24	Slovenia	322
9	Poland	5,500	25	Iceland	253
10	Sweden	5,422	26	Bulgaria	234
11	Spain	4,421	27	Cyprus	230
12	Denmark	4,282	28	Malta	185
13	Norway	4,221	29	Lithuania	138
14	Finland	2,383	30	Estonia	49
15	Portugal	2,155	31	Latvia	32
16	Czech Republic	1,630	32	Albania	5

Biggest earners
Earnings from tourism, $m

	1985	1990	1995
Italy	8,756	20,016	27,433
France	7,942	20,185	27,429
Spain	8,151	18,593	25,018
United Kingdom	7,120	14,940	18,805
Austria	5,084	13,410	14,633
Germany	4,748	11,471	12,290
Switzerland	3,145	6,769	7,250
Poland	118	358	6,400
Netherlands	1,661	3,636	5,762
Belgium	1,663	3,721	5,250
Turkey	1,482	3,225	4,957
Portugal	1,137	3,555	4,402
Greece	1,428	2,587	4,128
Denmark	1,326	3,322	3,674
Sweden	1,190	2,916	3,447
Czech Republic		419	2,875
Norway	755	1,570	2,386
Cyprus	380	1,258	1,788
Finland	543	1,170	1,716
Hungary	271	824	1,714
Ireland	531	1,453	1,677
Croatia		1,704	1,584
Russia			1,385
Slovenia		721	1,163
Malta	149	495	650
Slovakia		70	620
Romania	182	106	574

Earnings importance
Earnings from tourism as % of GDP, 1995

1	Belgium	23.93	19	Romania	2.06
2	Croatia	13.10	20	Iceland	1.96
3	Slovenia	8.16	21	Macedonia FYR	1.82
4	Poland	6.76	22	France	1.79
5	Austria	6.27	23	Azerbaijan	1.74
6	Slovakia	5.20	24	Luxembourg	1.72
7	Spain	4.47	25	United Kingdom	1.71
8	Hungary	4.39	26	Norway	1.63
9	Portugal	4.25	27	Sweden	1.50
10	Bulgaria	3.90	28	Netherlands	1.46
11	Greece	3.70	29	Finland	1.36
12	Turkey	3.01	30	Albania	0.57
13	Ireland	2.76	31	Germany	0.51
14	Italy	2.52	32	Russia	0.35
15	Lithuania	2.48	33	Latvia	0.32
16	Switzerland	2.39	34	Ukraine	0.29
17	Estonia	2.14	35	Moldova	0.05
18	Denmark	2.12	36	Czech Republic	0.01

Road transport

Longest road networks
Km

1	France	812,550	16	Ireland	92,345
2	Germany	639,805	17	Norway	90,178
3	Romania	461,880	18	Finland	77,644
4	Turkey	381,028	19	Czech Republic	73,776
5	Poland	370,510	20	Switzerland	71,348
6	United Kingdom	366,477	21	Denmark	71,255
7	Spain	341,230	22	Latvia	64,693
8	Italy	305,388	23	Lithuania	61,329
9	Austria	200,000	24	Azerbaijan	59,748
10	Ukraine	172,315	25	Belarus	50,964
11	Hungary	158,633	26	Bulgaria	36,911
12	Belgium	140,978	27	Croatia	26,929
13	Sweden	135,920	28	Albania	18,450
14	Greece	116,150	29	Slovakia	17,889
15	Netherlands	103,800	30	Estonia	14,754

Car congestion
Private cars per km of road

1	Italy	92
2	Germany	62
3	Netherlands	57
4	Slovakia	56
5	United Kingdom	55
6	Slovenia	45
7	Switzerland	44
8	Bulgaria	43
9	Luxembourg	42
10	Spain	40
	Czech Republic	40
12	Macedonia FYR	31
	France	31
14	Belgium	30
15	Sweden	26
	Croatia	26
17	Finland	24
18	Denmark	23
	Estonia	23
20	Cyprus	21
21	Poland	19
22	Norway	18
	Greece	18
24	Austria	17
25	Belarus	15
26	Moldova	14
	Hungary	14
28	Lithuania	11
29	Iceland	10
	Ireland	10
31	Turkey	8

Vehicle congestion
All vehicles per km of road

1	Italy	91
2	Ukraine	73
3	Germany	65
	Netherlands	65
	Slovakia	65
6	United Kingdom	63
7	Czech Republic	57
8	Bulgaria	49
	Spain	49
10	Switzerland	48
11	Slovenia	47
12	Luxembourg	45
13	France	37
14	Macedonia FYR	35
15	Belgium	33
	Romania	33
17	Cyprus	30
18	Austria	29
	Serbia	29
20	Croatia	28
	Sweden	28
22	Denmark	27
	Estonia	27
	Finland	27
25	Greece	23
	Hungary	23
	Poland	23
28	Norway	22
29	Moldova	20
30	Azerbaijan	15
31	Iceland	12

Road accidents
No. of accidents

1	Germany	392,400	16	Sweden	14,959
2	United Kingdom	234,101	17	Croatia	12,846
3	France	132,726	18	Netherlands	10,278
4	Spain	78,474	19	Romania	9,381
5	Ukraine	67,770	20	Norway	8,337
6	Turkey	59,409	21	Denmark	8,279
7	Poland	53,647	22	Bulgaria	7,288
8	Belgium	53,018	23	Belarus	7,144
9	Serbia	45,798	24	Slovakia	6,586
10	Portugal	45,404	25	Ireland	6,376
11	Austria	42,015	26	Finland	6,245
12	Czech Republic	27,590	27	Lithuania	3,902
13	Switzerland	23,526	28	Latvia	3,389
14	Greece	22,165	29	Cyprus	3,027
15	Hungary	20,723	30	Moldova	2,648

Injuries in road accidents
No. of injuries

1	Germany	516,000	16	Hungary	26,961
2	United Kingdom	315,189	17	Sweden	20,373
3	Italy	240,688	18	Croatia	17,679
4	France	180,382	19	Netherlands	11,735
5	Spain	113,716	20	Norway	11,124
6	Turkey	102,848	21	Ireland	9,831
7	Belgium	73,497	22	Denmark	9,757
8	Poland	64,573	23	Bulgaria	8,441
9	Serbia	61,426	24	Romania	8,198
10	Portugal	60,024	25	Finland	8,080
11	Austria	55,156	26	Belarus	7,296
12	Ukraine	45,881	27	Slovakia	6,081
13	Czech Republic	35,667	28	Cyprus	4,374
14	Greece	29,910	29	Lithuania	4,146
15	Switzerland	29,278	30	Latvia	3,721

Deaths in road accidents
No. of deaths

1	Germany	9,805	16	Hungary	1,562
2	France	8,533	17	Bulgaria	1,390
3	Ukraine	7,560	18	Austria	1,338
4	Italy	7,498	19	Netherlands	1,298
5	Poland	6,744	20	Croatia	804
6	Turkey	6,108	21	Lithuania	765
7	Spain	5,615	22	Switzerland	679
8	Serbia	4,619	23	Latvia	670
9	United Kingdom	3,650	24	Sweden	632
10	Romania	2,877	25	Denmark	546
11	Portugal	1,914	26	Moldova	540
12	Greece	1,830	27	Slovakia	505
13	Belgium	1,693	28	Finland	480
14	Belarus	1,670	29	Ireland	431
15	Czech Republic	1,637	30	Estonia	364

Rail transport

Railway networks
'000 km

Russia	87,469	Norway	4,023
Germany	40,355	Slovakia	3,661
France	32,275	Belgium	3,396
Poland	24,313	Switzerland	3,228
Ukraine	22,564	Netherlands	2,757
United Kingdom	16,536	Portugal	2,699
Italy	16,002	Greece	2,497
Spain	12,646	Latvia	2,413
Romania	11,374	Denmark	2,306
Sweden	9,661	Lithuania	2,002
Czech Republic	9,413	Ireland	1,944
Turkey	8,542	Croatia	1,907
Hungary	7,827	Moldova	1,318
Finland	5,880	Slovenia	1,201
Austria	5,636	Estonia	1,024
Belarus	5,543	Macedonia FYR	699
Bulgaria	4,291	Albania	674
Ex-Yugoslavia	4,281	Luxembourg	275
Algeria	4,246		

Passenger travel
m km

Albania	779	Lithuania	841
Armenia	435	Luxembourg	272
Austria	9,599	Macedonia FYR	66
Belgium	6,626	Malta	1,716
Belarus	19,500	Moldova	1,204
Bulgaria	5,059	Netherlands	14,400
Croatia	901	Norway	2,588
Cyprus	2,652	Poland	27,610
Czech Republic	8,481	Portugal	5,560
Denmark	4,784	Romania	18,313
Estonia	537	Russia	272,200
Finland	3,037	Slovakia	4,548
France	68,700	Slovenia	590
Germany	57,300	Spain	15,473
Greece	1,658	Sweden	5,600
Hungary	8,088	Switzerland	13,569
Iceland	2,304	Turkey	6,335
Ireland	1,273	Ukraine	70,882
Italy	49,493	United Kingdom	37,000
Latvia	2,359		

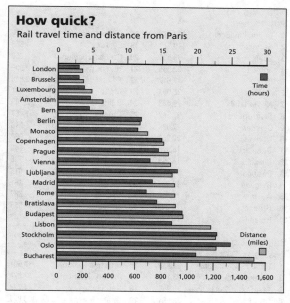

How quick?
Rail travel time and distance from Paris

Time (hours)

Distance (miles)

London
Brussels
Luxembourg
Amsterdam
Bern
Berlin
Monaco
Copenhagen
Prague
Vienna
Ljubljana
Madrid
Rome
Bratislava
Budapest
Lisbon
Stockholm
Oslo
Bucharest

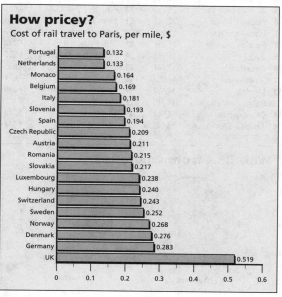

How pricey?
Cost of rail travel to Paris, per mile, $

Portugal	0.132
Netherlands	0.133
Monaco	0.164
Belgium	0.169
Italy	0.181
Slovenia	0.193
Spain	0.194
Czech Republic	0.209
Austria	0.211
Romania	0.215
Slovakia	0.217
Luxembourg	0.238
Hungary	0.240
Switzerland	0.243
Sweden	0.252
Norway	0.268
Denmark	0.276
Germany	0.283
UK	0.519

Air transport

Who flies most
'000s

1	United Kingdom	128,215		18	Finland	10,120
2	Germany	110,272		19	Cyprus	4,665
3	Spain	95,536		20	Czech Republic	3,358
4	France	87,255		21	Hungary	2,909
5	Italy	47,612		22	Poland	2,848
6	Turkey	26,097		23	Malta	2,541
7	Netherlands	25,488		24	Bulgaria	2,165
8	Switzerland	23,247		25	Croatia	1,487
9	Sweden	22,938		26	Luxembourg	1,210
10	Norway	22,253		27	Iceland	688
11	Denmark	15,878		28	Romania	642
12	Russia	14,295		29	Slovenia	638
13	Portugal	14,072		30	Macedonia FYR	616
14	Belgium	12,791		31	Latvia	491
15	Austria	11,040		32	Estonia	367
16	Greece	10,244		33	Lithuania	356
17	Ireland	10,126		34	Slovakia	187

Busiest airports
Passengers, '000s

1	Heathrow, London	54,453		16	Brussels National	12,601
2	Rhiem, Frankfurt	38,180		17	Ataturk, Istanbul	12,074
3	Charles de Gaulle, Paris	28,355		18	Barcelona	11,728
4	Orly, Paris	26,654		19	Linate, Milan	10,827
5	Schiphol, Amsterdam	25,355		20	Athinai, Athens	10,481
6	Gatwick, London	22,549		21	Fornebu, Oslo	9,695
7	Fiumicino, Rome	21,091		22	Vienna International	8,546
8	Barajas, Madrid	19,956		23	Tegel, Berlin	8,272
9	Zurich	15,340		24	Fühlsbuttel, Hamburg	8,201
10	Dusseldorf	15,147		25	Dublin	8,025
11	Manchester	14,988		26	Gran Canaria	7,877
12	Munich	14,868		27	Tenerife Sur, Tenerife	7,398
13	Palma de Mallorca	14,710		28	Vantaa, Helsinki	7,141
14	Copenhagen	14,667		29	Lisbon	6,376
15	Arlanda, Stockholm	13,540		30	Malaga	6,312

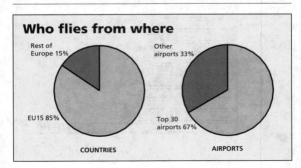

Who flies from where

Rest of Europe 15%

EU15 85%

COUNTRIES

Other airports 33%

Top 30 airports 67%

AIRPORTS

Sea transport

Largest merchant fleets
No. of vessels over 100 GRT[a]

1	Russia	5,160	20	Azerbaijan	296
2	Greece	1,863	21	Finland	274
3	Spain	1,724	22	Latvia	249
4	Cyprus	1,674	23	Lithuania	242
5	Norway	1,515	24	Estonia	235
6	United Kingdom	1,454	25	Croatia	210
7	Italy	1,397	26	Belgium	206
8	Malta	1,164	27	Bulgaria	202
9	Germany	1,146	28	Ireland	163
10	Ukraine	1,142	29	Georgia	85
11	Turkey	1,075	30	Luxembourg	42
12	Netherlands	1,059	31	Albania	32
13	France	739	32	Austria	29
14	Sweden	621	33	Switzerland	20
15	Denmark	558	34	Slovenia	11
16	Poland	516	35	Hungary	9
17	Romania	421	36	Czech Republic	8
18	Iceland	362	37	Slovakia	5
19	Portugal	304			

Largest ports
Total cargo, '000 tonnes

1	Rotterdam	293,794	21	Liverpool	29,265
2	Antwerp	109,494	22	Goteborg	28,755
3	Marseilles	91,062	23	Calais	25,419
4	Bergen	75,525	24	Gent	23,833
5	Hamburg	68,439	25	Tarragona	23,561
6	Le Havre	54,376	26	Venice	22,869
7	London	51,393	27	Felixstowe	22,116
8	Amsterdam	48,069	28	Sines	21,936
9	Forth	44,359	29	Gdansk	21,115
10	Tees and Hartlepool	42,994	30	Barcelona	20,390
11	Genoa	42,406	31	Lubeck	20,330
12	Grimsby-Immingham	40,921	32	Rouen	19,518
13	Sullom Voe	38,592	33	Livorno	19,338
14	Trieste	37,840	34	Ijmuiden	17,140
15	Dunkirk	37,168	35	Szczecin	15,667
16	Wilheimshaven	34,902	36	Medway	14,660
17	Algeciras	32,323	37	Orkney	14,097
18	Zeebrugge	32,134	38	Dover	14,089
19	Southampton	31,537	39	Narvik	13,554
20	Bremen-Bremerhaven	30,928	40	Lisbon	13,124

a GRT = gross tonnage, which is the total volume within the hull and above deck.
  1 GRT = 100 cubic feet.

Freight

Road importance
% inland freight carried by road

1	Greece	97.58	16	Sweden	52.92
2	Spain	93.45	17	Poland	49.01
3	Turkey	91.41	18	Austria	45.22
4	Portugal	89.37	19	Norway	43.14
5	Italy	89.08	20	Croatia	38.57
6	Macedonia FYR	79.39	21	Romania	35.60
7	Netherlands	75.48	22	Lithuania	34.00
8	Denmark	74.99	23	Bulgaria	30.92
9	France	74.28	24	Estonia	28.15
10	Belgium	67.62	25	Moldova	26.13
11	United Kingdom	67.15	26	Hungary	22.47
12	Albania	65.88	27	Latvia	14.71
13	Finland	65.48	28	Ukraine	14.61
14	Germany	63.54	29	Slovenia	8.61
15	Switzerland	54.93			

Rail importance
% inland freight carried by rail

1	Latvia	85.28	16	Macedonia FYR	20.61
2	Ukraine	83.06	17	Belarus	19.88
3	Hungary	76.75	18	Germany	19.79
4	Moldova	73.87	19	Austria	15.52
5	Estonia	71.85	20	Denmark	13.92
6	Bulgaria	69.08	21	Italy	10.88
7	Lithuania	65.78	22	Portugal	10.63
8	Romania	60.51	23	Norway	9.86
9	Poland	50.38	24	Slovenia	9.79
10	Croatia	49.41	25	Turkey	8.02
11	Switzerland	44.03	26	United Kingdom	6.89
12	Sweden	32.85	27	Spain	6.55
13	Albania	32.19	28	Netherlands	2.51
14	Finland	25.35	29	Greece	2.42
15	France	22.99			

Water importance
% inland freight carried by water

1	Slovenia	81.60	12	Romania	3.88
2	Norway	47.00	13	France	2.73
3	Austria	39.26	14	Ukraine	2.33
4	United Kingdom	25.96	15	Albania	1.93
5	Netherlands	22.00	16	Switzerland	1.03
6	Germany	16.67	17	Hungary	0.78
7	Sweden	14.23	18	Poland	0.61
8	Belgium	12.50	19	Turkey	0.56
9	Croatia	12.02	20	Lithuania	0.22
10	Denmark	11.09	21	Italy	0.04
11	Finland	9.17	22	Latvia	0.01

Life and death

Life expectancy
At birth, years

1994			2020–30		
1	Iceland	79.0	**1**	Sweden	82.1
2	France	78.0	**2**	Italy	81.7
	Greece	78.0	**3**	Iceland	81.2
	Italy	78.0	**4**	Belgium	81.1
	Monaco	78.0	**5**	Austria	80.9
	Netherlands	78.0		Switzerland	80.9
	Norway	78.0	**7**	Greece	80.7
	Sweden	78.0		Spain	80.7
	Switzerland	78.0	**9**	Netherlands	80.6
10	Austria	77.0	**10**	Cyprus	80.5
	Cyprus	77.0		France	80.5
	Malta	77.0	**12**	Luxembourg	80.0
	Spain	77.0		Malta	80.0
14	Belgium	76.0		United Kingdom	80.0
	Finland	76.0	**15**	Germany	79.8
	Germany	76.0	**16**	Finland	79.6
	Ireland	76.0	**17**	Ireland	79.4
	Luxembourg	76.0	**18**	Norway	79.2
	United Kingdom	76.0	**19**	Portugal	79.0
20	Denmark	75.0	**20**	Denmark	78.6
	Portugal	75.0	**21**	Slovenia	77.1
22	Slovenia	73.6	**22**	Georgia	76.9
23	Croatia	73.5	**23**	Armenia	76.7
24	Czech Republic	73.0	**24**	Bosnia & Hercegovina	76.6
	Georgia	73.0		Macedonia FYR	76.6
26	Albania	72.8	**26**	Albania	76.5
27	Macedonia FYR	72.7	**27**	Croatia	76.4
28	Slovakia	72.3		Serbia	76.4
29	Liechtenstein	72.0	**29**	Azerbaijan	76.1
30	Poland	71.7	**30**	Czech Republic	76.0
31	Bulgaria	71.2	**31**	Bulgaria	75.9
32	Armenia	71.1	**32**	Poland	75.8
	Bosnia & Hercegovina[a]	71.1	**33**	Slovakia	75.7
34	Estonia	70.1	**34**	Turkey	75.1

Infant mortality
Rates per 1,000 live births, 1985–90

1	Turkey	81	10	Georgia	21
2	Macedonia FYR	40	**11**	Bosnia & Hercegovina	20
3	Albania	31	**12**	Estonia	18
	Azerbaijan	31		Ukraine	18
5	Serbia	30	**14**	Hungary	17
6	Armenia	26		Poland	17
	Romania	26	**16**	Belarus	16
8	Moldova	25	**17**	Latvia	15
9	Russia	24		Lithuania	15

a 1985–90.

Death rate
Crude death rates per 100,000 population

1985–90			*2020–30*		
1	Hungary	13.8	1	Bulgaria	14.1
2	Czech Republic	12.9	2	Hungary	13.8
3	Latvia	12.3	3	Slovenia	13.6
4	Ukraine	12.0	4	Croatia	13.5
5	Bulgaria	11.9		Germany	13.5
	Estonia	11.9		Latvia	13.5
7	Germany	11.6	7	Russia	13.3
8	Denmark	11.5	8	Denmark	13.2
	United Kingdom	11.5		Estonia	13.2
10	Croatia	11.4		Italy	13.2
11	Austria	11.2	11	Greece	13.1
12	Sweden	11.1		Ukraine	13.1
13	Belgium	10.8	13	Romania	12.5
	Romania	10.8	14	Belarus	12.4
	Slovenia	10.8	15	Finland	12.3
16	Norway	10.7	16	Spain	12.2
	Russia	10.7	17	Czech Republic	12.1
18	Belarus	10.6	18	Lithuania	12.0
	Luxembourg	10.6	19	Luxembourg	11.9
20	Slovakia	10.5	20	Netherlands	11.7
21	Serbia	10.3		Portugal	11.7
	Lithuania	10.3	22	Switzerland	11.6
23	Moldova	10.1	23	Belgium	11.5
24	Poland	10.0		Bosnia & Hercegovina	11.5
25	Finland	9.8	25	Austria	11.4
	Portugal	9.8	26	Serbia	11.3
27	France	9.5	27	Norway	11.2
	Italy	9.5		Poland	11.2
29	Greece	9.3	29	France	11.1
30	Georgia	9.1		United Kingdom	11.1
	Ireland	9.1	31	Sweden	10.9
	Switzerland	9.1	32	Slovakia	10.6
33	Cyprus	8.6	33	Malta	10.4
34	Netherlands	8.5	34	Moldova	10.2

19	Bulgaria	14		United Kingdom	9
	Croatia	14	33	Denmark	8
	Portugal	14		France	8
	Slovakia	14		Germany	8
23	Cyprus	11		Ireland	8
	Czech Republic	11		Norway	8
	Greece	11		Spain	8
26	Italy	10	39	Netherlands	7
	Slovenia	10		Switzerland	7
28	Austria	9	41	Finland	6
	Belgium	9		Iceland	6
	Luxembourg	9		Sweden	6
	Malta	9			

Causes of death

Heart disease
Deaths per 100,000 population, 1992

1	Estonia[c]	752.4	14	Belarus[c]	498.8
2	Hungary	738.7	15	Norway[b]	488.5
3	Bulgaria	731.8	16	Greece[b]	484.7
4	Latvia[c]	721.5	17	Finland	482.4
5	Romania	707.5	18	Ex-Yugoslavia[c]	464.5
6	Lithuania[c]	594.1	19	Portugal	448.7
7	Ukraine[c]	567.9	20	Slovenia[b]	446.4
8	Sweden[c]	567.4	21	Luxembourg	432.6
9	Austria	555.4	22	Italy[b]	425.5
10	Russia[b]	543.7	23	Belgium[d]	412.9
11	Germany	542.6	24	Ireland[b]	403.3
12	Poland	537.4	25	Malta	361.9
13	United Kingdom	501.0	26	Spain[c]	348.0

Cancer
Deaths per 100,000 population, 1992

1	Hungary	349.2	14	Ireland[b]	240.4
2	United Kingdom	321.9	15	Germany	237.8
3	Denmark[a]	292.2	16	Luxembourg	236.4
4	Italy[b]	286.8	17	Russia[b]	232.3
5	Austria	278.5	18	Spain[c]	223.9
6	France[b]	271.9	19	Greece[b]	214.6
7	Netherlands[b]	271.5	20	Malta	204.0
8	Sweden[c]	264.4	21	Ukraine[c]	194.0
9	Norway[b]	258.4	22	Iceland	192.8
10	Latvia[c]	248.7	23	Lithuania[c]	185.9
11	Belgium[d]	248.2	24	Finland	181.3
12	Slovenia[b]	246.6	25	Ex-Yugoslavia[c]	179.1
13	Switzerland[a]	240.9	26	Estonia[c]	177.4

Injuries and poisons
Deaths per 100,000 population, 1992

1	Russia[b]	175.7	14	Romania	59.2
2	Latvia[c]	173.2	15	Poland	59.0
3	Lithuania[c]	148.7	16	Bulgaria	53.4
4	Ukraine[c]	135.8	17	Norway[b]	52.2
5	Belarus[c]	127.6	18	Austria	49.7
6	Hungary	104.0		Sweden[c]	49.7
7	Estonia[c]	95.0	20	Luxembourg	47.2
8	Finland	78.7	21	Belgium[d]	46.3
9	Slovenia[b]	70.9	22	Germany	42.9
10	France[b]	66.3	23	Ex-Yugoslavia[c]	41.7
11	Switzerland[a]	64.1	24	Portugal	38.7
12	Armenia[c]	62.1	25	Italy[b]	36.3
13	Denmark[a]	60.9	26	Iceland	32.9

a 1965.
b 1991.
c 1990.
d 1989.

Infectious diseases
Deaths per 100,000 population, 1992

1	Switzerland[a]	16.6		Poland	7.6
2	Romania	12.4	15	Portugal	7.5
3	France[b]	12.1	16	Luxembourg	7.4
4	Belgium[d]	10.7	17	Sweden[c]	7.3
5	Spain[c]	10.0	18	Albania	7.0
6	Ukraine[c]	9.9	19	Finland	6.9
7	Russia[b]	9.7	20	Germany	6.7
8	Ex-Yugoslavia[c]	9.5	21	Bulgaria	6.6
9	Denmark[a]	9.2	22	Norway[b]	6.1
	Hungary	9.2	23	Armenia[c]	5.9
11	Estonia[c]	8.6		Netherlands[b]	5.9
12	Lithuania[c]	8.1	25	Belarus[c]	5.8
13	Latvia[c]	7.6	26	Slovenia[b]	5.7

Motor vehicle traffic accidents
Deaths per 100,000 population, 1992

1	Latvia[c]	39.1	14	Belgium[d]	18.4
2	Estonia[c]	35.7	15	Armenia[c]	17.8
3	Lithuania[c]	30.8	16	Italy[b]	16.8
4	Portugal	28.1	17	Ex-Yugoslavia[c]	16.7
5	Russia[b]	26.0	18	France[b]	16.5
6	Ukraine[c]	23.0	19	Romania	15.0
7	Belarus[c]	22.8	20	Austria	14.9
8	Hungary	22.7	21	Germany	12.7
9	Greece[b]	22.0	22	Ireland[b]	12.1
10	Slovenia[b]	21.5	23	Bulgaria	11.9
11	Spain[c]	20.5	24	Albania	11.5
12	Luxembourg	19.5	25	Finland	11.3
13	Poland	19.2	26	Denmark[a]	11.1

AIDS
Cumulative deaths to June 1996

1	France	42,262	10	Belgium	2,142
2	Spain	40,061	11	Denmark	1,914
3	Italy	34,741	12	Austria	1,590
4	Germany	14,899	13	Sweden	1,406
5	United Kingdom	12,982	14	Greece	1,386
6	Switzerland	5,278	15	Norway	522
7	Netherlands	4,102	16	Russia	235
8	Romania	4,057	17	Turkey	207
9	Portugal	3,377	18	Czech Republic	77

Drinking and smoking

Pure alcohol

Litres per head per year, 1994

1	Luxembourg	12.5
2	France	11.4
3	Portugal	10.7
4	Germany	10.3
	Hungary	10.3
6	Czech Republic	10.1
7	Austria	9.9
	Denmark	9.9
9	Spain	9.7
	Switzerland	9.7
11	Belgium	9.0
12	Greece	8.9
13	Ireland	8.8
14	Italy	8.7
15	Bulgaria	8.3
16	Netherlands	7.9
17	Cyprus	7.8
18	Slovakia	7.5
	United Kingdom	7.5
20	Finland	6.6
21	Romania	6.5
22	Poland	6.1
23	Russia	5.7
24	Sweden	5.3
25	Norway	3.7
26	Iceland	3.5
27	Ukraine	2.0
28	Turkey	0.9

% change consumed per head, 1970–94

1	Cyprus	136.4
2	Turkey	80.0
3	Greece	67.9
4	Finland	53.5
5	Ireland	49.2
6	Denmark	45.6
7	United Kingdom	41.5
8	Netherlands	38.6
9	Luxembourg	25.0
10	Bulgaria	24.1
11	Czech Republic	20.2
12	Hungary	13.2
13	Poland	13.0
14	Iceland	9.4
15	Portugal	8.1
16	Norway	3.4
17	Romania	3.2
18	Belgium	1.1
19	Turkey	0.9
20	Germany[a]	0.0
21	Austria	-5.7
22	Sweden	-8.5
23	Switzerland	-9.3
24	Slovakia	-10.7
25	Russia	-12.3
26	Spain	-16.4
27	France	-29.6
28	Italy	-36.5

Wine

Litres consumed per head per year, 1994

1	France	62.5	15	Czech Republic	16.9
2	Luxembourg	60.5	16	Netherlands	15.7
3	Italy	58.5	17	Cyprus	13.8
4	Portugal	50.7	18	United Kingdom	12.7
5	Switzerland	44.3	19	Sweden	12.6
6	Greece	33.8	20	Ireland	12.1
7	Hungary	33.1	21	Slovakia	11.7
8	Austria	32.8	22	Finland	8.8
9	Spain	32.2	23	Poland	7.5
10	Denmark	26.2	24	Norway	6.0
11	Belgium	24.0	25	Iceland	4.8
12	Germany	22.6	26	Russia	3.3
13	Bulgaria	22.0	27	Ukraine	2.0
14	Romania	18.8	28	Turkey	0.7

a Western Germany for data prior to 1991.

Beer

Litres consumed per head per year, 1994

1	Czech Republic	160.0	15	Switzerland	64.3
2	Germany	139.6	16	Sweden	64.2
3	Ireland	135.2	17	Bulgaria	56.3
4	Luxembourg	122.9		Cyprus	56.3
5	Denmark	121.5	19	Norway	49.0
6	Austria	117.0	20	Greece	42.0
7	Slovakia	103.9	21	Romania	41.7
8	Hungary	103.0	22	France	40.0
9	United Kingdom	102.3	23	Poland	33.0
10	Belgium	101.6	24	Iceland	27.0
11	Netherlands	86.0	25	Italy	26.2
12	Finland	83.7	26	Russia	19.8
13	Portugal	77.1	27	Ukraine	10.8
14	Spain	66.2	28	Turkey	7.8

Heaviest smokers

Cigarettes smoked per head per day, 1994

1	Greece	7.70		Portugal	4.39
2	Poland	6.75	18	Italy	4.29
3	Estonia	6.39	19	Georgia	4.27
4	Bulgaria	6.35	20	France	4.26
5	Switzerland	6.21	21	Armenia	4.22
6	Hungary	5.93		Ukraine	4.22
7	Latvia	5.62	23	United Kingdom	4.10
8	Spain	5.61	24	Turkey	4.05
9	Czech Republic	5.05	25	Lithuania	3.61
10	Belarus	5.03	26	Russia	3.41
11	Austria	4.77	27	Denmark	3.39
12	Romania	4.58	28	Moldova	3.02
13	Ireland	4.52	29	Finland	2.99
14	Germany	4.51	30	Netherlands	2.94
15	Slovakia	4.48	31	Sweden	2.72
16	Belgium	4.39	32	Azerbaijan	1.67
	Luxembourg	4.39	33	Norway	1.63

Cutting back

% decrease of cigarettes smoked, 1989–94

1	Moldova	53.3	13	Latvia	9.3
2	Azerbaijan	48.3	14	Italy	9.0
3	Armenia	44.3	15	Georgia	8.0
4	Lithuania	35.3	16	France	7.9
5	Finland	29.7	17	Switzerland	7.4
6	Estonia	27.6	18	Denmark	6.2
7	Sweden	23.0		Belgium	6.2
8	Hungary	16.3	20	Austria	5.7
9	Norway	14.2	21	Russia	3.3
10	Germany	12.6	22	Netherlands	2.6
11	United Kingdom	11.9	23	Poland	1.7
12	Ukraine	9.7	24	Greece	0.6

Health matters

Population per doctor

1	Azerbaijan	256	16	Netherlands	412
2	Armenia	261	17	Macedonia FYR	425
3	Czech Republic	272	18	Iceland	433
4	Spain	279	19	Poland	450
5	Latvia	281	20	France	461
6	Slovakia	286	21	Luxembourg	508
7	Bulgaria	318	22	Romania	536
8	Hungary	330	23	Greece	587
9	Belgium	331	24	United Kingdom	613
10	Sweden	368	25	Ireland	630
11	Germany	369	26	Switzerland	641
12	Denmark	399	27	Malta	813
13	Portugal	402	28	Turkey	983
14	Finland	406	29	Cyprus	1,058
15	Norway	411	30	Albania	1,076

Population per nurse

1	Ukraine	86	16	Estonia	128
2	Iceland	87	17	Switzerland	130
3	Belarus	88	18	Ireland	139
4	Russia	90	19	Bulgaria	155
5	Lithuania	91	20	Netherlands	167
	Moldova	91	20	Hungary	172
7	Sweden	95	22	Austria	184
8	Armenia	101	23	Poland	189
9	Malta	104	24	Luxembourg	242
10	Azerbaijan	105	25	Italy	250
	Slovakia	105	26	Spain	258
12	Belgium	108	27	Romania	275
13	France	111	28	Cyprus	355
14	Latvia	119	29	Greece	453
15	United Kingdom	120	30	Turkey	1,106

Population per hospital bed

1	Latvia	83	17	Belgium	121
	Lithuania	83	18	Czech Republic	122
3	Luxembourg	84	19	Romania	127
4	Finland	93	20	Italy	132
5	Austria	94	21	United Kingdom	160
6	Georgia	95	22	Sweden	161
	Switzerland	95	23	Netherlands	170
8	Azerbaijan	96	24	Poland	179
9	Hungary	97	25	Cyprus	180
10	Ireland	101	26	Macedonia FYR	189
11	Denmark	103	27	Greece	199
12	Bulgaria	104	28	Spain	211
13	Estonia	105	29	Portugal	226
14	France	109	30	Albania	249
15	Germany	118	31	Turkey	406
16	Armenia	120			

Fighting measles

% of one-year-olds fully immunised against measles

1	Hungary	100	14	Albania	87
2	Iceland	99	15	Denmark	86
3	Bulgaria	97		Malta	86
	Finland	97	17	Spain	84
5	Poland	96	18	Ireland	78
	Portugal	96	19	Greece	76
7	Sweden	95		Turkey	76
8	Netherlands	94	21	Belgium	75
9	Romania	92	22	Cyprus	74
10	Germany	90	23	Luxembourg	71
	Norway	90	24	France	69
	Switzerland	90	25	Austria	60
13	United Kingdom	89	26	Italy	50

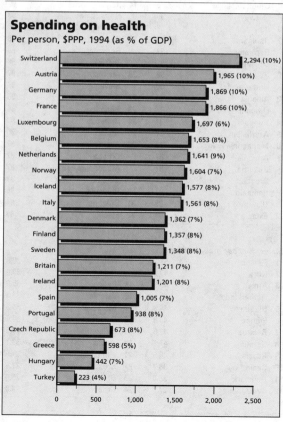

Spending on health

Per person, $PPP, 1994 (as % of GDP)

Switzerland	2,294 (10%)
Austria	1,965 (10%)
Germany	1,869 (10%)
France	1,866 (10%)
Luxembourg	1,697 (6%)
Belgium	1,653 (8%)
Netherlands	1,641 (9%)
Norway	1,604 (7%)
Iceland	1,577 (8%)
Italy	1,561 (8%)
Denmark	1,362 (7%)
Finland	1,357 (8%)
Sweden	1,348 (8%)
Britain	1,211 (7%)
Ireland	1,201 (8%)
Spain	1,005 (7%)
Portugal	938 (8%)
Czech Republic	673 (8%)
Greece	598 (5%)
Hungary	442 (7%)
Turkey	223 (4%)

0   500   1,000   1,500   2,000   2,500

Education enrolment ratios

Primary

Males, % of age group, 1993

1	Portugal	122
2	United Kingdom	112
3	France	107
	Russia	107
	Turkey	107
6	Spain	104
7	Austria	103
	Ireland	103
9	Slovakia	101
10	Finland	100
	Sweden	100
	Switzerland	100
13	Belgium	99
	Czech Republic	99
	Norway	99
16	Italy	98
17	Denmark	97
	Germany	97
	Slovenia	97
20	Belarus	96
	Netherlands	96
22	Albania	95
	Lithuania	95
24	Hungary	94
25	Azerbaijan	91
26	Macedonia FYR	88
27	Armenia	87
	Bulgaria	87
	Croatia	87
	Romania	87
	Ukraine	87
32	Estonia	84

Females, % of age group, 1993

1	Portugal	118
2	United Kingdom	113
3	Russia	107
4	France	105
	Spain	105
6	Austria	103
	Ireland	103
8	Switzerland	102
9	Slovakia	101
10	Belgium	100
	Czech Republic	100
	Finland	100
	Sweden	100
14	Italy	99
	Netherlands	99
	Norway	99
17	Denmark	98
	Germany	98
	Turkey	98
20	Albania	97
	Slovenia	97
22	Belarus	95
23	Hungary	94
24	Armenia	93
25	Lithuania	90
26	Azerbaijan	87
	Croatia	87
	Macedonia FYR	87
	Ukraine	87
30	Romania	86
31	Bulgaria	84
32	Estonia	83

Tertiary

Males, % of age group, 1993

1	Finland	58.2	13	Georgia[bd]	36.9
2	Norway	49.2		United Kingdom[c]	36.9
3	Armenia[ab]	48.9	15	Italy	35.9
4	Netherlands[c]	47.5	16	Estonia	35.3
5	Ukraine[a]	44.9	17	Moldova[b]	34.8
6	France	43.9	18	Sweden[c]	34.6
7	Belarus	42.5	19	Ireland[c]	34.5
8	Germany	41.1	20	Latvia	33.1
9	Russia	40.5	21	Lithuania	31.9
10	Spain[c]	38.7	22	Croatia	27.9
11	Denmark[c]	38.0	23	Bulgaria	25.9
12	Switzerland	37.7	24	Greece[d]	24.9

a 1991. b Males and females. c 1992. d 1990.

Secondary

Males, % of age group, 1993

1	Netherlands	126
2	Norway	118
3	Denmark	112
4	Finland	110
5	Austria	109
6	Spain	107
7	France	104
8	Belgium	103
9	Germany	101
	Ireland	101
11	Sweden	99
12	Switzerland	93
13	United Kingdom	91
14	Azerbaijan	89
	Belarus	89
16	Slovenia	88
17	Estonia	87
	Slovakia	87
19	Czech Republic	85
20	Latvia	84
	Russia	84
22	Romania	83
23	Italy	81
24	Armenia	80
	Croatia	80
26	Hungary	79
27	Lithuania	76
28	Turkey	74
29	Moldova	67
30	Bulgaria	66
31	Ukraine	65
32	Macedonia FYR	53

Females, % of age group, 1993

1	Finland	130
2	Netherlands	120
	Spain	120
4	Denmark	115
5	Norway	114
6	Ireland	110
7	France	107
8	Austria	104
	Belgium	104
10	Germany	100
	Sweden	100
12	Belarus	96
	Estonia	96
14	Ukraine	95
15	United Kingdom	94
16	Russia	91
17	Armenia	90
	Latvia	90
	Slovakia	90
	Slovenia	90
21	Switzerland	89
22	Azerbaijan	88
	Czech Republic	88
24	Croatia	86
25	Hungary	82
	Italy	82
	Romania	82
28	Lithuania	79
29	Moldova	72
30	Bulgaria	70
31	Macedonia FYR	55
32	Turkey	48

Females, % of age group, 1993

1	Finland	68.5	13	Netherlands[c]	42.1
2	Norway	59.9	14	Estonia	40.4
3	France	55.2	15	Italy	38.8
4	Russia	50.2	16	Bulgaria	38.7
5	Armenia[ab]	48.9	17	United Kingdom[c]	37.9
6	Ukraine[a]	46.9	18	Georgia[bd]	36.9
	Lithuania	46.6	19	Moldova[d]	34.8
8	Belarus	45.7	20	Ireland[c]	33.9
9	Latvia	44.7	21	Slovenia	32.0
10	Denmark[c]	44.0	22	Germany	29.7
11	Spain[c]	43.7	23	Poland	29.6
12	Sweden[c]	42.2	24	Portugal[a]	28.8

Spending and teachers

Spending on education

As % GDP, 1992			As % of govt. expenditure, 1992		
1	Sweden	8.8	1	Estonia	31.4
2	Norway	8.7	2	Moldova	26.4
3	Denmark[b]	7.4	3	Azerbaijan[b]	24.7
	Finland	7.4	4	Slovenia	23.2
5	Hungary	7.2	5	Lithuania	22.1
6	Slovakia	7.0	6	Armenia[c]	20.5
7	Bulgaria	6.4	7	Belarus	19.3
8	Netherlands[b]	6.2	8	Switzerland[b]	18.8
9	Ex-Yugoslavia[c]	6.1	9	Latvia[a]	16.1
	Ireland[b]	6.1	10	Andorra[e]	15.8
11	Austria	5.8	11	Romania	14.2
	Iceland[c]	5.8	12	Norway	14.1
13	France	5.7	13	Poland	14.0
	Slovenia	5.7	14	Sweden	12.7
15	Poland	5.6	15	Cyprus	12.5
16	Italy	5.4	16	Denmark[b]	11.8
17	Belgium	5.2	17	Finland	11.6
	Switzerland[b]	5.2	18	Ireland[b]	9.7
	United Kingdom[b]	5.2	19	Spain	9.3
20	Czech Republic	5.0	20	Germany[c]	8.6
21	Portugal[c]	4.8	21	Malta[c]	8.3
22	Spain	4.6	22	Austria	7.7
23	Luxembourg[d]	4.3		Hungary	7.7
24	Cyprus	4.0	24	Monaco	5.6
	Germany[c]	4.0			
	Malta[c]	4.0			
	Turkey	4.0			
28	Romania	3.6			
29	Greece[d]	3.1			

Pupil:teacher ratio

Primary, 1992			Secondary, 1992		
1	Moldova	32	1	Turkey	27
2	Turkey	28	2	Poland	20
3	Ireland	25	3	Albania	18
4	Slovakia	22	4	Spain	17
5	Czech Republic	21	5	Ireland	16
	Malta	21		Macedonia FYR	16
	Romania	21		Slovenia	16
	Spain	21	8	Greece	14
9	Macedonia FYR	20		Netherlands	14
	Russia	20		Romania	14
	United Kingdom	20		Slovakia	14
13	Cyprus	19	12	Bulgaria	13
	France	19		Croatia	13
	Greece	19		Cyprus	13
15	Croatia	18		France	13

a 1993.   b 1991.   c 1990.   d 1989.   e 1986.

Current expenditure

% of total spending on education allocated to current spending

Primary, 1992			Secondary, 1992	
1	Belarus	82.1	1 Monaco	61.7
2	Bulgaria	75.9	2 Moldova	53.1
3	Switzerland	75.2	3 Cyprus	49.6
4	Estonia	74.5	4 Austria	46.8
5	Ukraine	70.3	Spain	46.8
6	Lithuania	69.3	6 Greece	45.1
7	Denmark	67.4	7 Slovenia	44.1
8	Norway	62.6	8 United Kingdom	42.3
9	Iceland	59.5	9 Luxembourg	41.9
10	Sweden	59.4	10 Belgium	41.7
11	Macedonia FYR	56.5	11 France	40.4
12	Hungary	54.9	Malta	40.4
13	Romania	52.1	13 Ireland	39.4
14	San Marino	50.7	14 Portugal	37.5
15	Czech Republic	50.0	15 Netherlands	37.0
16	Poland	48.9	16 Finland	36.8
17	Luxembourg	44.4	17 San Marino	30.9
18	Portugal	39.6	18 Czech Republic	29.2
19	Slovakia	38.6	19 Iceland	25.6
20	Ireland	37.2	20 Hungary	24.5
21	Cyprus	35.6	21 Macedonia FYR	23.5
22	Greece	34.1	22 Romania	22.1
23	Slovenia	33.7	23 Poland	19.5
24	United Kingdom	29.8	24 Slovakia	18.5
25	Spain	28.7		
26	Finland	27.3		
27	France	26.4		
28	Austria	24.4		
29	Belgium	23.6		
30	Netherlands	22.6		
31	Malta	22.5		
32	Monaco	22.3		
33	Moldova	20.5		

Tertiary, 1992

1	Netherlands	31.9	14	Belgium	16.4
2	Finland	27.6	15	Spain	16.0
3	Ireland	20.9	16	Estonia	15.9
4	United Kingdom	20.7		Sweden	15.9
5	Greece	19.5	18	Portugal	15.5
6	Switzerland	19.4	19	Hungary	15.3
7	Slovenia	19.3	20	Slovakia	15.0
8	Austria	18.7	21	Iceland	14.9
9	Denmark	18.4		Lithuania	14.9
10	Malta	17.9	23	France	14.1
11	Macedonia FYR	17.1	24	Czech Republic	13.0
12	Norway	16.9	25	Ukraine	12.6
	Poland	16.9	26	Belarus	12.2

Years of education

Compulsory minimum
Compulsory no. of years of education

1	Belgium	12		Lithuania	9
	Germany	12		Luxembourg	9
3	Belarus	11		Norway	9
	Moldova	11		Portugal	9
	Netherlands	11		Russia	9
	Ukraine	11		Slovakia	9
	United Kingdom	11		Sweden	9
8	France	10	**29**	Albania	8
	Hungary	10		Bulgaria	8
	Malta	10		Croatia	8
	Monaco	10		Iceland	8
	Spain	10		Italy	8
13	Austria	9		Macedonia FYR	8
	Cyprus	9		Poland	8
	Czech Republic	9		Romania	8
	Denmark	9		San Marino	8
	Estonia	9		Serbia	8
	Finland	9		Slovenia	8
	Greece	9		Switzerland	8
	Ireland	9	**41**	Turkey	5
	Latvia	9			

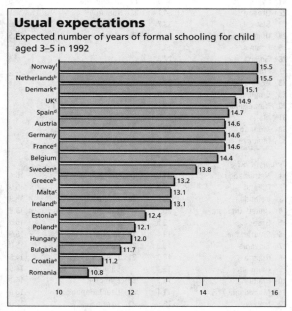

Usual expectations

Expected number of years of formal schooling for child aged 3–5 in 1992

Norway[f]	15.5
Netherlands[b]	15.5
Denmark[e]	15.1
UK[c]	14.9
Spain[d]	14.7
Austria	14.6
Germany	14.6
France[d]	14.6
Belgium	14.4
Sweden[a]	13.8
Greece[b]	13.2
Malta[c]	13.1
Ireland[b]	13.1
Estonia[a]	12.4
Poland[a]	12.1
Hungary	12.0
Bulgaria	11.7
Croatia[a]	11.2
Romania	10.8

a Age 3–6.   b Age 4–5.   c Age 3–4.   d Age 2–5.   e 6.   f Age 4–6.

Part IX
SOCIETY

Family matters

Tying the knot
Marriages per 1,000 population

1	Liechtenstein	12.9	24	Czech Republic	5.7
2	Azerbaijan	10.1		Serbia	5.7
3	Moldova	9.0	26	Germany	5.5
4	Turkey	8.0	27	Austria	5.4
5	Ukraine	7.7		Belgium	5.4
6	Albania	7.6		Poland	5.4
7	Macedonia FYR	7.5	30	Hungary	5.3
	Russia	7.5		Slovakia	5.3
9	Belarus	7.3	32	Estonia	5.1
10	Georgia	7.0	33	Italy	5.0
11	Malta	6.9		Spain	5.0
	Monaco	6.9	35	Finland	4.9
	Portugal	6.9		Iceland	4.9
14	Cyprus	6.8	37	Croatia	4.8
	Denmark	6.8	38	Ireland	4.6
	Romania	6.8	39	Bulgaria	4.5
17	Lithuania	6.3		Latvia	4.5
18	Switzerland	6.1		Norway	4.5
19	Greece	6.0	42	France	4.4
20	United Kingdom	5.9	43	Slovenia	4.2
21	Armenia	5.8	44	Sweden	3.9
	Luxembourg	5.8	45	Andorra	2.2
	Netherlands	5.8	46	Bosnia & Hercegovinia	0.7

Breaking up
Divorces per 1,000 population

1	Latvia	5.5		Netherlands	2.0
2	Russia	4.3	21	France	1.9
3	Ukraine	4.2	22	Germany	1.7
4	Belarus	3.9	23	Azerbaijan	1.6
5	Estonia	3.7	24	Slovakia	1.5
	Lithuania	3.7	25	Georgia	1.4
7	Moldova	3.4	26	Bulgaria	1.3
8	United Kingdom	3.0		Portugal	1.3
9	Czech Republic	2.9		Romania	1.3
10	Denmark	2.5	29	Armenia	0.9
	Sweden	2.5	30	Albania	0.7
12	Finland	2.4		Greece	0.7
	Norway	2.4		Poland	0.7
14	Austria	2.2		Slovenia	0.7
	Switzerland	2.2	34	Cyprus	0.6
16	Belgium	2.1		Spain	0.6
	Hungary	2.1	36	Turkey	0.5
18	Iceland	2.0	37	Italy	0.4
	Luxembourg	2.0	38	Macedonia FYR	0.3

Sex and contraception
%

	Sexually active	Condom	Pill	Steriliz-ation (F)	Steriliz-ation (M)	IUD
				Methods used		
France	81	4	30	7		26
United Kingdom	81	16	19	15	16	8
Finland	80	32	11	4	1	29
Belgium	79	5	46	11	8	5
Denmark	78	22	26	5	5	11
Italy	78	13	14	1		2
Sweden	78	25	23	2	1	20
Bulgaria	76	2	2	1	1	2
Netherlands	76	8	41	4	11	7
Norway	76	14	18	10	4	24
Germany	75	4	59	1	1	6
Slovakia	74	21	5	4		11
Hungary	73	4	39			19
Austria	71	4	40	1	0.3	8
Switzerland	71	8	28	8	8	11
Czech Republic	69	19	3	3		15
Portugal	66	6	19	1	0.1	4
Spain	59	12	16	4	0.3	6
Romania	57	4	3	1		4

Abortion

No. per 1,000 women of child-bearing age

1	Romania	172
2	Russia	120
3	Belarus	114
4	Ukraine	93
5	Moldova	83
6	Bulgaria	77
7	Latvia	70
8	Bosnia & Hercegovina	58
9	Macedonia FYR	57
10	Czech Republic	56
	Estonia	56
12	Croatia	44
13	Hungary	40
14	Slovakia	38
15	Slovenia	36
16	Lithuania	30
17	Sweden	20
18	Norway	17
19	Denmark	15
	United Kingdom	15
21	France	13
	Italy	13
23	Iceland	12
24	Finland	11
25	Germany	9
	Switzerland	9
27	Belgium	5
	Ireland[a]	5
	Netherlands	5
	Spain	5
31	Greece	4
	Poland	4

a Only to preserve mothers' lives.

Age factors

Legal sex
Age of consent

	Heterosexuals	Lesbians	Gay men
Albania	14	14	18
Austria	14	14	18
Belgium	16/18	16/18	16/18
Bulgaria	14	14	14
Croatia	14	18	18
Cyprus	16	16	18
Czech Republic	15	15	15
Denmark	15/18	15/18	15/18
Estonia	14	14	16
Finland	16	18	18
France	15/18	15/18	15/18
Germany	14	14	14/18
Greece	15	15	15
Hungary	14	18	18
Iceland	14	14	14
Ireland	17	17	17
Italy	14/16	14/16	14/16
Liechtenstein	14	14	18
Luxembourg	16	16	16
Malta	12/18	12/18	12/18
Netherlands	12/16	12/16	12/16
Norway	16	16	16
Poland	15	15	15
Portugal	16	16	16
San Marino	14/16	14/16	14/16
Serbia	14	14	18
Slovakia	15	15	15
Spain	12/18	12/18	12/18
Sweden	15	15	15
Switzerland	16/20	16/20	16/20
Turkey	18	18	18
United Kingdom	16	16	18

Notes
Male homosexuality is banned in Armenia, Azerbaijan, Bosnia & Hercegovina, Georgia,
Macedonia FYR and Romania. Female homosexuality is also banned in Romania.
When two ages are shown this is either because a higher age applies where the older
person is in a position of authority or influence over the younger, or because sexual
activity is legal at the lower age unless the younger person subsequently complains.

Voting age

Monaco	25	Liechtenstein	18
Turkey	21	Lithuania	18
Albania	18	Luxembourg	18
Andorra	18	Macedonia FYR	18
Armenia	18	Malta	18
Austria	18	Moldova	18
Azerbaijan	18	Netherlands	18
Belarus	18	Norway	18
Belgium	18	Poland	18
Bulgaria	18	Portugal	18
Cyprus	18	Romania	18
Czech Republic	18	Russia	18
Denmark	18	San Marino	18
Estonia	18	Slovakia	18
Finland	18	Spain	18
France	18	Sweden	18
Georgia	18	Switzerland	18
Germany	18	Ukraine	18
Greece	18	United Kingdom	18
Hungary	18	Bosnia & Hercegovinia[b]	16
Iceland	18	Croatia[b]	16
Ireland	18	Serbia[b]	16
Italy[a]	18	Slovenia[b]	16
Latvia	18		

Retirement age
EU15

	Men	Women
Austria	65	60
Belgium	60–65	60–65
Denmark	67	67
Finland	65	65
France	60	60
Germany	65	65
Greece	65	65
Ireland	65	65
Italy	62	57
Luxembourg	65	65
Netherlands	65	65
Portugal	65	63
Spain	65	65
Sweden	65	65
United Kingdom	65	60

a Senatorial elections, minimun age 25.
b If employed, otherwise 18.

Religion

Who belongs to which faith
% of total population

Albania

| Muslim 70 | Orthodox 20 | Other 10 |

Andorra

| Roman Catholic 99 | | Other 1 |

Armenia

| Orthodox 94 | | Other 6 |

Austria

| Roman Catholic 85 | Protestant 6 | Other 9 |

Azerbaijan

| Muslim 87 | Orthodox 6 | Other 7 |

Belgium

| Roman Catholic 75 | Protestant 20 | Other 5 |

Bosnia & Hercegovina

| Muslim 40 | Orthodox 31 | Other 29 |

Bulgaria

| Orthodox 85 | Muslim 13 | Other 2 |

Croatia

| Roman Catholic 77 | Orthodox 11 | Other 12 |

Cyprus

| Orthodox 78 | Muslim 18 | Other 4 |

Czech Republic

| Atheist 40 | Roman Catholic 39 | Other 21 |

Denmark

| Evangelical Lutheran 91 | Protestant 2 | Other 7 |

Finland

| Evangelical Lutheran 89 | Orthodox 1 | Other 10 |

France

| Roman Catholic 90 | Protestant 2 | Other 8 |

Georgia

| Orthodox 65 | Muslim 11 | Other 24 |

Germany

| Protestant 45 | Roman Catholic 37 | Other 18 |

Greece

| Orthodox 98 | Muslim 1 | Other 1 |

Hungary

| Roman Catholic 68 | Calvinist 20 | Other 12 |

Iceland

| Evangelical Lutheran 96 | Protestant 2 | Other 2 |

Ireland

| Roman Catholic 93 | Anglican 3 | Other 4 |

Italy

Roman Catholic 100

Liechtenstein

| Roman Catholic 87 | Protestant 8 | Other 5 |

Luxembourg

| Roman Catholic 97 | Jewish 2 | Other 1 |

Macedonia FYR

| Eastern Orthodox 59 | Muslim 26 | Other 15 |

Malta

| Roman Catholic 98 | | Other 2 |

Moldova

| Eastern Orthodox 98 | Jewish 2 |

Monaco

| Roman Catholic 95 | | Other 5 |

Netherlands

| Roman Catholic 36 | Protestant 27 | Other 37 |

Norway

| Evangelical Lutheran 88 | Roman Catholic 3 | Other 9 |

Poland

| Roman Catholic 95 | Eastern Orthodox 2 | Other 3 |

Portugal

| Roman Catholic 97 | Protestant 1 | Other 2 |

Romania

| Orthodox 70 | Roman Catholic 6 | Other 24 |

Serbia

| Orthodox 65 | Muslim 19 | Other 16 |

Slovakia

| Roman Catholic 60 | Protestant 8 | Other 32 |

Slovenia

| Roman Catholic 96 | Muslim 1 | Other 3 |

Spain

| Roman Catholic 99 | | Other 1 |

Sweden

| Evangelical Lutheran 94 | Roman Catholic 2 | Other 4 |

Switzerland

| Roman Catholic 48 | Protestant 44 | Other 8 |

Turkey

| Muslim 99.8 | | Other 0.2 |

United Kingdom

| Anglican 47 | Roman Catholic 16 | Other 37 |

Income and savings

Poor shares
% of income
Lowest 20% share, 1993

Russia[cd]	3.7	*Lowest 10% share, 1993*	
United Kingdom[hik]	4.6	Russia[cd]	1.2
Switzerland[him]	5.2	Estonia[ef]	2.4
Denmark[hin]	5.4	Moldova[efg]	2.7
France[hij]	5.6	Bulgaria[efg]	3.3
Norway[hio]	6.2	Lithuania[ef]	3.4
Finland[hin]	6.3	Romania[efg]	3.8
Estonia[ef]	6.6	Hungary[cd]	4.0
Italy[hil]	6.8	Poland[cdg]	4.0
Moldova[efg]	6.9	Ukarine[efg]	4.1
Germany[hik]	7.0	Slovenia[ef]	4.1
Belgium[hip]	7.9	Latvia[ef]	4.3
Sweden[hin]	8.0	Czech Republic[ef]	4.6
Lithuania[ef]	8.1	Belarus[ef]	4.9
Netherlands[hik]	8.2	Slovakia[efg]	5.1
Bulgaria[efg]	8.3		
Spain[hik]	8.3		
Romania[efg]	9.2		
Poland[cdg]	9.3		
Slovenia[ef]	9.5		
Ukraine[efg]	9.5		
Hungary[cd]	9.5		
Latvia[ef]	9.6		
Czech Republic[ef]	10.5		
Belarus[ef]	11.1		
Slovakia[efg]	11.9		

Rich shares
% of income, highest 10% share, 1993

Russia[cd]	38.7	Denmark[hin]	22.3
Estonia[ef]	31.3	Latvia[ef]	22.1
Switzerland[him]	29.8	Poland[cdg]	22.1
Lithuania[ef]	28.0	Netherlands[hik]	21.9
United Kingdom[hik]	27.8	Spain[hik]	21.8
France[hij]	26.1	Finland[hin]	21.7
Moldova[efg]	25.8	Belgium[hip]	21.5
Italy[hil]	25.3	Norway[hio]	21.2
Bulgaria[efg]	24.7	Sweden[hin]	20.8
Germany[hik]	24.4	Ukraine[efg]	20.8
Slovenia[ef]	23.8	Romania[efg]	20.2
Czech Republic[ef]	23.5	Belarus[ef]	19.4
Hungary[cd]	22.6	Slovakia[efg]	18.2

a Gross savings.   b Excludes mandatory savings through pension schemes.
c Spending shares by fractiles of persons.   d Ranked by spending per person.
e Income shares by fractiles of persons.   f Ranked by income per person.
g 1992.   h Income shares by fractiles of households.
i Ranked by household income.
j 1991.   k 1988.   l 1986.   m 1982.   n 1981.   o 1979.   p 1978–79.

Distribution of income
Gini index[q], 1993

Russia[cd]	49.6	Hungary[cd]	27.0
Estonia[ef]	39.5	Latvia[ef]	27.0
Moldova[efg]	34.4	Czech Republic[ef]	26.6
Lithuania[ef]	33.6	Ukraine[efg]	25.7
Bulgaria[efg]	30.8	Romania[efg]	25.5
Slovenia[ef]	28.2	Belarus[ef]	21.6
Poland[cd]	27.2	Slovakia[efg]	19.5

Household savings rates
% of disposable income

1980

1	Portugal	25.5
2	Italy[a]	23.0
3	Belgium	18.7
4	France[a]	17.6
5	United Kingdom[a]	13.4
6	Germany	12.8
7	Ireland	11.6
8	Spain[a]	10.8
9	Austria	10.5
10	Sweden	6.7
11	Finland	5.4
12	Norway	3.4
13	Switzerland	3.3
14	Netherlands[b]	1.8

1985

1	Portugal	24.6
2	Italy[a]	18.9
3	Belgium	14.0
4	France[a]	14.0
5	Germany	11.4
6	Spain[a]	11.2
7	Ireland	10.9
8	United Kingdom[a]	10.7
9	Austria	8.3
10	Switzerland	5.7
11	Finland	3.8
12	Sweden	2.3
13	Netherlands[b]	0.1
14	Norway	-2.7

1990

1	Italy[a]	18.2
2	Belgium	17.1
3	Portugal	15.3
4	Germany	13.8
5	Austria	13.7
6	France[a]	12.5
7	Switzerland	12.2
8	Spain[a]	10.5
9	Ireland	9.7
10	United Kingdom[a]	8.1
11	Netherlands[b]	5.8
12	Norway	0.9
13	Finland	0.4
14	Sweden	-0.6

1995

1	Belgium	19.3
2	France[a]	14.3
3	Austria	13.4
4	Italy[a]	13.1
5	Ireland	12.0
6	Spain[a]	11.7
7	Germany	11.6
8	Portugal	11.0
9	United Kingdom[a]	10.2
10	Switzerland	9.9
11	Sweden	8.2
12	Norway	5.2
13	Finland	5.0
14	Netherlands[b]	1.8

q The Gini index is a measure of income inequality. 0 means all households have the same income, 100 means one household has all the income.

Consumer spending

Who spends how much on what
1995, % of household budget spent on

Food and drink		Clothing and footwear	
Russia	45.9	Poland	10.6
Czech Republic	44.1	Russia	10.3
Slovakia	43.2	Italy	9.4
Poland	38.1	Czech Republic	9.2
Hungary	35.7	Slovakia	9.2
Norway	25.7	Spain	8.8
Sweden	22.7	Hungary	8.7
Denmark	22.6	Sweden	7.9
Spain	21.7	Germany	7.5
Italy	20.9	Belgium	7.1
Germany	20.0	Netherlands	7.1
United Kingdom	19.5	United Kingdom	6.6
Belgium	19.3	Norway	6.2
France	18.5	France	5.7
Netherlands	14.7	Denmark	5.6

Housing and energy		Household	
Sweden	24.5	Belgium	10.3
Denmark	23.1	Poland	9.7
Germany	21.2	Slovakia	9.6
France	18.8	Czech Republic	9.2
Netherlands	18.6	Germany	9.1
Norway	18.6	Italy	9.1
United Kingdom	17.6	France	7.6
Belgium	17.0	Hungary	7.6
Spain	16.0	Spain	7.4
Italy	14.5	Netherlands	7.2
Russia	13.0	Sweden	7.1
Hungary	9.5	United Kingdom	7.0
Slovakia	8.0	Norway	6.9
Czech Republic	7.9	Denmark	6.0
Poland	7.9	Russia	4.6

Health		Personal transport	
France	13.1	United Kingdom	17.8
Netherlands	13.1	Germany	16.6
Belgium	10.5	France	15.9
Poland	7.9	Spain	15.5
Italy	6.8	Sweden	15.4
Slovakia	6.2	Denmark	15.1
Czech Republic	6.1	Norway	13.5
Norway	5.2	Belgium	13.0
Spain	5.1	Netherlands	12.7
Hungary	4.8	Italy	12.6
Germany	3.3	Poland	10.8
Sweden	2.9	Hungary	8.7
Denmark	2.3	Slovakia	8.2
Russia	2.2	Russia	8.2

Growth in consumer spending
Average growth, %

1980–92		1995	
United Kingdom	3.6	Poland	6.0
Spain	3.4	Russia	6.0
Italy	3.0	Denmark	3.8
Germany	2.6	Norway	3.7
France	2.4	Czech Republic	3.0
Belgium	2.0	Spain	2.6
Hungary	1.9	France	2.1
Netherlands	1.8	Sweden	2.0
Sweden	1.8	Netherlands	1.8
Denmark	1.6	Slovakia	1.8
Poland	1.0	United Kingdom	1.8
Norway	0.9	Belgium	1.5
		Italy	1.5
		Hungary	1.2
		Germany	0.2

Working time to buy

By steel worker		*By car worker*	
1 kilo bread, minutes		*Refrigerator (hours)*	
Hungary	29	Turkey	474
Sweden	29	Greece	239
Finland	26	Malta	182
Czech Republic	23	Hungary	128
Italy	23	France	87
France	19	Portugal	84
Portugal	19	Sweden	79
Greece	17	Italy	73
Austria	13	Austria	54
Germany	13	Spain	44
Spain	13	Finland	35
Switzerland	13	Ireland	35
Belgium	12	Belgium	31
Cyprus	12	Germany	31
Ireland	11	United Kingdom	19
Netherlands	11		
Norway	11		
Denmark	8		
United Kingdom	7		

Wired world

Televisions
% of households, 1994

1	Italy	100		Hungary	97
2	Austria	99		Ireland	97
	Slovakia	99		Turkey	97
	Spain	99		United Kingdom	97
5	Czech Republic	98	18	Belgium	96
	Denmark	98		Greece	96
	Netherlands	98		Sweden	96
	Norway	98	21	Bulgaria	95
	Poland	98	22	France	94
	Portugal	98	23	Slovenia	93
	Russia	98	24	Switzerland	87
12	Finland	97	25	Romania	85
	Germany	97			

Video cassette recorders
% of households

1	United Kingdom	74.5	13	Norway	57.5
2	Sweden	71.5	14	Luxembourg	56.4
3	Finland	68.9	15	Spain	55.5
4	France	66.4	16	Italy	47.4
5	Germany	64.6	17	Portugal	37.5
6	Switzerland	64.5	18	Hungary	34.9
7	Denmark	63.4	19	Greece	32.6
8	Ireland	62.8	20	Slovakia	30.1
9	Netherlands	61.8	21	Poland	27.9
10	Belgium	61.0	22	Russia	13.5
11	Iceland	58.5	23	Czech Republic	9.1
12	Austria	58.1			

Internet
Hosts by country, July 1996

1	United Kingdom	579,492	16	Russia	32,022
2	Germany	548,168	17	Hungary	25,109
3	Finland	277,207	18	Ireland	21,464
4	Netherlands	214,704	19	Portugal	17,573
5	France	189,786	20	Greece	12,689
6	Sweden	186,312	21	Turkey	7,743
7	Norway	120,780	22	Estonia	6,605
8	Italy	113,776	23	Ukraine	4,499
9	Switzerland	102,691	24	Latvia	2,932
10	Denmark	76,955	25	Luxembourg	2,877
11	Austria	71,090	26	Romania	2,725
12	Spain	62,447	27	Croatia	2,480
13	Belgium	43,311	28	Bulgaria	2,254
14	Poland	38,432	29	Yugoslavia	1,631
15	Czech Republic	32,219	30	Lithuania	1,335

Cable
% of households

1994			2005		
1	Belgium	94	1	Belgium	96
2	Luxembourg	93	2	Netherlands	94
3	Netherlands	91	3	Switzerland	82
4	Switzerland	79	4	Denmark	76
5	Denmark	60	5	Germany	65
6	Sweden	49	6	Ireland	61
7	Germany	46	7	Sweden	54
8	Ireland	38	8	Norway	53
	Norway	38	9	Austria	51
10	Austria	36	10	finland	48
	Finland	36	11	Spain	33
12	Iceland	31	12	France	29
13	Hungary	26	13	United Kingdom	27
14	Poland	17	14	Turkey	23
15	Czech Republic	15	15	Portugal	12
16	Slovakia	14			
17	Spain	10			
	Russia	10			
19	France	8			
20	United Kingdom	4			
21	Portugal	2			
22	Turkey	1			

Satellite dishes
% of households

1994			2005		
1	Austria	16	1	Austria	28
2	Germany	14	2	Portugal	20
3	United Kingdom	13	3	Norway	18
4	Denmark	10	4	United Kingdom	17
	Norway	10	5	Germany	16
6	Portugal	9		Sweden	16
7	Sweden	8	7	Finland	14
8	Belgium	6	8	France	13
9	Finland	4		Spain	13
	Ireland	4	10	Turkey	12
	Netherlands	4	11	Denmark	8
12	France	3		Ireland	8
	Spain	3		Switzerland	8
	Switzerland	3	14	Belgium	4
15	Italy	1	15	Netherlands	3
	Turkey	1	16	Greece	1

a 1995.   b 1993.

Books and newspapers

Books sales: by value

Total, $m, 1995			Per head, $, 1995		
1	Germany	9,962	1	Norway	137
2	United Kingdom	3,650	2	Germany	122
3	France	3,380	3	Belgium	117
4	Spain	2,992	4	Switzerland	114
5	Italy	2,246	5	Austria	101
6	Netherlands	1,200	6	Denmark	81
7	Belgium	1,189	7	Netherlands	78
8	Austria	809	8	Spain	76
9	Switzerland	805	9	United Kingdom	63
10	Russia	634	10	France	58
11	Norway	602	11	Sweden	56
12	Sweden	491	12	Ireland	55
13	Denmark	425	13	Finland	52
14	Finland	267	14	Italy	39
15	Portugal	217	15	Portugal	22
16	Czech Republic	199	16	Slovenia	20
	Poland	199	17	Greece	16
18	Ireland	198	18	Hungary	14
19	Greece	172	19	Czech Republic	10
20	Hungary	142	20	Slovakia	9
21	Slovakia	48	21	Poland	5
22	Slovenia	40	22	Russia	4
23	Turkey	23	23	Turkey	<1

Fiction or non-fiction

Fiction book sales, $m, 1995			Non-fiction book sales, $m, 1995		
1	Germany	2,789	1	Germany	7,173
2	United Kingdom	1,095	2	United Kingdom	2,556
3	France	967	3	France	2,433
4	Spain	688	4	Spain	2,304
5	Italy	427	5	Italy	1,819
6	Netherlands	348	6	Belgium	856
7	Belgium	333	7	Netherlands	852
8	Russia	247	8	Austria	591
9	Switzerland	242	9	Switzerland	564
10	Austria	218	10	Norway	404
11	Norway	199	11	Russia	387
12	Sweden	162	12	Sweden	329
13	Denmark	128	13	Denmark	297
14	Finland	75	14	Finland	192
15	Portugal	74	15	Portugal	143
16	Hungary	63	16	Ireland	141
17	Poland	62	17	Greece	137
18	Ireland	58		Poland	137
19	Czech Republic	36	19	Hungary	80
20	Greece	34	20	Czech Republic	62
21	Slovakia	17	21	Slovakia	31
22	Slovenia	15	22	Slovenia	25
23	Turkey	2	23	Turkey	21

Newspaper circulation
Per 1,000 population, 1992

1	Liechtenstein	653		21	Lithuania	225
2	Norway	607		22	France	205
3	Czech Republic	583		23	Belarus	186
4	Croatia	532			Ireland	186
5	Iceland	519		25	Bulgaria	164
6	Finland	512		26	Slovenia	160
7	Sweden	511		27	Poland	159
8	Austria	398		28	Malta	150
9	Russia	387		29	Greece	135
10	United Kingdom	383		30	Bosnia & Hercegovina	131
11	Switzerland	377		31	Ukraine	118
12	Luxembourg	372		32	Italy	106
13	Denmark	332		33	Spain	104
14	Romania	324		34	Latvia	98
15	Germany	323		35	Andorra	67
16	Slovakia	317		36	Albania	49
17	Belgium	310		37	Moldova	47
18	Netherlands	303			Portugal	47
19	Hungary	282		39	Macedonia FYR	27
20	Monaco	258				

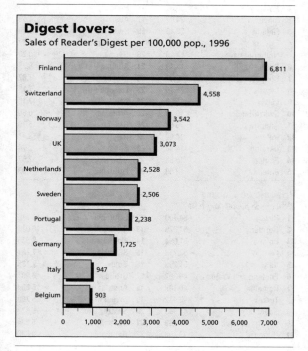

Digest lovers
Sales of Reader's Digest per 100,000 pop., 1996

- Finland — 6,811
- Switzerland — 4,558
- Norway — 3,542
- UK — 3,073
- Netherlands — 2,528
- Sweden — 2,506
- Portugal — 2,238
- Germany — 1,725
- Italy — 947
- Belgium — 903

Crime and punishment

Offensive records
Total criminal offences per 100,000 population

1	Finland	16,189	18	Estonia	2,750
2	Sweden	13,750	19	Slovenia	2,739
3	United Kingdom	11,483	20	Ireland	2,710
4	Denmark	10,399	21	Malta	2,697
5	Netherlands	10,180	22	Spain	2,402
6	Germany	7,838	23	Bulgaria	2,255
7	Luxembourg	7,044	24	Poland	2,020
8	Andorra	7,000	25	Russia	1,856
9	France	6,660	26	Lithuania	1,199
10	Austria	6,421	27	Portugal	900
11	Norway	5,466	28	Ukraine	781
12	Switzerland	5,457	29	Cyprus	667
13	Hungary	4,326	30	Romania	636
14	Monaco	4,277	31	Armenia	437
15	Italy	4,165	32	Azerbaijan	305
16	Greece	3,699	33	Albania	231
17	Belgium	3,591	34	Turkey	209

Juvenile crime
% of total crime committed by people under age 21 yrs

1	Norway	35.00	16	Hungary	11.80
2	Slovenia	24.62	17	Austria	11.50
3	Finland	20.40	18	Sweden	11.30
4	Estonia	17.00	19	Romania	10.37
	Netherlands	17.00	20	Germany	10.20
6	Russia	16.40	21	Albania	8.25
7	Bulgaria	15.80	22	Monaco	7.87
8	Cyprus	15.70	23	Luxembourg	7.13
9	Latvia	15.60	24	Azerbaijan	7.10
10	Switzerland	15.30	25	Armenia	6.80
11	Andorra	15.00	26	Greece	5.70
12	Ireland	14.60	27	Italy	3.71
13	Ukraine	14.40	28	Spain	2.74
14	France	13.88	29	Denmark	2.67
15	Poland	13.50	30	Lithuania	1.93

Prisoners en masse
Total prison population, 1994

1	Russia	664,700	12	Lithuania	11,776
2	Germany	67,626	13	Portugal	10,023
3	Poland	61,694	14	Netherlands	8,535
4	France	53,758	15	Slovakia	7,781
5	Italy	51,299	16	Belgium	7,138
6	England and Wales	49,392	17	Greece	6,881
7	Romania	46,189	18	Austria	6,806
8	Turkey	43,432	19	Sweden	5,780
9	Spain	41,169	20	Switzerland	5,627
10	Czech Republic	18,199	21	Scotland	5,594
11	Hungary	13,196	22	Denmark	3,828

Prisoners in proportion
Prisoners per 100,000 population

1	Russia	443.0	16	Austria	85.0
2	Lithuania	342.0	17	Germany	83.0
3	Romania	200.0	18	Switzerland	81.0
4	Czech Republic	181.6	19	Turkey	72.4
5	Poland	163.6	20	Denmark	72.0
6	Slovakia	139.0	21	Greece	71.0
7	Hungary	128.1	22	Sweden	66.0
8	Northern Ireland	117.0	23	Belgium	64.8
9	Scotland	109.0	24	Norway	62.0
	Luxembourg	109.0	25	Finland	59.0
11	Spain	105.9	26	Ireland	58.6
12	Portugal	101.0	27	Netherlands	55.0
13	England and Wales	96.0	28	Iceland	38.2
14	France	90.3	29	Cyprus	24.7
15	Italy	89.7			

Prison capacity
Total prison capacity

1	Russia	781,800	15	Austria	7,614
2	Turkey	80,502	16	Sweden	6,306
3	Germany	70,702	17	Switzerland	6,097
4	Poland	67,087	18	Belgium	6,002
5	England and Wales	49,085	19	Scotland	5,635
6	France	48,109	20	Greece	4,087
7	Italy	39,896	21	Finland	4,053
8	Romania	30,886	22	Denmark	3,913
9	Czech Republic	17,139	23	Norway	2,817
10	Hungary	16,867	24	Northern Ireland	2,207
11	Lithuania	13,400	25	Ireland	2,174
12	Netherlands	8,305	26	Luxembourg	466
	Slovakia	8,305	27	Cyprus	240
	Portugal	8,305	28	Iceland	114

How crowded prisons are
Prison population per 100 places

1	Greece	168.4	15	Luxembourg	93.8
2	Romania	149.5	16	Slovakia	93.7
3	Italy	128.6	17	Switzerland	92.3
4	Portugal	126.9	18	Poland	92.0
5	Belgium	118.9	19	Sweden	91.7
6	France	111.5	20	Iceland	89.5
7	Czech Republic	106.2	21	Austria	89.4
8	Netherlands	102.8	22	Lithuania	87.9
9	England and Wales	100.6	23	Northern Ireland	86.6
10	Scotland	99.3	24	Russia	85.0
11	Denmark	97.8	25	Hungary	78.2
12	Germany	95.6	26	Finland	73.4
13	Norway	95.5	27	Cyprus	65.4
14	Ireland	94.4	28	Turkey	54.0

Music and gambling

Album sales
Sales of LPs, CDs and music cassettes per head, 1995

1	Switzerland	3.8	13	Spain	1.3
	United Kingdom	3.8	14	Portugal	1.2
3	Denmark	2.9	15	Latvia	0.9
4	Germany	2.8	16	Czech Republic	0.8
	Sweden	2.8		Greece	0.8
6	Austria	2.5		Italy	0.8
	Netherlands	2.5	19	Hungary	0.7
8	France	2.3	20	Poland	0.6
9	Belgium	2.2		Russia	0.6
10	Iceland	2.1	22	Slovakia	0.3
11	Finland	2.0	23	Bulgaria	0.2
	Ireland	1.3		Romania	0.2

CD popularity
Penetration of CDs as % of total album sales of LPs, CDs and music cassettes, 1995

1	Netherlands	96.2	14	Finland	64.7
2	Belgium	95.7		Italy	64.7
3	Iceland	94.3	16	Ireland	58.4
4	Denmark	93.3	17	Portugal	56.4
5	Sweden	90.0	18	Hungary	46.8
6	Norway	88.7	19	Czech Republic	45.7
	Switzerland	88.7	20	Slovakia	32.7
8	Austria	88.3	21	Poland	17.9
9	Germany	84.8	22	Russia	7.1
10	France	80.6	23	Romania	5.3
11	United Kingdom	70.9	24	Latvia	4.1
12	Greece	70.2	25	Bulgaria	2.7
13	Spain	64.9			

Classical business
Sale of classical records as % of market value, 1995

1	Romania	15.0	12	Belgium	7.0
2	Hungary	11.2	13	Norway	6.8
3	Netherlands	11.0		United Kingdom	6.8
	Slovakia	11.0	15	Latvia	6.7
5	Switzerland	10.1	16	Italy	5.8
6	Germany	9.5	17	Portugal	5.3
7	Finland	9.0	18	Sweden	4.0
8	Austria	8.6	19	Denmark	3.9
9	Spain	8.4	20	Ireland	3.7
10	Czech Republic	8.2	21	Greece	3.6
11	France	7.9	22	Russia	2.0

Pirates

Piracy level as % of total value of sales, 1995

1	Bulgaria	80		Switzerland	4
2	Romania	73	14	Germany	3
3	Latvia	63		Sweden	3
4	Russia	62	16	Finland	2
5	Hungary	23		France	2
6	Italy	20		Ireland	2
7	Greece	19		Norway	2
	Poland	19	20	Austria	1
9	Slovakia	7		Denmark	1
10	Netherlands	6		Spain	1
11	Czech Republic	5		United Kingdom	1
12	Belgium	4			

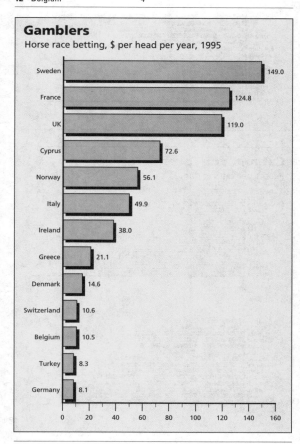

Gamblers

Horse race betting, $ per head per year, 1995

Sweden	149.0
France	124.8
UK	119.0
Cyprus	72.6
Norway	56.1
Italy	49.9
Ireland	38.0
Greece	21.1
Denmark	14.6
Switzerland	10.6
Belgium	10.5
Turkey	8.3
Germany	8.1

Pets

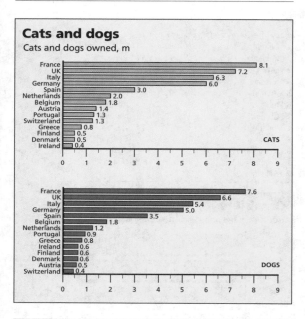

Cats and dogs
Cats and dogs owned, m

CATS

France	8.1
UK	7.2
Italy	6.3
Germany	6.0
Spain	3.0
Netherlands	2.0
Belgium	1.8
Austria	1.4
Portugal	1.3
Switzerland	1.3
Greece	0.8
Finland	0.5
Denmark	0.5
Ireland	0.4

0 1 2 3 4 5 6 7 8 9

DOGS

France	7.6
UK	6.6
Italy	5.4
Germany	5.0
Spain	3.5
Belgium	1.8
Netherlands	1.2
Portugal	0.9
Greece	0.8
Ireland	0.6
Finland	0.6
Denmark	0.6
Austria	0.5
Switzerland	0.4

0 1 2 3 4 5 6 7 8 9

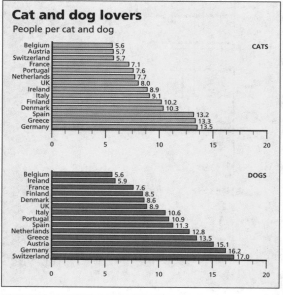

Cat and dog lovers
People per cat and dog

CATS

Belgium	5.6
Austria	5.7
Switzerland	5.7
France	7.1
Portugal	7.6
Netherlands	7.7
UK	8.0
Ireland	8.9
Italy	9.1
Finland	10.2
Denmark	10.3
Spain	13.2
Greece	13.3
Germany	13.5

0 5 10 15 20

DOGS

Belgium	5.6
Ireland	5.9
France	7.6
Finland	8.5
Denmark	8.6
UK	8.9
Italy	10.6
Portugal	10.9
Spain	11.3
Netherlands	12.8
Greece	13.5
Austria	15.1
Germany	16.2
Switzerland	17.0

0 5 10 15 20

GOVERNMENT AND DEFENCE

Europe's national governments

Albania

Parliamentary republic with an interim constitution adopted in 1991. Legislative power is vested in the People's Assembly, a single chamber of 140 deputies with elections held every four years. The People's Assembly elects the president of the republic as head of state whose term of office is five years. Executive power is the responsibility of a council of ministers, the chairman of which is the head of government. The chairman is appointed by the president as are ministers, after recommendation by the chairman and subject to approval by the People's Assembly.

Andorra

Parliamentary monarchy with a constitution adopted in 1993. Andorra is uniquely a co-principality. Its joint heads of state are the Bishop of Urgel and the President of the French Republic, though since 1993 the positions have been almost entirely honorary. The legislature is the General Council (*Conseil General*) whose 28 councillors are elected for four-year terms. Executive authority resides with the head of government (*Cap du Govern*) elected by a majority of the General Council. Government ministers are nominated by the head of government.

Armenia

Parliamentary republic with a constitution adopted in 1995. Legislative authority resides with the National Assembly, made up of 131 deputies elected for terms of four years. The president, directly elected for five years, is head of state and exercises executive power. In addition the president appoints the prime minister and, subject to the prime minister's recommendation, members of the government.

Austria

Federal parliamentary republic with a constitution adopted in 1920. The bicameral legislature, the Federal Assembly, consists of the National Council (*Nationalrat*) and the Federal Council (*Bundesrat*). The former has 183 members elected for four-year terms by a system of proportional representation. The latter has 64 members with seats allocated according to the strengths of the parties in the provincial assemblies and terms corresponding to the terms of the provincial government represented. The president is elected directly every six years as head of state and appoints the head of the federal executive branch, the chancellor and other ministers on the chancellor's advice.

The provincial assemblies (*landtage*) of the nine states elect state governments consisting of a provincial governor and councillors.

Azerbaijan

Presidential republic with a constitution adopted in 1995. The National Assembly (*Milli Majlis*) is the supreme legislative body and has 125 members elected directly for terms of five years, one-fifth by proportional representation from a party list and the remainder in single member constituencies. Executive power is held by the head of state, the president, who is also elected for five years. The president appoints and exercises executive power through a council of ministers headed by a prime minister. The president retains the right to call legislative elections.

Belarus

Presidential republic with a constitution adopted in 1994. The foremost body of legislative power is the Supreme Council of the Republic of Belarus which has 260 deputies directly elected for five-year terms. The president, also directly elected for five years, is head of state. He has executive authority but exercises it on the advice of the chairman and cabinet of ministers who are responsible to the Supreme Council.

Belgium

Parliamentary monarchy with a constitution adopted in 1831 but subsequently considerably revised. Legislative power is exercised by the bicameral parliament and the monarch who is head of state. Parliament comprises a Chamber of Representatives with 150 members elected by proportional representation and a Senate with 71 members, of whom 40 are elected directly by proportional representation and 31 are appointed by the elected senators. Members of both houses are elected for terms of up to four years. Supreme executive power is nominally held by the monarch but is exercised by the cabinet headed by a prime minister. Considerable autonomy is exercised by assemblies representing the three regions of Flanders, Wallonia and Brussels, and the three linguistic communities.

Bosnia and Hercegovina

The envisioned post-war government has been taking shape. A three man presidency representing the Croats, Bosnian Serbs and muslims exercises executive authority through a council of ministers. A 42-member House of Representatives acting as a constituent assembly was expected to authorise the creation of a highly decentralised federal system of government.

Bulgaria

Parliamentary republic with a constitution adopted in 1991. A single chamber National Assembly holds legislative power. It has 240 members elected for four-year terms. Executive power is exercised by a council of ministers headed by a chairman who is also prime minister. The president, who is directly elected as head of state for five years, appoints the prime minister, usually from one of the two largest parties.

Croatia

Presidential republic with a constitution adopted in 1990. The Assembly (*Sabor*) exercises legislative power through the Chamber of Representatives (*Zastupnicki dom*) and the Chamber of Municipalities (*Zupanijski dom*), both of which are directly elected for four-year terms. The former comprises at least 100 members and no more than 160. The latter has three members from each of the 21 counties. The president, prime minister and ministers have executive authority. The prime minister and members of the government are appointed by the president and are responsible both to the president and the Chamber of Representatives. The president is elected directly for five-year terms and is head of state.

Cyprus

The island of Cyprus is divided between two administrations. The southern (Greek-Cypriot) presidential republic has an executive president who exercises power through a council of ministers. The legislative House of Representatives nominally contains 80 members according to the 1960 power-sharing constitution but in 1963 the 24 members elected by the Turkish-Cypriot minority stopped attending. Members are elected for five-year terms by proportional representation.

The Turkish Republic of Northern Cyprus, which is not recognised internationally, has a 50-seat Legislative Assembly and an executive president as head of state who exercises power through a council of ministers.

Czech Republic

Parliamentary republic with a constitution adopted in 1992. A bicameral legislature consists of the 200-member Chamber of Deputies, elected for four-year terms, and an 81-member Senate directly elected for six-year terms. The president is head of state and is elected by a joint session of both chambers for five years. Executive power is vested in a council of ministers under a prime minister.

Denmark

Parliamentary monarchy with a constitution adopted in 1849 and last revised in 1953. The unicameral parliament (*Folketing*) holds legislative power jointly with the monarch though the latter's powers are nominal. Parliament's 179 members, including 2 each for Greenland and the Faroe Islands, are elected by proportional representation for terms of four years. The monarch is head of state. The prime minister is head of government.

Estonia

Parliamentary republic with a constitution adopted in 1992. The legislative 101-member State Assembly (*Riigikogu*) is elected every four years by proportional representation. It elects the president of the republic, who is head of state, for a five-year term. The president nominates the prime minister for approval by the State Assembly.

Finland

Parliamentary republic with a constitution adopted in 1919. Legislative power is the responsibility of the unicameral 200-member parliament (*Eduskunta*) elected for four year terms by proportional representation. The president, elected directly for six years, is head of state and holds supreme executive power. The president appoints the council of state, which includes the prime minister and other ministers.

France

Presidential republic with a constitution adopted in 1958. The 577-member National Assembly is directly elected for five-year terms. The Senate has 321 members elected for nine-year terms, one third every three years, by an electoral college in each Department. The president, directly elected for seven years, holds executive power and is head of state. A council of ministers headed by the prime minister is appointed by the president and is responsible to parliament.

Georgia

Presidential republic with a constitution adopted in 1995. Legislative power is vested in the unicameral parliament elected for four years. Of its 235 members, 150 are elected by proportional representation and 85 by a simple majority. A bicameral legislature is planned. The head of state and holder of supreme executive power is the president, who is directly elected for five years. Ministers are appointed by the president with the approval of parliament.

Germany

Federal parliamentary republic with a constitution adopted in 1949. A bicameral legislature comprises the Federal Assembly (*Bundestag*) and the Federal Council (*Bundesrat*). The former contains 672 members elected for terms of four years by a system combining simple majority and proportional representation. The latter contains 68 members appointed by the 16 state (*Land*) governments each having between three and six seats in proportion to state population. The head of state is the federal president who is elected for five years by a special federal convention. The federal government exercises executive authority and is headed by the federal chancellor, elected by the Federal Assembly. The chancellor proposes federal ministers who are appointed by the federal president.

Greece

Parliamentary republic with a constitution adopted in 1975. Legislative authority resides with a unicameral parliament of between 200 and 300 members elected for terms of four years by proportional representation. Executive power is vested in the prime minister and cabinet. The president is head of state and is elected by parliament for five years.

Hungary

Parliamentary republic with a constitution adopted in 1949 but greatly revised in 1989. The single chamber national assembly (*Orszaggyules*) contains 386 members who are elected for terms of four years. 176 are elected by simple majority, 120 by proportional representation and 90 from a national list. Executive power is held by a council of ministers, which is responsible to the national assembly. The head of state is the president, who is elected by the national assembly for five years.

Iceland

Parliamentary republic with a constitution adopted in 1944. Legislative authority is vested jointly in the president and parliament (*Althing*). The president is elected directly for four-year terms and is head of state. Parliament comprises 63 members and is elected every four years by a system principally based on proportional representation. Executive authority is held by a cabinet appointed by the president. The cabinet and prime minister are responsible to parliament. The president has supreme executive authority under the constitution but in practice waives it in favour of the cabinet.

Ireland

Parliamentary republic with a constitution adopted in 1937. A bicameral parliament consisting of a senate (*Seanad*) and a house of representatives (*Dail*) holds legislative power. The senate has 60 members of which 11 are nominated by the prime minister, 6 elected by the universities and the remainder elected from vocationally based panels by other branches of the Irish polity. The house of representatives has 166 members elected for five-year terms by the single transferable vote system of proportional representation. The president, directly elected for seven years, is head of state, and the prime minister (*taoiseach*) is head of government.

Italy

Parliamentary republic with a constitution adopted in 1948. A bicameral parliament holds legislative authority. The senate has 315 members of whom 10 are life members. The chamber of deputies has 630 members. Elected members of both houses – 75% of whom are elected by simple majority and the remainder by proportional representation – serve five-year terms. Executive power is vested in a council of ministers headed by the prime minister who is appointed by the president. The president is head of state and is elected by a specially convened electoral college comprising both houses of parliament and 58 regional representatives.

Liechtenstein

Parliamentary monarchy with a constitution adopted in 1921. Legislative authority is the joint reponsibility of the prince and the 25-member parliament (*Landtag*). Members of parliament are elected by a system of proportional representation for four year terms. In addition legislation can be proposed by citizen's groupings and referendums can be applied to parliamentary legislation. The prince is head of state and appoints the executive, comprising a prime minister and four councillors, for four-year terms subject to the approval of parliament.

Lithuania

Parliamentary republic with a constitution adopted in 1992. A unicameral parliament (*Seimas*) has legislative power. Of its 141 members, 71 are elected by simple majority and the remainder by a system of proportional representation for four-year terms. A council of ministers headed by a prime minister holds executive authority.

The prime minister is appointed by the president who is elected directly for a five-year term and is head of state.

Luxembourg

Parliamentary monarchy with a constitution adopted in 1868 but subsequently considerably revised. A unicameral parliament (*Chambre des Deputés*) exercises legislative authority, its 60 members are elected for five-year terms by a system of proportional representation. The Grand Duke is head of state and is nominally the constitutional executive head. However a council of ministers under a prime minister has assumed executive resposibility.

Macedonia (Former Yugoslav Republic of)

Parliamentary republic with a constitution adopted in 1991. Legislative power is exercised by an assembly (*Sobranje*) of between 120 and 140 members directly elected for four-year terms. Executive authority resides with the prime minister, assisted by other ministers. The president, elected directly for 5 years, is head of state.

Malta

Parliamentary republic with a constitution adopted in 1974. Legislative authority resides with a 65-member House of Representatives elected for five-year terms by a system of proportional representation. The executive comprises a prime minister appointed by the president and a cabinet appointed by the president on the prime minister's advice. The president is head of state and is appointed for five years by the House of Representatives.

Moldova

Presidential republic with a constitution adopted in 1994. A 104-member unicameral legislature is directly elected for terms of four years. Executive authority resides jointly with the president of the republic and a council of ministers headed by a prime minister. The president, elected directly for four years, is head of state.

Monaco

Parliamentary monarchy with a constitution adopted in 1962. Legislative authority is held by the reigning monarch in conjunction with a legislature (*Conseil National*) elected by a system of proportional representation for terms of five years. Executive authority is exercised by a four member Council of Government under the authority of the reigning monarch. The Council of Government is headed by a minister of state, a French civil servant selected by the monarch from a short list of three people nominated by the French government. The monarch is head of state. Under agreements established in 1918 and 1919, if the reigning prince dies without leaving a male heir, Monaco will be incorporated into France.

Netherlands

Parliamentary monarchy with a constitution adopted in 1814 and most recently revised in 1983. The bicameral *Staten-Generaal* is the legislative authority. The first chamber has 75 members elected for four-year terms by the provincial councils. The second chamber has 150 members and is elected for four-year terms by a system of proportional representation. The first chamber can only approve or reject bills. Executive authority resides with a council of ministers lead by the prime minister. The monarch is head of state.

Norway
Parliamentary monarchy with a constitution adopted in 1814. Legislative authority resides with a unicameral parliament (*Storting*) of 165 members elected for four-year terms by a system of proportional representation. A quarter of the members are elected by parliament to form an upper house (*Lagting*). The remainder make up the lower house (*Odelsting*). Legislation is decided by both houses or in the event of deadlock by the entire parliament. Constitutional questions are decided by parliament as a unified body. Executive power is exercised by a state council headed by a prime minister. The monarch is head of state.

Poland
Presidential republic based on a constitution adopted in 1952 but subsequently heavily amended. Under the 1992 revised but interim constitution legislative authority is vested in a bicameral national assembly comprising a 100-member upper chamber (*Senat*) and a 460-member lower chamber (*Sejm*). The former is elected directly at provincial level for terms of four years. The latter is elected for four-year terms by a system of proportional representation. The head of state is the president, who is elected directly for five-year terms.

Portugal
Parliamentary republic with a constitution adopted in 1976 and revised fundamentally in 1982 and 1989. Legislative authority is vested in a unicameral assembly comprising between 230 and 235 members elected for four-year terms by a system of proportional representation. Executive authority resides with a prime minister appointed by the president and a council of ministers appointed by the president on the recommendation of the prime minister. The president, who is elected directly for five years, is head of state.

Romania
Presidential republic with a constitution adopted in 1991. Legislative authority is the responsibility of a bicameral parliament comprising a 341-member Chamber of Deputies and a 143-member Senate. Members of both houses are elected for terms of four years by a system of proportional representation. The president of the republic has executive authority and is directly elected for four-year terms. As head of state the president appoints a prime minister who in turn appoints a council of ministers.

Russia
Presidential republic with a constitution adopted in 1993. The bicam-

eral federal assembly is the supreme legislative body comprising a 178-member upper chamber, the federal council, and a 450-member lower chamber (*Duma*). The federal council is appointed by the regional assemblies: two members from each territorial unit. The lower chamber is elected directly for terms of four years. The president, directly elected for four-year terms, is head of state and holds executive authority in tandem with a prime minister and ministers. The prime minister and ministers have competence in budgetary matters and law and order. The president appoints the prime minister with the approval of the lower chamber.

Serbia

Federal republic with a constitution adopted in 1992 to cover Serbia and Montenegro – the rump of the Federal Republic of Yugoslavia. Legislative authority resides with the bicameral federal assembly. The Chamber of Citizens contains 138 members directly elected for terms of four years; the Chamber of the Republics has 40 members from Serbia and Montenegro. The federal president is head of state and is elected for a four-year term by a joint session of the federal assembly. The president is responsible for appointing a federal prime minister. Legislative authority is shared with the directly elected republican assemblies of Serbia and Montenegro. The republics also have their own elected executive presidents.

Slovakia

Parliamentary republic with a constitution adopted in 1992. The National Council for the Slovak Republic has supreme legislative authority, comprising a single chamber of 150 members elected directly for terms of four years. Executive power is vested in a prime minister and ministers responsible to the National Council. The president is elected by the National Council for five years and is head of state.

Slovenia

Parliamentary republic with a constitution adopted in 1991. Legislative authority resides with the unicameral national assembly (*Drzavni Zbor*) comprising 90 members serving terms of four years. Of these 50 are elected by a system of proportional representation and 38 are directly elected by simple majority. The remaining two are elected by the minority ethnic Italian and Hungarian communities. Some legislative powers are shared with the national council (*Drzavni Svet*) comprising 18 members elected by social, economic and local constituencies and 22 members directly elected for five-year terms. Executive authority is vested in a prime minister, elected by a majority vote of the national assembly, and ministers appointed by the national assembly on the prime minister's recommendation. The head of state is the president who is directly elected for five years but whose powers are largely nominal.

Spain

Parliamentary monarchy with a constitution adopted in 1978. A bicameral parliament (*Cortes Generales*) is the legislative authority where both chambers are elected for four-year terms. The senate contains 256 members, 208 directly elected, the remainder elected by the regional assemblies. The Congress of Deputies has 350 members elected by proportional representation. Executive power is in the hands of a prime minister and a council of ministers appointed by the monarch, who is head of state. Regional parliaments have some autonomy subject to state law and are elected for four-year terms.

Sweden

Parliamentary monarchy with a constitution adopted in 1975 formalising and revising former basic laws which previously served as a constitution. A unicameral parliament (*Riksdag*) holds legislative power, comprising 349 members elected for four-year terms by a system of proportional representation. Executive authority rests with the cabinet (*Regeringen*) headed by a prime minister nominated by the speaker and subject to the approval of parliament. The monarch is head of state but has only a limited ceremonial role.

Switzerland

Federal republic with a constitution adopted in 1874. The legislature, a bicameral federal assembly, comprises the Council of States and the National Council. The former contains 46 members elected for three to four-year terms, two members from each of the 23 Cantons (three cantons are divided, so each half Canton sends one member). The latter contains 200 members elected for terms of four years by proportional representation. Executive authority resides with a federal council of 7 members elected for four years by the federal assembly. One member of the federal council is then elected president of the confederation by the federal assembly for a one-year term and is head of state. Each Canton has its own legislature and executive and power is further devolved by the relative ease with which referendums can be called to propose or mandate legislation.

Turkey

Presidential republic with a constitution adopted in 1982. The unicameral Turkish Grand National Assembly holds legislative authority; its 550 members are directly elected for five-year terms. The president who holds executive power and is head of state is elected for a seven-year term by the assembly. The president appoints a prime minister.

Ukraine

Presidential republic with a constitution adopted in 1996. Legislative authority is vested in a 450-member Supreme Council elected directly for four-year terms. Executive authority is jointly held by a prime minister and a president. The president is directly elected for five years and appoints a prime minister and cabinet. The president is head of state.

United Kingdom

Parliamentary monarchy without a formal written constitution. The system of government is defined by convention, the common law, acts of parliament and tradition. Legislative authority is vested in a bicameral parliament. The pre-eminent chamber, the House of Commons, contains 651 members elected directly for five years, though elections can be held more frequently. The upper chamber, the House of Lords has power to delay or modify legislation and is composed of hereditary members, political appointees and senior members of the judiciary and the Church of England. Executive power is vested in a prime minister, usually the leader of the largest party in the House of Commons, who appoints a cabinet. The monarch is head of state.

Defence

Spending on defence

	\$bn (1995 prices)		% of GDP	
	1985	1995	1985	1995
NATO Europe				
Belgium	5.6	4.6	3.0	1.7
Denmark	2.9	3.1	2.2	1.8
France	44.6	48.0	4.0	3.1
Germany	48.1	41.8	3.2	2.0
Greece	3.2	5.1	7.0	4.6
Iceland	...	...	...	...
Italy	23.5	20.0	2.3	1.8
Luxembourg	0.1	0.1	0.9	0.9
Netherlands	8.1	8.5	3.1	2.2
Norway	2.8	3.8	3.1	2.6
Portugal	1.7	2.8	3.1	2.9
Spain	10.3	8.5	2.4	1.5
Turkey	3.1	6.0	4.5	3.6
United Kingdom	43.5	34.2	5.2	3.1
Total	**197.5**	**186.4**	**3.1**	**2.3**
Non-NATO Europe				
Armenia	...	0.1	...	4.4
Austria	1.8	2.1	1.2	1.0
Azerbaijan	...	0.1	...	5.0
Belarus	...	0.5	...	3.3
Bosnia & Hercegovina	...	0.9	...	18.8
Bulgaria	7.9	0.4	14.1	3.3
Croatia	...	1.9	...	12.6
Cyprus	0.1	0.4	3.6	4.5
Czech Republic	...	1.1	...	2.8
Ex-Czechoslovakia	6.6	...	4.7	...
Estonia	...	0.1	...	5.3
Finland	2.1	2.1	2.8	2.0
Macedonia FYR	...	0.1	...	7.8
Georgia	...	0.1	...	3.4
Hungary	5.2	0.6	7.2	1.4
Ireland	0.4	0.7	1.8	1.2
Latvia	...	0.1	...	3.2
Lithuania	...	0.1	...	2.4
Poland	7.9	2.6	8.1	2.5
Romania	1.9	0.9	4.5	3.1
Slovakia	...	0.4	...	2.8
Slovenia	...	0.3	...	1.5
Sweden	4.4	6.0	3.3	2.9
Switzerland	2.6	5.1	2.1	1.9
Ukraine	...	1.0	...	3.0
Serbia	4.6	3.1	3.8	22.1
Russia	...	82.0	...	7.4
Soviet Union	329.4	...	16.1	...
Total Europe	**572.7**	**299.2**		

Armed forces
'000s

	1985	1995		1985	1995
NATO Europe					
Belgium	91.6	47.2	Netherlands	105.5	74.4
Denmark	29.6	33.1	Norway	37.0	30.0
France	464.3	409.0	Portugal	73.0	54.2
Germany	478.0	339.9	Spain	320.0	206.0
Greece	201.5	171.3	Turkey	630.0	507.8
Iceland	...	...	United Kingdom	327.1	239.6
Italy	385.1	328.7			
Luxembourg	0.7	0.8	**Total**	**3,143.4**	**2,442.0**

	1985	1995		1985	1995
Non-NATO Europe					
Albania	40.4	73.0	Ireland	...	12.9
Armenia	...	60.0	Latvia	...	7.0
Austria	54.7	55.8	Lithuania	...	4.9
Azerbaijan	...	86.7	Malta	0.8	1.9
Belarus	...	98.4	Moldova	...	11.9
Bosnia & H'govina	...	92.0	Poland	319.0	278.6
Bulgaria	148.5	101.9	Romania	189.5	217.4
Croatia	...	105.0	Slovakia	...	47.0
Cyprus	10.0	10.0	Slovenia	...	8.4
Czech Republic	...	86.4	Sweden	65.7	64.0
Ex-Czechoslovakia	203.3	...	Switzerland	20.0	31.4
Estonia	36.5	3.5	Ukraine	...	452.5
Finland	...	31.0	Serbia	241.0	126.5
Macedonia, FYR	...	10.4	Russia	...	1,520.0
Georgia	106.0	9.0	Ex-Soviet Union	5,300.0	...
Hungary	13.7	70.5			

Conscripts
1995

1	Turkey	528,000	16	Austria	25,000
2	Russia	381,000	17	Finland	23,100
3	France	182,250	18	Albania	22,050
4	Germany	164,550	19	Portugal	17,600
5	Italy	163,800	20	Norway	16,900
6	Poland	147,100	21	Netherlands	13,135
7	Spain	128,800	22	Moldova	11,000
8	Romania	127,200	23	Cyprus	8,700
9	Greece	119,200	24	Macedonia FYR	8,000
10	Bulgaria	50,300	25	Denmark	7,810
11	Serbia	43,000	26	Slovenia	5,500
12	Sweden	42,100	27	Estonia	3,450
13	Croatia	41,400	28	Latvia	3,000
14	Hungary	41,200	29	Lithuania	2,000
15	Czech Republic	38,500			

Military equipment
1995

	Tanks	*Combat aircraft*
Albania	721	98
Armenia	102	6
Austria	170	53
Azerbaijan	300	46
Belarus	2,320	349
Belgium	132	132
Bosnia & Hercegovina	675	0
Bulgaria	1,550	272
Croatia	250	25
Cyprus	52	0
Czech Republic	953	126
Denmark	353	66
Finland	232	118
France	880	616
Georgia	70	0
Germany	2,988	543
Greece	1,735	388
Hungary	835	127
Ireland	0	19
Italy	1,164	319
Netherlands	734	108
Norway	170	80
Poland	1,721	467
Portugal	186	90
Romania	1,375	368
Russia	17,650	5,494
Serbia	1,360	204
Slovakia	478	125
Slovenia	109	0
Spain	698	207
Sweden	664	413
Switzerland	742	153
Turkey	4,280	434
Ukraine	4,026	789
United Kingdom	2,462	538

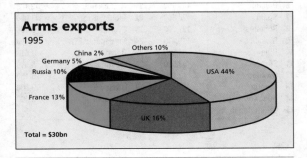

Arms exports
1995

China 2%
Germany 5%
Russia 10%
France 13%
Others 10%
USA 44%
UK 16%

Total = $30bn

Part XI

THE EUROPEAN UNION

Members and votes

Who joined when

ECSC 1951		EEC Treaty of Rome 1957	EC 1973
Belgium		Belgium	Denmark
W. Germany		W. Germany	Ireland
France		France	United Kingdom
Italy		Italy	
Luxembourg		Luxembourg	
Netherlands		Netherlands	

EC 1981	EC 1986	EC 1990	EU 1995
Greece	Spain	E. Germany	Austria
	Portugal		Finland
			Sweden

Other applications: Morocco and Turkey (1987), Malta and Cyprus (1990), Norway (1961, 1967, 1992), Switzerland (1992), Hungary and Poland (1994).

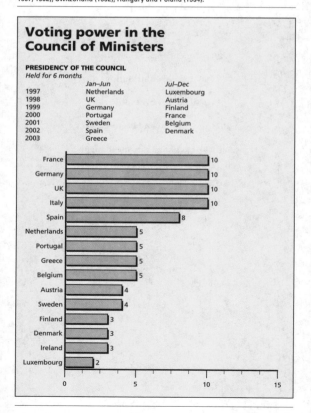

Voting power in the Council of Ministers

PRESIDENCY OF THE COUNCIL
Held for 6 months

	Jan–Jun	Jul–Dec
1997	Netherlands	Luxembourg
1998	UK	Austria
1999	Germany	Finland
2000	Portugal	France
2001	Sweden	Belgium
2002	Spain	Denmark
2003	Greece	

Country	Votes
France	10
Germany	10
UK	10
Italy	10
Spain	8
Netherlands	5
Portugal	5
Greece	5
Belgium	5
Austria	4
Sweden	4
Finland	3
Denmark	3
Ireland	3
Luxembourg	2

EMU: the Maastricht criteria

Inflation, interest rates and ERM membership

	Inflation, % Consumer price index August 1996	Interest rates Long-term, % August 1996	Exchange rates ERM participation October 1996
Reference value:	**2.9**	**8.4**	
Belgium	1.9	6.6	Yes
Denmark	2.4	7.3	Yes
Germany	1.4	6.3	Yes
Greece	8.5	14.2	No
Spain	3.7	8.9	Yes
France	1.6	6.4	Yes
Ireland	1.4	7.3	Yes
Italy	3.3	9.5	No
Luxembourg	1.4	6.6	Yes
Netherlands	1.9	6.3	Yes
Austria	1.8	6.4	Yes
Portugal	3.6	8.7	Yes
Finland	0.4	7.1	Yes
Sweden	0.3	8.1	No
United Kingdom	2.1	7.8	No
EU15	**2.3**	**7.5**	

Budget deficits and debt[a]
1995

	Deficit as % of GDP		Debt as % of GDP
		Cyclically adjusted	
Reference value:	**3.0**	**3.0**	**60.0**
Belgium	4.5	4.0	133.8
Denmark	2.0	2.2	73.6
Germany	3.6	3.2	58.8
Greece	9.3	8.9	114.4
Spain	5.9	4.9	64.8
France	5.0	4.5	51.5
Ireland	2.5	3.3	85.9
Italy	7.2	6.8	124.9
Luxembourg	-0.4	-0.6	6.3
Netherlands	3.1	3.0	78.4
Austria	5.5	5.4	68.0
Portugal	5.2	4.6	70.5
Finland	5.6	3.5	60.3
Sweden	7.0	5.4	81.4
United Kingdom	5.1	4.5	52.5
EU15	**4.7**	**4.2**	**71.1**

a General government.

The European Parliament

Political groups in the European Parliament[a]
As at November 11th 1996

	PES	EPP	UFE	ELDR
Belgium	6	7		6
Denmark	4	3		5
Germany	40	47		
Greece	10	9	2	
Spain	21	30		2
France	16	12	17	1
Ireland	1	4	7	1
Italy	18	14	27	6
Luxembourg	2	2		1
Netherlands	7	10	1	10
Austria	6	7		1
Portugal	10	9	3	
Finland	4	4		5
Sweden	7	5		3
United Kingdom	63	19		2
Total	215	182	57	43

PES	Party of European Socialists.
EPP	European People's Party, comprising mainly Christian Democrat parties but including British Conservatives and one Ulster Unionist and Fine Gael members from Ireland.
UFE	Union for Europe comprises representatives of Mr Berlusconi's party plus one Lega Nord and one Social Democrat member (Italy), 17 French MEPs, 7 Irish Fianna Fail, 2 Greek Political Spring party and 3 Portuguese centre party members.
ELDR	European Liberal, Democratic and Reformist Group, largely from the Netherlands also Lega Nord members, 2 British Liberals and one Irish independent.
EUL/NGL	Confederal Group of the European United Left/Nordic Green Left. Comprises representatives of Green/Left parties from Denmark, Finland, Greece, Italy, Spain and Sweden plus member of Communist parties from France, Greece and Portugal.
ERA	European Radical Alliance. Based on the French Radical Party and includes 2 Scottish Nationalists. A progressive left party, supporting the idea of a Federal Europe.
IND	Independents, including French and Belgian National Front members and Ian Paisley, and the ex-European of the Nations members.

a The European Parliament has monthly plenary sessions in Strasbourg and committee meetings in Brussels. Its administrative secretariat is based in Luxembourg.

EUL/NGL	Greens	ERA	IND	Total
	2	1	3	25
			4	16
	12			99
4				25
9		2		64
7		12	22	87
	2			15
5	4	2	11	87
		1		6
	1		2	31
	1		6	21
3				25
2	1			16
3	4			22
		2	1	87
33	27	20	49	626

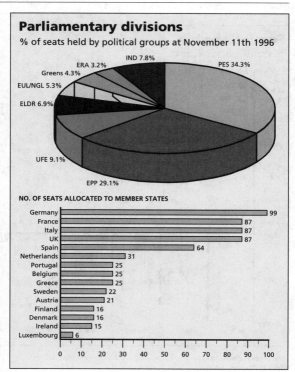

Parliamentary divisions

% of seats held by political groups at November 11th 1996

ERA 3.2%
IND 7.8%
Greens 4.3%
EUL/NGL 5.3%
ELDR 6.9%
PES 34.3%
UFE 9.1%
EPP 29.1%

NO. OF SEATS ALLOCATED TO MEMBER STATES

Germany	99
France	87
Italy	87
UK	87
Spain	64
Netherlands	31
Portugal	25
Belgium	25
Greece	25
Sweden	22
Austria	21
Finland	16
Denmark	16
Ireland	15
Luxembourg	6

0 10 20 30 40 50 60 70 80 90 100

Budget contributions

Who pays what and receives what
Ecus, m

	1980		1985	
	Contributions to Brussels	Receipts from Brussels	Contributions to Brussels	Receipts from Brussels
Germany	4,610	2,940	7,504	4,185
United Kingdom	3,168	1,803	5,090	3,107
France	2,992	3,372	5,319	5,416
Italy	1,929	2,611	3,630	4,480
Netherlands	1,273	1,667	1,889	2,232
Belgium	951	677	1,293	1,070
Denmark	346	680	620	913
Ireland	139	827	296	1,549
Luxembourg	20	15	51	9
Greece			388	1,703
Spain				
Portugal				
Miscellaneous		12		40
Total	**15,428**	**14,604**	**26,080**	**24,704**

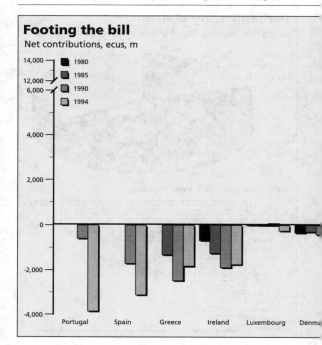

Footing the bill
Net contributions, ecus, m

- 1980
- 1985
- 1990
- 1994

Note: Presentational changes in the EU budget mean that different years are not strictly comparable.

	1990		1994	
	Contributions to Brussels	*Receipts from Brussels*	*Contributions to Brussels*	*Receipts from Brussels*
	10,358	4,807	21,366	7,729
	6,534	3,147	6,417	5,259
	8,090	6,285	12,551	9,924
	6,098	5,681	7,760	5,219
	2,615	2,984	4,246	2,416
	1,764	990	2,822	2,513
	775	1,198	1,296	1,495
	368	2,261	639	2,391
	75	14	165	419
	564	3,034	1,216	3,043
	3,671	5,383	4,718	7,835
	502	1,103	992	4,844
		391		7,218
	41,413	**37,278**	**64,188**	**60,305**

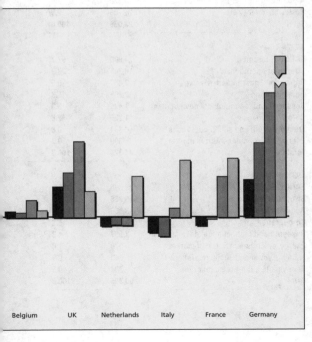

Belgium   UK   Netherlands   Italy   France   Germany

Budget breakdown

Payments to member states by sector

	ecus, m	% of total
1980		
EAGGF-Guarantee	11,283	69.3
Regional policy and transport	1,103	6.8
Repayments	846	5.2
Administration	820	5.0
Social policy	772	4.7
Agricultural structures, fisheries	646	4.0
Co-operation with developing countries	509	3.1
Research, energy etc	312	1.9
Total	**16,290**	**100.0**
1985		
EAGGF-Guarantee	19,726	70.2
Regional policy and transport	1,726	6.2
Social policy	1,491	5.3
Administration	1,296	4.6
Repayments	1,248	4.4
Co-operation with developing countries	1,085	3.9
Agricultural structures, fisheries	820	2.9
Research, energy etc	708	2.5
Total	**28,099**	**100.0**
1990		
EAGGF-Guarantee	24,980	57.7
Structural operations	10,368	23.9
Repayment, guarantees, reserves	2,381	5.5
Administration	2,298	5.3
Research and technological development	1,429	3.3
Co-operation	1,225	2.8
Training, youth and social operations	334	0.8
Energy, environment, internal market	309	0.7
Total	**43,325**	**100.0**
1994		
EAGGF-Guarantee	33,605	55.7
Structural operations	15,966	26.5
Administration	3,566	5.9
Co-operation	3,152	5.2
Research and technological development	2,587	4.3
Energy, environment, internal market	578	1.0
Training, youth and social operations	543	0.9
Repayment, guarantees, reserves	308	0.5
Total	**60,305**	**100.0**

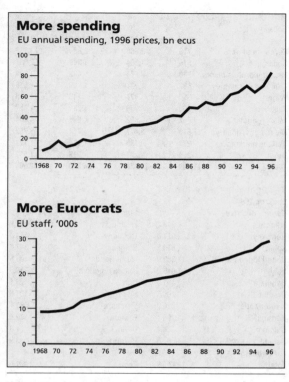

More spending
EU annual spending, 1996 prices, bn ecus

More Eurocrats
EU staff, '000s

Where the money comes from

Ecus, m

1980	
Agricultural levies	1,535
Sugar and isoglucose levies	467
Customs duties	5,906
VAT own resources	7,520
Total	**15,428**

1990	
Agricultural levies	1,173
Sugar and isoglucose levies	911
Customs duties	11,428
VAT own resources	28,968
GNP resources	285
Costs incurred in collection	-1,351
Total	**41,413**

1985	
Agricultural levies	1,122
Sugar and isoglucose levies	1,057
Customs duties	8,310
VAT own resources	15,592
Total	**26,080**

1994	
Agricultural levies	923
Sugar and isoglucose levies	1,382
Customs duties	12,420
VAT own resources	33,280
GNP resources	17,657
Costs incurred in collection	-1,472
Total	**64,188**

Agricultural and regional aid

Agricultural aid by product[a]
Ecus, m

	1980	1985	1990	1994
Cereals and rice	1,719	2,360	3,881	12,656
Sugar	575	1,804	1,388	2,062
Fats and protein plants	748	2,174	5,482	2,204
Fruit and vegetables	687	1,231	1,253	1,556
Wine	300	921	745	1,176
Tobacco	309	863	1,232	1,057
Milk products	4,752	5,933	4,895	4,484
Meat, eggs, poultry	1,618	3,477	4,711	5,752
Various markets	277	736	1,174	1,117
Other	299	227	219	1,542
Total	**11,284**	**19,726**	**24,980**	**33,606**

Who got what for what
Ecus, m, 1994

Cereals and rice		Sugar	
France	4,248.1	France	554.9
Germany	2,911.0	Germany	474.0
Spain	1,610.5	Belgium	347.6
United Kingdom	1,362.9	Netherlands	186.8
Italy	1,046.0	United Kingdom	158.0
Denmark	491.9	Italy	126.1
Greece	299.5	Spain	108.0
Netherlands	226.9	Denmark	82.1
Portugal	198.1	Greece	12.4
Belgium	188.4	Ireland	7.8
Ireland	67.0	Portugal	3.9
Luxembourg	5.5		
Total	**12,655.8**	**Total**	**2,061.6**

Fats and protein plants		Fruit and vegetables	
Spain	819.2	Greece	441.0
Italy	707.7	Spain	421.2
Greece	416.6	Italy	341.7
France	129.2	France	222.1
Portugal	44.5	Netherlands	44.4
Germany	34.2	Portugal	41.9
Denmark	20.7	Belgium	19.8
Netherlands	19.5	Germany	13.8
United Kingdom	9.9	United Kingdom	6.0
Belgium	1.6	Denmark	3.6
Ireland	0.4	Ireland	0.1
Total	**2,203.5**	**Total**	**1,555.6**

a Payments from the European Agricultural Guidance and Guarantee Fund (EAGGF).

Wine		Tobacco	
Italy	477.0	Greece	426.1
Spain	379.3	Italy	394.5
France	230.3	Spain	119.7
Greece	38.7	France	78.1
Portugal	38.3	Germany	28.8
Germany	8.0	Belgium	5.2
Netherlands	3.3	Portugal	5.1
United Kingdom	1.1		
Belgium	0.1		
Denmark	0.1		
Luxembourg	0.0		
Total	**1,176.2**	**Total**	**1,057.5**

Milk products		Meat, eggs, poultry	
Netherlands	1,011.4	France	1,165.5
France	962.2	Ireland	970.7
Germany	762.7	United Kingdom	849.2
Denmark	386.5	Germany	732.8
Ireland	364.2	Spain	581.6
United Kingdom	347.6	Italy	346.2
Belgium	313.2	Netherlands	306.6
Italy	190.7	Belgium	224.9
Spain	76.0	Greece	218.8
Portugal	58.6	Denmark	211.0
Greece	7.8	Portugal	141.2
Luxembourg	3.1	Luxembourg	3.8
Total	**4,484.0**	**Total**	**5,752.3**

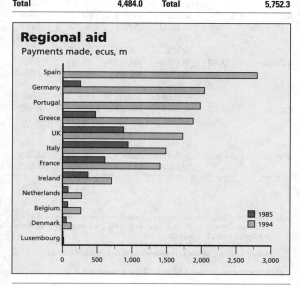

Regional aid
Payments made, ecus, m

The exchange rate mechanism

Central rates, with upper and lower intervention limits
As at October 14th 1996

Currency	1 ecu =	BFr100 =	DKr100 =	DM100 =	Pta100 =
		-	627.880	2395.20	28.1525
Belgian franc	39.3960	-	540.723	2062.55	24.2447
		-	465.665	1776.20	20.8795
		21.4747	-	442.968	5.20640
Danish krone	7.28580	18.4938	-	381.443	4.48376
		15.9266	-	328.461	3.86140
		5.63000	30.4450	-	1.36500
D-mark	1.91007	4.84837	26.2162	-	1.17548
		4.17500	22.5750	-	1.01230
		478.944	2589.80	9878.50	-
Peseta	162.493	412.461	2230.27	8507.18	-
		355.206	1920.70	7326.00	-
		18.8800	102.100	389.480	4.57780
French franc	6.40608	16.2608	87.9257	335.386	3.94237
		14.0050	75.7200	288.810	3.39510
		2.33503	12.6261	48.1696	0.566120
Punt	0.792214	2.01090	10.8734	41.4857	0.487537
		1.73176	9.36403	35.7143	0.419859
		6.34340	34.3002	115.235[a]	1.53793
Guilder	2.15214	5.46286	29.5389	112.673[a]	1.32445
		4.70454	25.4385	110.1675[a]	1.14060
		39.6089	214.174	816.927	9.60338
Schilling	13.4383	34.1107	184.444	703.550	8.27008
		29.3757	158.841	605.877	7.12200
		577.090	3120.50	11903.3	139.920
Escudo	195.792	496.984	2687.31	10250.5	120.493
		428.000	2314.30	8827.70	103.770
		17.1148	92.5438	353.008	4.14938
Markka	5.80661	14.7391	79.6976	304.000	3.57345
		12.6931	68.6347	261.801	3.07740

Notes: Italy and the United Kingdom left the exchange rate mechanism in September 1992
but on November 24th 1996 Italy re-joined the ERM at a central rate of 990 lire to
the D-mark with a 15% fluctuation band.
Greece and Sweden have not participated in the ERM.
Central banks are obliged to intervene to keep rates within their limits.

a Bilateral agreement between German and Dutch monetary authorities.

FFr100 =	I£1 =	FI100 =	ASch100 =	Esc100 =	Fmk100 =
714.030	57.5445	2125.60	340.420	23.3645	787.830
614.977	49.7289	1830.54	293.163	20.1214	678.468
529.660	42.8260	1576.45	252.470	18.3285	584.290
132.066	10.6792	393.105	62.9561	4.32100	145.699
113.732	9.19676	338.537	54.2170	3.72119	125.474
97.9430	7.92014	291.544	46.6910	3.20460	108.057
34.6250	2.8000	90.7700ª	16.5050	1.13280	38.1970
29.8164	2.4111	88.7526ª	14.2136	0.975561	32.8948
25.6750	2.0760	86.7800ª	12.2410	0.840100	28.3280
2945.40	238.175	8767.30	1404.10	96.3670	3249.50
2536.54	205.113	7550.30	1209.18	82.9927	2798.41
2184.40	176.641	6502.20	1041.30	71.4690	2410.00
-	9.38950	345.650	55.3545	3.79920	128.107
-	8.08631	297.661	47.6706	3.27188	110.324
-	6.96400	256.350	41.0533	2.81770	95.0096
14.3599	-	42.7439	6.84544	0.469841	15.8424
12.3666	-	36.8105	5.89521	0.404620	13.6433
10.6500	-	31.7007	5.07668	0.348453	11.7494
39.0091	3.15450	-	18.5963	1.27637	43.0378
33.5953	2.71662	-	16.0149	1.09920	37.0636
28.9381	2.33952	-	13.7918	0.94661	31.9187
243.586	19.6971	725.065	-	7.97000	268.735
209.773	16.9629	624.417	-	6.86356	231.431
180.654	14.6082	537.740	-	5.91086	199.305
3549.00	286.983	10564.0	1691.80	-	3915.40
3056.35	247.145	9097.55	1456.97	-	3371.88
2632.10	212.838	7834.70	1254.70	-	2903.80
105.253	8.51107	313.30	50.1744	3.44376	-
90.6422	7.3296	269.81	43.2094	2.96570	-
78.0597	6.31217	232.35	37.2114	2.55402	-

The ecu

The ecu basket
Composition of the ecu basket

March 3rd 1979		Sept 17th 1984		Sept 21st 1989	
DM	0.828	DM	0.719	DM	0.6242
FFr	1.15	FFr	1.31	FFr	1.332
Fl	0.286	FL	0.256	FL	0.2198
BFr	3.66	BFr	3.71	BFr	3.301
LuxFr	0.14	LuxFr	0.14	LuxFr	0.13
Lire	109	Lire	140	Lire	151.8
DKr	0.217	DKr	0.219	DKr	0.1976
I£	0.00759	I£	0.00871	I£	0.008552
£	0.0885	£	0.0878	£	0.08784
		Dr	1.15	Dr	1.44
				Pta	6.885
				Esc	1.393

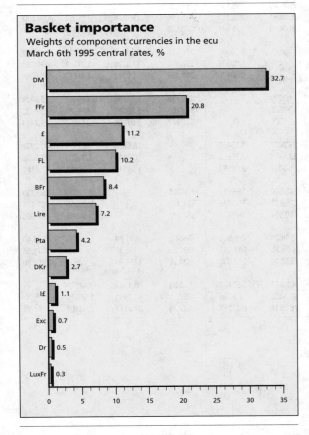

Basket importance
Weights of component currencies in the ecu
March 6th 1995 central rates, %

DM	32.7
FFr	20.8
£	11.2
FL	10.2
BFr	8.4
Lire	7.2
Pta	4.2
DKr	2.7
I£	1.1
Exc	0.7
Dr	0.5
LuxFr	0.3